Praise for *The Way of Heaven and Earth*

"This book is like a many-jeweled crown. It is a rich treasury of thousands of pieces of wonderfully unoriginal Catholic wisdom arranged in an original and unforgettable 'big picture' that reveals the Catholic (universal) 'both/and' mind in contrast to all its 'either/or' alternatives. It shows how Christ is a matchmaker who marries (not compromises) all the spiritual couples that the world divorces."

—**Peter Kreeft**, Professor of Philosophy, Boston College, and author of *Socrates' Children*

"Pursuing holiness requires a type of suffering that many are not able to bear. It includes a radical transformation in the way we see God, ourselves, and the world. In *The Way of Heaven and Earth*, Becklo masterfully leads us down the road that Scripture calls 'narrow' and 'constricted' by breaking through the false dichotomies that distract many today and teaching us how to be holy, how to see, how to understand, and simply how to be human. If you're tired of wrestling with the either/or scenarios that plague the human heart or tired of sitting in the tension of polarization and extremes, this book is an invitation to be free of the paradoxes by diving deeper into them through the lens of the Incarnation. Everyone should read it."

—**Rachel Bulman**, author, speaker, and editor of *With All Her Mind: A Call to the Intellectual Life*

"I am so happy that Matthew Becklo has written *The Way of Heaven and Earth*. Why? Because when people discover that I teach philosophy at a seminary, they often share with me their deep desire to study philosophy in the light of the Catholic faith to better understand God, themselves, the Church, the world, and their participation in it. Whether he intended it or not, in *The Way of Heaven and Earth*, Becklo covers all the major philosophical themes required by the *Program for Priestly Formation* in a well-written, thoroughly researched, and challenging yet accessible book. As our world, our country, and even at times our Church become more polarized, Becklo reminds us that the fullness of truth is usually found in the Catholic both/and, and that heaven and earth ought not be opposed."

—**Fr. Damian Ference**, Vicar for Evangelization and Secretary for Parish Life in the Diocese of Cleveland, Professor of Philosophy at Borromeo Seminary, and author of *Understanding the Hillbilly Thomist: The Philosophical Foundations of Flannery O'Connor's Narrative Art*

THE WAY OF HEAVEN AND EARTH

THE WAY OF HEAVEN AND EARTH

From
EITHER/OR
to the Catholic
BOTH/AND

MATTHEW BECKLO

Published by Word on Fire, Elk Grove Village, IL 60007

Printed in the United States of America

Cover design, typesetting, and interior art direction
by Rozann Lee, Nic Fredrickson, Marlene Burrell, and Cassie Bielak

Minor adjustments have occasionally been made on excerpted material for consistency and readability

ISBN: 978-1-68578-106-4

Library of Congress Control Number: 2023946609

For Elizabeth

How can we know the way? . . .

I Am the Way.

—John 14:5–6

Contents

ACKNOWLEDGMENTS xi

INTRODUCTION The Great Both/And 1

PRELUDE The Things: The Heavens or the Earth 9

Part I: The Dilemmas of Life

1. Life: Heaven or Earth 19
2. The People: God or Man 28
3. The Places: God's Place or Man's Place 39
4. Man's Place: The Spiritual or the Physical 49
5. Man: The Spirit or the Flesh 61

Part II: The Dilemmas of Philosophy

6. Philosophy: Essence or Existence 75
7. Being: The One or the Many 86
8. The Good Life: Discipline or Passion 97
9. History: Divine Providence or Human Freedom 108
10. The Self: The Soul or the Body 116

11. Knowledge: Thought or Experience 125
12. Action: Subjective Freedom or Objective Causation 134
13. The Good: Values or Facts 144
14. The Soul Power: The Intellect or the Will 154
15. Society: Order or Openness 164

Part III: The Dilemmas of Christianity

16. Christianity: The Not Here and Not Yet or the Here and Now 177
17. The Light: Faith or Reason 185
18. Christ: The Word or the Flesh 195
19. God: Transcendence or Immanence 203
20. The Church: The Holy Spirit or the Body of Christ 214
21. Mission: Contemplation or Action 224
22. Conversion: Grace or Nature 233
23. Morality: Rigor or Relaxation 242
24. The Christian Life: Abstinence or Indulgence 253
25. Salvation: The Elect or the World 265
26. Reformation: The Solas or the Alsos 276
CONCLUSION The Great Either/Or 291
APPENDIX Illustrations of the Way 296
SCRIPTURE INDEX 331

Acknowledgments

In February 2015, several years after my reversion to the Catholic faith, I began to think about a book on the "Catholic both/and." For the next six years, I continued to think about it, occasionally scribbling down paragraphs, notes, and quotations. Word on Fire has given me the great gift of finally turning this dream into a reality, and in February 2025—a decade later—it arrives in print.

The cultivation of these ideas over this decade has been the graced work of my life up to this point, and it wouldn't have been possible without the help and encouragement of so many along the way.

I would first like to thank Bishop Robert Barron, whose teaching and preaching on the beauty and truth of Catholicism have shaped me since discovering Word on Fire on YouTube in 2009. It was Bishop Barron who taught me the Way, and anyone familiar with his work will see his influence all over this book from start to finish.

Thank you to Fr. Steve Grunow, a spiritual father who has given me the great honor of contributing to Word on Fire's mission. And thank you to Brandon Vogt, who reached out and encouraged me when I was a fledgling writer, and changed the course of my life. So many of the wonderful opportunities and experiences I've been given stem from his example, friendship, and support.

Thank you also to Sean and Rozann Lee for their dedication to Word on Fire and kindness to me; to the whole Publishing team, especially Daniel Seseske and James O'Neil for their careful reviews of the book and many valuable suggestions; to the Design team, especially Cassie Bielak and Nic Fredrickson for a beautiful cover design; and to the rest of the Word on Fire family and all their families, whose cooperation with the Spirit continues to set the world ablaze.

To Peter Kreeft, whose philosophical lectures and writings have also done so much to shape me and teach me the Way: thank you for sharing your wisdom and wonder.

My gratitude also goes to Sally Read, Tod Worner, and Daniel McInerny, all of whom generously provided helpful input on different portions of an earlier draft, and to the Canons Regular of St. Augustine in New York for their spiritual fatherhood, especially Fr. Elias Carr, who also offered valuable feedback on the book, and Fr. Gabriel Rach, who generously loaned me a space in the parish office to do some focused writing.

Thank you to my mother, Catherine, for giving me life and teaching me service and prayer; my father, Alan, for keeping the faith and teaching me wisdom and fatherhood; my brothers, Wes, Brady, and Nate, for their inspiring camaraderie and creativity; my uncle Fred for first passing the torch of the life of the mind—and the works of Balthasar, de Lubac, and Ratzinger—to our family; Janet and Alex for welcoming me as a son into their beautiful family; and all my sisters-in-law and brothers-in-law for their kindness and encouragement.

Thank you to our children, Grace, Teresa, Alexandria, and Jude, for their love, joy, and wonder; for praying for their father and for being patient with him when he disappeared into his office to write; and for being the four greatest gifts we've ever experienced.

Finally, thank you to my wife, best friend, and first editor, Elizabeth, to whom this book is dedicated, for her steadfast love for me—a "little trip to heaven" on earth—and steadfast support for this book. "Am I rambling incoherently," I asked her once in one of our many conversations about the Way, "or did that make sense?" A good Catholic and a good wife, she responded, "It's a both/and."

INTRODUCTION

The Great Both/And

Man is a divided animal. Division, of course, has always been with us. But the speed, frequency, and intensity with which we can now share ideas has brought us to a crisis of polarization—one that more and more threatens the future of civilization. Whether it's religion, philosophy, culture, politics, or art, we find ourselves in a fiercely divided world: divided countries, divided states, divided communities, divided families, divided minds. The variety of ideas on a given subject always seems to boil down to some overarching dichotomy, some inevitable showdown. "The world is broken, sundered, busted down the middle, self ripped from self."[1]

Polarization requires the choice between two poles, and behind all of our divisions, we find dilemmas. Do we believe in the conservative or the liberal cause? Tradition or progress? High culture or pop culture? Religion or science? Is man a soul or a body? Is the good life in discipline or passion? Should we be religious or spiritual? Is reality spiritual or material? Should we follow the light of faith or reason? Are we saved by faith or works? Everywhere we turn, we're tempted into an either/or, our vision split in two like

1. Walker Percy, *Love in the Ruins* (New York: Picador, 1971), 382–383.

the double-faced Roman god Janus. We can't bear the tension, and inevitably we choose one way at the expense of the other, narrowing our eyes at those who chose the opposite way.

How we make the choice, of course, varies: sometimes we go to war with the opposing element, and sometimes we deny that it exists at all; sometimes we keep a respectful distance from it, and sometimes we absorb it; sometimes we push it down, and sometimes we rise up to take its place. But we choose—and the stakes are high. Seizing one element at the expense of the other tends toward extremes, and these extremes—whether by common cause or opposite charge—tend to attract one another. In fact, in the ultimate punishment, one extreme often leads right into the clutches of its direct opposite. This is what Carl Jung, borrowing from Heraclitus, called "enantiodromia" (in the Greek, an "opposite-running"). When one side of a dilemma dominates our thinking, the other side will eventually build up, explode through our conscious control, and wreak new havoc.

Social media—so carefully engineered to affirm what we choose, and to addict us to that affirmation—has clearly contributed to this crisis of division and extremism. But the dilemmas behind it have always been with us, and the digital revolution has at least forced us to face them all at once. Can we overcome them before they overcome us? Can we even understand them at all?

This book finds new hope in a forgotten Way. It hinges on three closely related ideas. The first is this: *Our greatest dilemmas are heaven-earth dilemmas.* But what does "heaven and earth" mean? There are layers of meaning to these terms, which come down to the West through the Bible. The surface layer is the *things* of heaven and earth: the guiding metaphor of the sky above and the ground below.

But these surface meanings orient us to four deeper meanings of the terms. The first two look at the big picture: the *people* of heaven and earth (God and man) and the *places* of heaven and earth (God's place and man's place). The second two zoom in on the earth side, where the heavenly and earthly intersect: *man's place* (the spiritual and the physical) and *man himself* (the spirit and the flesh).

The great dilemmas in the history of ideas in the West are heaven-earth dilemmas. The most prominent are these four ultimate dilemmas of life, which all extend out of "heaven or earth": God or man, God's place or man's place, the spiritual or the physical, and the spirit or the flesh. Surrounding these are the great dilemmas of philosophy and theology, which extend out of these same four pairs. And each dilemma that we encounter plays out the same dynamics: on one side, we find a *heavenward* way that chooses the heavenly element at the expense of the earthly; on the other side, we find an *earthward* way that chooses the earthly element at the expense of the heavenly. Man is a creature "pulled two ways like between two teams of horses,"[2] and these two ways are heaven and earth. We find ourselves falling into this same pattern time and time again. Heaven and earth crack the code of our deepest divisions.

This leads to a second idea: *Our heaven-earth dilemmas are only resolved in Christ, the Way of heaven and earth.* From the beginning of Genesis to the end of Revelation, "heaven and earth" is the great mantra of the Bible. And heaven and earth—in all four meanings of those terms—reach their fulfillment in Jesus of Nazareth. He is the Way in person; in him, "the sky did really come down and

2. William Faulkner, "Barn Burning," in *Selected Short Stories of William Faulkner* (New York: Modern Library, 2012), 18.

join the earth,"[3] and his spired churches all over the world reach up into the heavens. He says as much, calling himself "the way" (John 14:6)—and not as a road to some other place, but as both the journey and the destination. In Christ, heaven and earth are *contrasted*; heaven is higher than the earth and has the primacy. Yet they're also *connected*; heaven has come down to the earth, drawing the two together in an intimate union. In a word, heaven and earth are in *communion* (together-as-one) in Jesus. God gathers "all things in him, things in heaven and things on earth," "to reconcile to himself all things" (Eph. 1:10; Col. 1:20). In Christ, both heaven and earth are full of God's glory (Isa. 6:3).

When we look at our great dilemmas in the light of the Way, they become false dilemmas. Christ frees us from having to choose between heaven and earth, and offers safe passage between the Scylla and Charybdis of each without the other. But this is no mere intellectual or spiritual program; the more we open ourselves to the truth of Christ, the more we're drawn into his life. We don't claim the Way; the Way claims us. And from within it, we find again and again that the heavenward and earthward each get something right, but that neither gets the whole picture; that the Wayward hold together what the wayward separate or confuse.

This leads to the third and final idea: *The fullness of the Way is in the Catholic Church, which is defined by the principle of "both/and."* Early Christians took Jesus at his word, often describing their newfound faith as "the Way" (Acts 9:2; 19:9, 23; 22:4; 24:14, 22)—a participation, soul and mind and body, in the life of Jesus. Most Christians walk together on the first stretch of his Way—a "mere

3. C.S. Lewis, *The Voyage of the Dawn Treader* (New York: Scholastic, 1987), 214.

Christianity"—but the Catholic Church has the temerity to see it all the way through to the end. This is the "Catholic both/and."

This phrase has been popularized today through the evangelical work of Bishop Robert Barron, and in the twentieth century, was a preoccupation of various theologians of the Society of Jesus, including Hans Urs von Balthasar, Henri de Lubac, and many others. But this *et-et* (and-and) theme stretches back through the whole of Catholic literature—from Flannery O'Connor and G.K. Chesterton, back through Aquinas and Augustine, all the way to Irenaeus of Lyons and Ignatius of Antioch—and into the Sacred Scriptures. The Church's dogmas, doctrines, and condemnations, its sacraments, saints, and social teachings—all of it comes back to the both/and.

What is it? It's simply an insistence on the Way—an instinct for seeing it and choosing it, for inhabiting the creative tension of paradoxes rather than falling into simplistic solutions. Like the young girl in the Old El Paso commercial about the choice between hard or soft taco shells, now made famous by a meme, it's a knack for responding, "Por que no los dos?" *Why not both?* It seeks dualities without dualism, binaries without bifurcation, dyads without dichotomy. Like some of the saints, it bilocates. Catholics use various images for this both/and: harmony, marriage, sanity, tension, balance, fullness, wholeness ("catholic" meaning *kata holos*, according to the whole). And they frame it using various principles: analogical, sacramental, dialectical, incarnational. But ultimately, the great image and principle is Christ himself. The both/and is just *Christocentric*: it centers on the Way incarnate. Like the *mandorla*, it sees the spheres of heaven and earth intersecting and integrating. Like the Mandalorian, it declares, "This is the Way."

But isn't there a fatal flaw in this whole project? Doesn't the Bible also talk, time and time again, about the *dangers* of the earthly? Aren't the great enemies of the soul, as Christian tradition has it, "the world, the flesh, and the devil"? If so, how can we talk of a "Way of heaven and earth"?

Here, we have to make a key distinction between two very different meanings of the earthly. The first, which we might call "the true earth," is the earthly insofar as it *exists*. But the second, which we might call "the false earth," is the earthly insofar as it's *evil*. Earth in the first sense—the body, the human being, God's "very good" creation (Gen. 1:31)—is the opposite pole of heaven, and these opposites come together on the Way. But earth in the second sense—St. Paul's "works of the flesh" (Gal. 5:19–21), St. Augustine's "City of Man," St. John's "the world" (1 John 2:15–17)—isn't the opposite pole of heaven. In fact, it isn't even a pole at all: evil is an absence, a privation, a lacuna—a sinking downward into nothingness. In the topographical poetry of the Bible, it leads to Sheol, which is under the earth, and Gehenna, a cavernous valley; it's the way not to life but to everlasting death.

Thus, this false earth has no place on the Way of heaven and earth; on the contrary, it's what stirs up all our divisions between them. God is the great gatherer; the devil (*diabolos*, from *diaballein*, "to scatter") is the great divider. Where there is holiness, there is wholeness—two words that share the same etymological root; by contrast, "where there are sins, there is multiplicity, there are schisms, there are heresies, there are dissensions."[4] C.S. Lewis rightly saw a spiritual darkness behind our collapses into extremes

4. Origen, *Homilies 1–14 on Ezekiel*, trans. Thomas P. Scheck (New York: Newman, 2010), 117.

and enantiodromias: "all extremes, except extreme devotion," are playthings of the devil, who "always sends errors into the world in pairs—pairs of opposites," and "relies on your extra dislike of one error to draw you gradually into the opposite one."[5]

The Church doesn't say "both/and" to good and evil—only to good. It also doesn't say "both/and" to truth and falsehood—only to truth. It doesn't even properly say "both/and" to the countless pairs of arbitrarily or closely related things—beautiful as they might be. Instead—with eyes fixed on Christ, who is goodness, truth, and beauty itself—its "both/and" is to heaven and earth, that radiant unity-in-difference that molds and moves its people.

Of course, none of this is to say that the Way is tidy or easy. It's neither. The Way comes with principles, but not with a script; it requires careful discernment and constant prudence. Those who walk it bring a great variety of gifts—temperaments, experiences, insights—and tend to stress one element in a given dilemma, even as all those gifts are drawn together in the unity of the Church, where "iron sharpens iron" (Prov. 27:17). The Catholic both/and doesn't shut down conversation; on the contrary, it's where things really get interesting. It's a path of tension and drama, of self-assessment and self-correction, of fine-tuning and hair-splitting—one that always makes the oversimplifications of the either/or look so tempting. Indeed, while the "either/or" is often associated with Protestant thought, the debates of the Reformation are just one chapter—in this book, the last chapter—in a broader story, one that very much involves Catholic history.

You will, I hope, see your own journey and the journeys of

5. C.S. Lewis, *The Screwtape Letters* and *Mere Christianity*, in the *Signature Classics* (New York: HarperOne, 2002), 204, 150.

those you know all over these case studies of heavenward and earthward ways, just as I have, even though so many of them are from long ago. "There is nothing new under the sun"—nothing but the Way "making all things new" (Eccles. 1:9; Rev. 21:5). And the methodical yet brisk approach will hopefully keep the journey from being either too cursory or too cumbersome. It will involve passing through old and difficult arguments, but not for long—because the argument of this book is the arguments themselves.

But my greatest hope is that this book will bring the reader closer to answering that greatest question: *What does it mean to be human?* All of our questions, even that of God, pivot off this question, because even our search for God is inescapably a human search. Man himself is the question. Nothing is as common, familiar, or obvious, yet as precious, distant, or mysterious. And whether we succeed or fail in our attempt at an answer, Joseph Ratzinger was right: "There is no escape from the dilemma of being a man."[6]

6. Joseph Ratzinger, *Introduction to Christianity*, 2nd ed., trans. J.R. Foster (San Francisco: Ignatius, 2004), 45.

PRELUDE

The Things: The Heavens or the Earth

We've been born into a world of heaven and earth. No matter where we go, and no matter what we do, we're always oriented by the sky above and the ground below. If we go outside, we see the sun and the stars above us and the ground under and around us. If we stay inside, the roof and walls above our head shield us from the rain and snow, and the foundation beneath our feet digs into the dirt and rock. Even when we soar above the clouds in a plane, there remain the heavens above and the earth below. Modern technology has distanced us from this basic truth, but it's always there: the heavens and the earth shape all that we do and all that we are. There is nothing more basic to our experience of the world.

Science, of course, has changed how we think about these surroundings, purifying us of primitive notions. We now know that there's no real "sky," but only the scattering of blue light in earth's atmosphere, and no real "above," but only the vast space of the cosmos surrounding a spherical earth. Yet the essential thing remains: a polarity between "up there" and "down here." In fact, even if we become an interplanetary species, as bodily creatures we'll always experience a given space and the greater space beyond it.

And we'll always be faced with the choice between looking at one or the other in any given moment. We can't so much as glance at the heavens above and the earth below at one and the same time. We can look at the horizon line connecting them, and we can look back and forth between them, but we can't fully hold them together in view. We can either gaze upward at the sky or around and down at the earth; we can either look along a vertical plane or a horizontal plane. They are divided in a zero-sum game: the more we fill our field of vision with the heavens, the less we see of the earth, and vice versa.

The Latin root of "decision," *decidere*, means to cut: and to decide to look one way is necessarily to cut off the other way. In any given moment, we're making a decision: Should we ignore the world around us for a moment and take in the power and glory of the sky? Or should we ignore the sky above us and hit the ground running? We can't do both; we're only human.

|

Faced with this dilemma, we might go the *heavenward* way: we decide to look up at the sky. We keep our gaze vertical and our posture fixed, contemplating the stars above in a kind of rapture.

When we gaze at the sky like this—which ancient people so often did—we're transported, even transformed. We seem to be in orbit around our cares. Unlike life on the ground, the sky is majestic, fixed—a beautiful and orderly procession of light moving in predictable patterns. It's also distant and mysterious. What we look at isn't an everyday object within our reach. It's not like a mug of coffee that we can pick up, smell, and sip. Its objects are remote—the most remote things, in fact, that we'll ever see in this life. The stars are even separated from us by time as well as the vastness of space. Yet this celestial realm shines down and affects our world. We can't hold the sun, lasso the moon, or reach the stars; yet the sun burns our skin, the moon moves the sea, and the stars flicker in our eyes. This heavenly show, however remote, is ours; all we need to do is look up.

But the rapture of the heavenward gaze, grand and glorious though it may be, comes at a cost. It takes us up and out of the earth around us—not only the physical earth itself, but also the particular people and concrete things we experience on it. All of it falls outside of our vision. We look at the sky, but we cease to care for the ground. The bright heavens become true reality—the earth, a shadowy distraction.

—

On the other hand, we can take the *earthward* way: we can keep our eyes and hands fixed on what's in front of us, and our bodies on the move horizontally.

Here, we don't stop and gaze up to the lunar, but instead enter the rhythm and energy of the sublunary. If the first way was common in the ancient world, the second is the defining feature of postmodern life: we see, we feel, we react, we go. Life on the ground isn't majestic and fixed, but messy and ever in flux; the only thing that stays the same is change, and we change with it, coping with all of the earth's ambiguities and uncertainties. And what we experience isn't distant or mysterious, but immediate and familiar; it's a whirlpool that pulls us into itself, a parade of places and names and things and voices that enters into us as surely as we step out and enter into it.

But this earthward movement also has its price. By narrowing our focus to the earth, we ignore and forget the glory of the heavens. The world up above would have lifted us up, but we remain too sunk in our own cares to really see it at all. We make progress on practical matters, but the mystery of the universe remains outside of our worried mind. The sky even becomes a kind of artificial painting—a mere backdrop to the stage of earth. The shifting ground becomes true reality—the heavens, an abstract illusion.

All of us in the West today have been shaped, through and through, by the Christian faith; Christianity, for its part, has been shaped, through and through, by the Bible; and the Bible is shaped, through and through, by a singular image that appears throughout its pages, beginning with the very first line of the very first book: "the heavens and the earth" (Gen. 1:1).

The familiarity of this phrase obscures its great power. What the Bible offers us here is a revolution in human perception: we're not looking at the heavens alone, or the earth alone, or the space between them, or one and then the other: we're looking at both at once. The "heavens and the earth" was for the ancient Israelites what *kosmos* was for the Greeks: the term for "the universe," for everything. The limitations of our visual gaze remain, of course—we still can't look fully at one or the other—but Scripture expands that gaze out to the whole, drawing us into the vantage point of the Creator of all things. Our world teaches us that we can't occupy two sights in one look or trod two paths with one step. But right from the beginning, the Bible invites us into a radical new space.

The phrase itself is mysterious—a paradox of twoness and oneness, the ultimate merism uniting two poles into one whole. On the one hand, the heavens and the earth are a duality: they *contrast* with each other. The sky and the ground are clearly not the same thing; if they were, the constant repetition of that lengthy phrase—*hashamayim ve'et ha'aretz* in the Hebrew—would be a lot of unnecessary work. The heavens are above, while the earth is below; they are distinct. In fact, creation involves a whole sequence of orderly contrasts—light and darkness, day and night, dry land and the sea—but it all begins with this first contrast of the heavens and the earth. If one or the other were ignored, the great drama of the Bible would never get underway.

On the other hand, the heavens and the earth are a unity: they *connect* with each other. Despite the clear contrast, they can't be neatly divided, each in its own separate, self-contained space. The sky and the ground are ordered to each other, reach out for each other, participate in each other. This connection is established by a top-down movement, with heaven first lowering itself: the "lights in the dome of the sky" shine down as "signs" and give light to the earth (Gen. 1:14–15), and the land is "watered by rain from the sky" (Deut. 11:11). But the earth doesn't just passively receive this shower of light and water; it responds by growing upward and outward: "The land shall yield its produce, and the tress of the field shall yield their fruit" (Lev. 26:5). The prophet Isaiah captures this down-and-up dance: "The rain and the snow come down from heaven, and do not return there until they have watered the earth, making it bring forth and sprout, giving seed to the sower and bread to the eater" (Isa. 55:10).

The simultaneous contrast and connection of the heavens and the earth is *communion*. And both are necessary: without contrast, there's no *com* (together), no distinction of one from the other; but without connection, there's no *union*, no oneness bridging the distance. The heavens and the earth are neither one indistinct substance nor two separate substances; they're like a lover and beloved in a dance of mutual attraction, the two becoming "one flesh" in marriage (Gen. 2:24). In the biblical vision, all of physical reality begins with this great both/and.

Then again, we now know that the cosmology of Genesis—which imagined a flat earth surrounded by a bowl-shaped dome, the "firmament," separating an ocean above the sky from the oceans around the earth—was mostly wrong. What's more, all of this sky talk was in the service of telling a story about God. Doesn't this make the God of the Bible just another mythological god, like Zeus reigning on Mount Olympus as the god of sky and thunder? Doesn't it confirm the atheist trope that the Bible is just a nice story about a bearded father figure sitting above the clouds? Why does the Bible, and Christianity to this day, put such an emphasis on the sky?

The answer lies neither in science nor in mythology but in poetry. We can't help but think and speak in the symbols of the above and the below: we approach the transcendent with the imagery of the sky, and we approach the mundane with the imagery of the ground. Even the words themselves bear witness to this: "transcendent" comes from the Latin for "climbing over" and "mundane" from the Latin for "world." One person has their head in the clouds; another is grounded. One idea dawns on us; another gets murky. An aspiration is lofty; a resentment is buried. We sing of higher loves and of friends in low places. We gaze at Hollywood stars and praise the down-to-earth. We write of our better angels and of man underground. No one ever wrote of everlasting love using the imagery of grit and mud; it's always the moon and the stars. No one ever spoke of everyday struggle using the imagery of the moon and the stars; it's always grit and mud. The sky and ground are always orienting us, always helping us find our way.

This deeply human impulse reaches a high point in the Scriptures, where "the heavens and the earth" takes us beyond the "everything" of physical reality and into the greater everything of all reality. The sky and the ground are the master metaphor for this greater story—and the heavenward and earthward ways the master metaphors for failing to enter into it.

PART I
The Dilemmas of Life

CHAPTER I

Life: Heaven or Earth

The history of man is haunted by the religious sense: the search for the ultimate meaning of life.

And just as sight throws us into a dilemma of the sky and the ground, life throws us, time and again, into four great dilemmas of heaven and earth: God or man, God's place or man's place, the spiritual or the physical, and the spirit or the flesh. The same zero-sum game between the local vertical and horizontal is in play, but now, we're pulled between an absolute vertical and horizontal: the vertical axis of all things heavenly, and the horizontal axis of all things earthly.

Is the meaning of life in heaven or on earth?

|

The heavenward way is heaven at the expense of earth.

Between the eighth and third centuries BC, something strange happened to humanity, and it was the emergence of this heavenward way. The philosopher Karl Jaspers called it "the Axial Age." It was a time of religious and philosophical awakening in both East and West. From Zarathustra to Plato, the Axial Age produced mystical sages, wild prophets, and lovers of wisdom. All of this spiritual combustion collectively set humanity in a new direction—and that direction was *upward.* Man was becoming aware of "being as a whole," setting for himself "the highest aims" and experiencing his own depths "in the clarity of transcendence."[1]

This heavenward zeitgeist came to fruition with Gnosticism, a strange but captivating constellation of religious sects combining Greek thought and Eastern religion. Gnostic teachings appeared on the earth like the monolith of *2001: A Space Odyssey*—ominous, alien, and utterly vertical. A line from Robert Frost captures the Gnostic view of life: after seeing a spider with a dead moth on a flower, the poet asks, "What but design of darkness to appall? / If design govern in a thing so small."[2] For the Gnostics, this earth is an appalling design of darkness and death, right down to its smallest details. God, on the other hand, is spiritual light and life, completely transcendent and unknowable. He dwells eternally in the highest heights, surrounded by various divine beings. Sparks of divinity are trapped here below, including deep within us: this is the *pneuma* (spirit)—the true self. But God didn't create this world and wants nothing to do with it; rather, it's the work of a lesser god who rules over man with an iron fist. We're caught in this world like a moth in a spider web. What binds us here isn't sin, but ignorance, and the way out isn't salvation, but *gnosis* (knowledge).

1. Karl Jaspers, *Way to Wisdom: An Introduction to Philosophy*, trans. Ralph Manheim (New Haven: Yale University Press, 1954), 100.

2. Robert Frost, "Design," in *Anthology of Modern American Poetry*, ed. Cary Nelson (Oxford: Oxford University Press, 2000), 96.

Gnosticism has been called the first great Christian heresy, but the father of all Gnostics, Simon Magus, was already busy proclaiming his own gospel in Samaria when St. Philip arrived there to proclaim Jesus. The Acts of the Apostles tells us that he was dazzling people with magic, and that they called him "the power of God that is called Great" (Acts 8:9–10). The Church Father Irenaeus gives us more detail: Simon presented himself as "the Being who is the Father over all," and his companion, a prostitute called Helena, as the latest physical dwelling of his own divine mind, which had fallen from the spiritual realm above down into this deteriorated world below, "passing from body to body."[3]

Gnostic movements, fresh from the Axial Age, eventually latched onto the story of Jesus and assimilated it. Many taught that Jesus was a divine messenger from above, not God himself, and that his humanity was really just an illusion; therefore, he didn't really suffer and die as a human being at all, but only *seemed* to. St. John warns the early Christians about these "Docetists" (from the Greek *dokeo*, "to seem"): "Many deceivers have gone out into the world, those who do not confess that Jesus Christ has come in the flesh; any such person is the deceiver and the antichrist!" (2 John 7).

The Gnostics capture something vital, something that speaks to us in the deepest recesses of our being—namely, the fascination with and longing for heaven above. They affirm, with great religious zeal, the reality and superiority of the vertical. That the Apostles and the Fathers had to protest so frequently and so firmly against these movements is telling: Gnosticism was the ultimate heavenward challenger to Christianity for the heart of the world.

3. Irenaeus, *Against the Heresies* 1.23.1–2. Unless otherwise indicated, Church Fathers quotations are from the Ante-Nicene or Nicene and Post-Nicene Fathers series, available at newadvent.org.

But this heavenward way leaves us in a high-strung dualism of heaven and earth. We learn the knowledge of God, but a rejection of man; the longing for a pure place above, but a rejection of this place below; the pursuit of the spiritual, but a rejection of the physical; and the release of the spirit in death, but a rejection of the flesh in life. But there's no escape; all these earthly things surround and assault us on the way up—and disgust and dread deaden the very spirit we long to liberate.

—

The earthward way is earth at the expense of heaven.

Something just as gradual, universal, and transformative as the Axial Age has been happening to humanity in our time, and it's a reorientation toward this earthward way. We're too immersed in it to really see it, but we can confidently call it something like a New Axial Age. It's an age not of transcendental vision, but of practical revolution—of rapid technological, cultural, and political change. The themes of the New Axial Age are the polar opposite of the Axial: man lays aside being as a whole for being in its parts, the highest aims for the most practical, and the clarity of transcendence for "the iron grip of immanence."[4] An instinct for the vertical no longer comes naturally to us, and even if we strive for it, it often remains an affectation, a live action role-play. All of us—religious and nonreligious alike—are children of this horizontal worldview.

Is there a counterpoint to Gnosticism in the New Axial Age? It's tempting to say agnosticism (a-gnostic). But the agnostic

4. Walker Percy, *Lost in the Cosmos: The Last Self-Help Book* (New York: Picador, 1983), 124.

only refrains from making any knowledge claims about God and heaven; he doesn't close himself off to them, and certainly not to the spiritual. Instead, the ultimate counterpoint to Gnosticism is secularism—from the Latin *saeculum* meaning "world" or "age." The secularist doesn't believe in God, but turns his attention instead to exalting man; he doesn't believe in a world beyond this one, but turns his attention instead to social progress; he doesn't believe in the spiritual, but defaults to science in explaining everything; and he doesn't believe in the spirit, but finds happiness in life's little pleasures and victories. Secularists, like the Gnostics, claim Jesus as their own, but in their hands, he isn't a divine messenger from above, but a purely human teacher from below. His life is about his message, and his message is earthly: feeding the poor, unsettling the establishment, not judging others, being kind to one another.

Secularism is the new ultimate challenger to Christianity—and it's not without its merits. Its great virtue is affirming what so many heavenward souls have denied: the inherent goodness of man, the world, and the body. Where the heavenward spurn the earthly with pessimistic disgust, the earthward embrace it with optimistic hope.

But that optimism leaves us dissatisfied and restless. We look for happiness all around us—in people and places, in pleasures and passions—but we never quite find it. The earth, beautiful as it can be, only disappoints in the end: the delight we take in things fades away, and if it doesn't, they do. And over time, the weight of the world—man's cruelty, society's injustice, the fragility of the physical, the frailty of the flesh—is too much to bear. Without a light from heaven, we can only plod deeper into the mud—a darkening path of confusion and sorrow that leads to a dead end.

+

The Way is both heaven and earth.

The Bible opens with the heavens and earth we see, but only to open us to the heaven and earth we live: God and man, God's place and ours, the spiritual and the physical, the spirit and the flesh. Yet rather than leave the associations of sky and ground behind, it leans into them. Like a wise teacher, God's Word meets us where we are—in a world of the vertical and horizontal—to take us both higher and deeper.

This happens first through language itself, which connects the sky to God and his "place." "Heaven," "the heavens," and "sky" are all translations of the exact same Hebrew word: the plural *shamayim* (the root of which means "lofty"). God's "place" is the heaven beyond all heavens, "the heaven of heavens" (Deut. 10:14). "Heaven," in line with rabbinic tradition, is also sometimes used as a metonymy for God to show respect to his name, as when Matthew speaks of "the kingdom of heaven" in place of "the kingdom of God." The terms "God" and "heaven" are so closely related that we can even speak of God himself as heaven, and heaven itself as God.

Likewise, the Scriptures connect the ground to man and his world. The word for "ground" (*erets*) is also translated as "earth," "world," or "territory." *Erets* isn't just the clumps of dirt under our feet; it's our *place*, the place into which we're all born: "The heavens [*shamayim*] are the LORD's heavens, but the earth [*erets*] he has given to human beings" (Ps. 115:16). The Hebrew *adam* (human being) is also a play on words with *adamah* (meaning "red soil" or "ground"): "The LORD God formed man [*adam*] from the dust of the ground [*adamah*]" (Gen. 2:7). *Adamah* can also be translated as "earth" and even "land." Genesis later equates man with *apar* (dust): "You are dust, and to dust you shall return" (Gen. 3:19). Even our word "human" comes from the Latin *humus* (earth).

But this is just the beginning: the connections are not only linguistic but also symbolic. God and heaven are constantly associated with sky images in the Old Testament, most especially light. But we also hear of what appears in the sky (the stars, the moon, and especially the sun), what emerges from the sky (clouds and rain, lightning and thunder, storms and whirlwinds, falling fire and soaring rainbows), and of what rises to the sky (eagles and their wings, the cedars of Lebanon, and the many biblical mountains). The vision of heaven in the book of Revelation, the last book of the Bible, is a sort of climactic finale in which all of these sky images reappear.

The ground images the Bible uses to describe man and the world are no less varied and constant. We hear of what makes up the earth (clay and soil, dust and ashes), of what rises from and sinks back to the earth (grass and flowers, worms and beasts), and of what runs along the earth (fading shadows and fleeting winds). All three categories of earth appear in Psalm 103, which also contrasts them with the height of heaven:

> For as the heavens are high above the earth,
> so great is his steadfast love toward those who fear him. . . .
> For he knows how we were made;
> he remembers that we are dust.
> As for mortals, their days are like grass;
> they flourish like a flower of the field;

for the wind passes over it, and it is gone,
   and its place knows it no more. (Ps. 103:11, 14–16)

The same associations link the spiritual to heaven and the physical to earth. God and his place are pure spirit; thus, spirits, blessings, and all kinds of invisible realities—especially angels, those spiritual creatures so often associated with the sky—have a close kinship with heaven. By contrast, waters, fields, plants, flowers, and especially animals are closely associated with earth.

Thus, in the Bible, the sky and the ground are the great images for heaven and earth, in all their meanings. And the point of all this—the upshot of this great pattern—is that the communion we observe in the first pair is an image of what God intends for all the others. Heavenly things keep their primacy, but earthly things are being drawn into union with them. Communion, with the same tension of contrast and connection, is the heart of biblical religion.

We see all of this come together in the twenty-eighth chapter of Genesis. Jacob stops in the middle of a journey to lay down on the ground for the night, resting his head on a stone. In his horizontal posture on the earth, he has a vertical vision of heaven: "He dreamed that there was a ladder set up on the earth, the top of it reaching to heaven; and the angels of God were ascending and descending on it." God speaks to him, promising him that "the land on which you lie I will give to you and to your offspring." Jacob arises in the morning, declaring, "How awesome is this place! This is none other than the house of God, and this is the gate of heaven."

This is the famous "Jacob's ladder." The word behind "ladder," *sullam*, really means more of a stairway or a stepped ramp, but the idea is the same: a path, a connection, a way. And it's a way connecting heaven and earth. Jacob, a visionary on the move, sees heaven and earth commune: God and man, paradise and the world, angels and rocks, spirit and flesh—all through the lens of the sky above and the ground below. This is the biblical dream: that heaven and earth would become one.

And in first-century Palestine, an itinerant rabbi declared this dream fulfilled in himself: "Very truly, I tell you, you will see heaven opened and the angels of God ascending and descending upon the Son of Man" (John 1:51).

CHAPTER 2

The People: God or Man

The heart of man is a search for God. This experience is written into our history, both personal and collective. But from it comes a fatal distortion: God and man appear divided, rivals in a zero-sum game. We're thus thrown into the primary dilemma between heaven and earth. It seems like we have to embrace either the way of divinity or the way of humanity; there's no other way.

Is ultimate reality in God or man?

I

The heavenward way is God at the expense of man.

We see this impulse in the Gnostic sect of Manichaeism. Mani, under the influence of Zoroastrian dualism, taught that behind reality there stand two opposite forces, the "Father of Greatness" and the "King of Darkness," which dwell in eternally separated realms of good and evil, light and darkness. The first is associated with *pneuma* (spirit) and the second with *hyle* (matter), though spirit and matter are ultimately composed of the same "stuff." The world,

Mani taught, began with a clash between these two realms: the darkness rushed up to the light and launched an attack against it. Eventually, some of the powers of darkness devoured some of the light, mingling the two substances together. The powers of light then struck back and conquered them, forming the world from their mixed corpses. The world is thus a vast chamber of death confining the swallowed light. This cosmic prison is ruled by the "archons," evil powers of that same dark kingdom.

But what is man? In Manichaean teaching, he is, quite literally, the spawn of Satan. In a devious plan to hold on to as much of the light as possible, the King of Darkness had two of his demons devour other light-infused demons and then mate with each other, and their offspring became the first human beings: Adam and Eve. But the *pneuma*, the light of spirit, remains buried within this creature of darkness, and it needs to be liberated—making humanity a key battleground in the cosmic war.

This is where Jesus, on the Manichaean reading, enters the picture: not as a savior, but as a messenger of light from above. Jesus is sent to liberate the sparks of divinity—fragments of his own light substance—which are being endlessly devoured and trampled in the darkness here below. Through spiritual acts of self-denial and ritual purity—and also through the rays of the sun—the light is released and lifted up and out of the world. The moon, for the Manichaeans, is a celestial ferryboat: when it waxes, it's filling up with spiritual light from below, and when it wanes, it's delivering that light to the sun, and from the sun, to its home above with the Father of Greatness. Once all the spiritual light is freed, this world will burn up and disappear.

Manichaeism speaks not only to our longing to find divine

perfection but also to our longing to escape a raging sea of wickedness and ignorance. However bizarre its teachings may sound today, it was one of the most popular religions of the first millennium, cropping up again and again in new forms well into the medieval era: the Bogomils of Bulgaria, the Cathars or "pure ones," and, most notoriously, the Albigensian branch of the Cathars. The world can be a very dark, foreboding, and unforgiving place, and human history—so glutted on greed, lust, cruelty, and pride—at times appears a macabre parade that we're forced to march in yet helpless to change. Manichaeism gives voice to this great anguish at ourselves.

But can we escape our own humanity so easily? For the heavenward, the true man of God is a man beyond men, deeply suspicious of all things human. But this heavenward narrative puts us in a strange bind: its very refusal of man is itself a deeply human act, midwifed by the mind and heart. Even as we resist humanity, our own humanity does the resisting. We can utterly separate the *pneuma* from our own lives—our thoughts, our desires, our choices—but in that case, "we" seem to disappear altogether. We're not so much elevated as extinguished.

Even setting aside this theoretical problem, the heavenward campaign against man delivers us, on a practical level, into inhuman heights. It offers us a sense of direction, but at the cost of a profound alienation. We're stripped of our innate goodness, becoming so much devilish rubbish; a mood of terror and paranoia engulfs the human experience here below; and the spiritual journey becomes brutal and colorless. We have to escape ourselves, but until we die, we can't; we can't embrace what's human, but if we're really to live at all, we have to.

—

The earthward way is man at the expense of God.

There are many trails on this earthward side, but we find the polar opposite of Manichaeism in modern atheistic humanism. For the atheistic humanist, all talk of divinity has to be left behind as an illusion, and the true humanist has to be a man beyond God.

This earthward path was forged by the titans of modern atheism: Friedrich Nietzsche in philosophy, Sigmund Freud in psychology, Karl Marx in politics. But all of these titans were shaped by the same German thinker before them: Ludwig Feuerbach. "God," for Feuerbach, is simply man's outward and upward projection of his own greatness: "The more empty life is, the fuller, the more concrete is God. The impoverishing of the real world and the enriching of God is one act. Only the poor man has a rich God."[1] To arrive at intellectual maturity, we have to reclaim everything we gave to God for ourselves.

Like Manichaeism, atheistic humanism has gone from an arcane doctrine to a popular phenomenon. A growing number of Western denizens identify as atheists and regard God as an illusion. Even where religious identity prevails, a de facto atheism often operates under the surface: when push comes to shove, man edges out God.

And like its ancient heavenward counterpoint, the way of man has its attractions and even its merits. It digs beneath the reality of man's wickedness to find his inherent goodness, exalting as noble everything that the Gnostic rejects as hopelessly corrupted: the human body with its desires and passions, human experience with

1. Ludwig Feuerbach, *The Essence of Christianity*, trans. Marian Evans (London: Trübner, 1881), 73.

its ambiguities and complexities, human creativity with its questions and advances. Where Gnosticism says no to man, atheistic humanism says yes.

But can man live without worshiping? David Foster Wallace answered no: "In the day-to-day trenches of adult life, there is actually no such thing as atheism. There is no such thing as not worshiping. Everybody worships. The only choice we get is *what* to worship."[2] In the absence of God, every man still treats something as his sky. Worship is our spiritual energy: it's neither created nor destroyed—only converted. And its most alluring form in the New Axial Age—and the height of human folly—is self-worship. This is often more covert than overt, but for Feuerbach, "Man is the true God and Savior of man";[3] through religion, we were really adoring ourselves all along, and to truly go beyond God, we have to embrace it.

The earthward depths also risk becoming every bit as inhuman as the heavenward heights. We tunnel through the caverns of our own minds, but with no ultimate sense of direction or purpose. Nietzsche powerfully captured this heavenless vertigo with his parable of the madman, who proclaims the death of God not as a triumphant victory but as a disorienting plummet: "What were we doing when we unchained this earth from its sun? Where is it moving to now? Where are we moving to? Away from all suns? Are we not continually falling? And backwards, sidewards, forwards, in all

2. David Foster Wallace, *This Is Water: Some Thoughts, Delivered on a Significant Occasion, about Living a Compassionate Life* (New York: Little, Brown, 2009), 98–101.

3. Feuerbach, *Essence of Christianity*, 277.

directions? Is there still an up and a down?"[4] Any turn is now possible, even justifiable: without God, "everything is permitted."[5] The atheist can still do good and know truth, but only from within a freefall beyond both. On the way of man, man loses his way.

+

The Way is both God and man.

"He came down from heaven." This line of the ancient Nicene Creed holds a unique importance in the liturgy of the Catholic Church. After the word "heaven" and through the following line ("And by the Holy Spirit was incarnate of the Virgin Mary, and became man"), the faithful are instructed to bow—and then, only after "heaven" has reached "man," do they again raise their eyes. It's the only formal gesture called for during the entire recitation of the Creed.

This profound bow is meant to signal humility and awe before the "distinctive sign" of Christianity: the Incarnation.[6] "For us men and for our salvation"—finite and fallen though we are—God *became* man in Jesus of Nazareth: "In the beginning was the Word, and the Word was with God, and the Word was God. . . . And the Word became flesh and lived among us" (John 1:1, 14). More stunning still, he became a helpless baby: "God's infinity / Dwindled to infancy / Welcome in womb and breast / Birth, milk,

4. Friedrich Nietzsche, *The Gay Science*, trans. Josefine Nauckhoff (Cambridge: Cambridge University Press, 2003), 120.

5. Fyodor Dostoevsky, *The Brothers Karamazov*, trans. Richard Pevear and Larissa Volokhonsky (New York: Farrar, Straus and Giroux, 1990), 589.

6. *Catechism of the Catholic Church* 463.

and all the rest."[7] This is the "fullness of time" (Gal. 4:4), the final revelation of the God of Israel, whose exalted titles—the Lord of heaven and earth, who is "God in heaven above and on the earth beneath" (Deut. 4:39)—burst open into a resplendent and shocking new meaning. The heart of God, it turns out, is a search for man: we couldn't work our way up to God, so God climbed down to us. This is how the Good News begins: "The kingdom of God has come near" (Mark 1:15). Christ is "'Emmanuel,' which means, 'God is with us'" (Matt. 1:23).

We see the full power of the Incarnation by turning back to the first three chapters of Genesis, where we find five key "originals." First, there is an original blessing: creation is "good," and with the creation of man, "very good" (Gen. 1:28–31). Adam and Eve are commissioned to populate the earth and invited to eat freely of all the garden's trees except one—a tree that, by refusing the contrast between God and man, would destroy man. Everything that God has is theirs. In Eden, heaven and earth, in all their meanings, are in communion.

Then comes the original lie, spewed by "the father of lies" (John 8:44): that Creator and creature are in competition with each other. "God knows that when you eat of it," the serpent says of the tree, "your eyes will be opened, and you will be like God" (Gen. 3:5). We hear in this lie a heavenward whisper: a rejection of our status as creatures. In fact, the Gnostic Ophites even taught that the serpent (*ophis*) wasn't a tempter at all, but rather a heavenly messenger from above trying to free Adam and Eve through *gnosis*. But we also feel

7. Gerard Manley Hopkins, "The Blessed Virgin compared to the Air we Breathe," in *As Kingfishers Catch Fire*, ed. Holly Ordway (Elk Grove Village, IL: Word on Fire Institute, 2023), 67.

here an earthward nudge: a rejection of the authority of the Creator. The serpent challenges man to reject both his own humanity and God's divinity. Thus, in the serpent's lie, man is drawn—simultaneously—into the errors of both sides.

Adam and Eve accept the lie as the truth, and fall into it—and original sin enters the world. This is the "false earth"—a corruption of God's good creation and the loss of holiness and harmony—and it's passed on to all their descendants, not as a personal act but as a general state, a wretchedness contracted just by virtue of being human.

Out of this original sin also comes an original division: the division between God and man. And out of this division comes *all* division. It's not only that Adam and Eve have divided themselves from God; they've also divided God's place from man's place, themselves from the world, and each from the other. They've even divided their spirits from their bodies—a division that ends in death, which is "the wages of sin" (Rom. 6:23). After the fall, man looks out at a world torn asunder.

But division isn't where the story ends; this is the message of the "protoevangelium"—the original Gospel, proclaimed by God himself: "I will put enmity between you and the woman, and between your offspring and hers; he will strike your head, and you will strike his heel" (Gen. 3:15). A mysterious descendent of the woman will conquer both Satan and sin by suffering their torments, and reunify God and man. This is God's promise, even as he casts man outside the garden and places a cherubim with flaming sword to guard "the way to the tree of life" (Gen. 3:24).

The whole Old Testament is filled with rumblings of this reunion: God's covenants with Noah, Abraham, Moses, and David; his formation of the people Israel through the Law and the prophets; the tabernacle and the temple in Jerusalem, where God made his dwelling among the Israelites (Exod. 25:8; 1 Kings 6:13). But it's in the small village of Nazareth that God and man finally become one again. The angel Gabriel visits the Virgin Mary, inviting her to become the mother of Jesus, "Son of the Most High" (Luke 1:32). Through her *fiat*, her "let it be" (Luke 1:38), the Way bursts forth into the world, beginning in a humble family.

Jesus wasn't (as the Gnostics held) God *seeming* like a man, nor (as the atheistic humanists hold) a man *seeming* like God. He was true God: "You are from below," he says, "I am from above; you are of this world, I am not of this world" (John 8:23). But he was also true man: "Jesus Christ has come in the flesh" (1 John 4:2). Christ was the Son of God, and whoever saw him saw the heavenly Father (John 14:9). But he was also the Son of Man, and whoever saw him saw his earthly mother (Mark 6:3). Jesus is neither God alone nor man alone, nor is he half man and half God; he's fully God and fully man. He's the communion of the heavenly God and earthly man without any competition between them—a scandal to both the Axial and New Axial Ages.

Why the Incarnation? St. Athanasius beautifully articulated the Christian answer: *theosis*, or divinization. "The Son of God became man so that we might become God."[8] Out of sheer love, God wants humanity to become one with him—to become, by faith and participation in his divine life, "gods" (John 10:34). Christ is both God's descent to man and man's ascent to God; he became a participant of our human nature that we might become "participants of the divine nature" (2 Pet. 1:4).

8. *Catechism* 460; Athanasius, *On the Incarnation* 54.3.

But Jesus is not only the Way, the *hodos*, to divine life, but also the Way out, the *Ex-hodos*, from sin and death. Thus, the Incarnation culminates in the Crucifixion. In the Nicene Creed, the bow of the Incarnation is immediately followed by this stunning blow, the sore wounding of this sacred head: "For our sake he was crucified under Pontius Pilate." God sends his Son all the way into godforsakenness, allowing him who knew no sin or death to become sin and die—and "by his wounds you have been healed" (1 Pet. 2:24). The cross is the tree of life that wrought our salvation.

This is the trajectory of divine love, two movements that can't be separated: "Love by its very nature tends to an incarnation, and an incarnation by its very nature tends to a crucifixion."[9] The wood of the crib leads to the wood of the cross, and the vertical and the horizontal that meet in Bethlehem lead to the two beams on Calvary:

> Let the same mind be in you that was in Christ Jesus,
> who, though he was in the form of God,
> did not regard equality with God
> as something to be exploited,
> but emptied himself,
> taking the form of a slave,
> being born in human likeness.
> And being found in human form,
> he humbled himself
> and became obedient to the point of death—
> even death on a cross. (Phil. 2:5–8)

9. Fulton J. Sheen, *The Mystical Body of Christ* (Elk Grove Village, IL: Word on Fire, 2023), 174.

This is the Christian vision of ultimate reality. And it has devastating consequences for both sides of the God-man dilemma. Christianity resists a heavenward anti-humanism because God has brought the divine down to the human. The Psalmist asked, "What are human beings that you are mindful of them?" (Ps. 8:4). But the Christian poses a far more radical question: What are human beings that you have *become* one of them? Christ was without sin, but otherwise, nothing human was alien to him; he can "sympathize with our weaknesses" and was in every respect "tested as we are" (Heb. 4:15). The heavenward man who denies man on behalf of God is reduced to silence before the God who became man on behalf of men.

But just as we can choose God without dispensing with man (since Christ is fully human), we can also choose man without dispensing with God (since Christ is fully divine). Thus, Christianity also resists an earthward humanism, because in Christ, man has been "invaded" by God; there's no longer a purely human sphere—again, aside from sin—where God can't be found. God still has an absolute primacy over man—and indeed "first place in everything" (Col. 1:18)—but the whole great drama of human existence is now one with him. Man is now a child of God and sibling of his Son, grafted onto his Body and brought into relationship with him forever. And when we receive Christ, we're transformed and elevated, but not destroyed: "It is no longer I who live, but it is Christ who lives in me" (Gal. 2:20). Waving the banner of "humanity" is of no avail; God is the ultimate humanist.

The heavenward and the earthward both try to kick away this Jacob's ladder connecting heaven and earth—one from above, the other from below. But the world has been forever changed; it lives in the strange gaze of the God-man.

CHAPTER 3

The Places: God's Place or Man's Place

Man's great search for God is also a search for God's "place"—a world beyond our broken world. This experience, too, comes naturally to us, and it throws us into a second great heaven-earth dilemma: the pull between rising to an eternal realm above and reforming the temporal realm below.

Are we oriented toward God's place or our own?

I

The heavenward way is God's place at the expense of man's place.

This impulse marks Gnosticism as a whole, but we find a prime example in Valentinianism. For this sect, the world didn't start with a divine civil war, but rather with a kind of divine fall. The trouble began when Sophia, one of thirty "aeons" or emanations from God—collectively, the *pleroma* (fullness)—tried to know the unknowable God. She failed, and with devastating consequences: she gave birth to Achamoth or Lower Sophia, a kind of formless daughter, and looked upon her strange progeny with a mix of grief, fear, bewilderment, and ignorance. Lower Sophia and these negative passions then gave rise to the Demiurge, and the Demiurge to the world, shadow upon shadow being cast further and further away from the *pleroma*. But this Lower Sophia secretly injected something of the light from above into the darkness: the *pneuma*, buried deep in man.

In this system, too, Christ is an angelic messenger, a manifestation of the aeons above—one who "came by means of fleshly appearance" but not as true man.[1] When we come to know our tragic origins, we cancel out the cosmic curse begun with Sophia's infraction; our knowledge saves us, lifting us up, here and now, into the light of God's place. And when we die, our liberated spirits rise out of this world to the "middle" realm of Lower Sophia, who, at the end of time, will return to God's place with her spiritual children. As for the world, it will, once again, eventually go up in flames and vanish.

The upshot of this strange story—perhaps less dark and more sophisticated than the Manichaean account, but no less strange—is that this world is one great mistake, one that can't be redeemed, but only evaded. Earth is a lost cause at the furthest reaches from the divine dwelling, linked to it only by a series of accidental shadows. God's place and man's place are utterly foreign to each other—and never the twain shall meet. At best, the world is a distraction keeping our minds off of heaven; at worst, it's a kind of prison of the soul. We're all E.T. stranded on earth and trying to get back home.

1. *The Gospel of Truth*, in *The Nag Hammadi Library in English*, trans. Members of the Coptic Gnostic Library Project of the Institute for Antiquity and Christianity (Leiden: E.J. Brill, 1984), 43.

On this vertical way, the whole goal of life on earth is summarized in one word: *escape*.

Valentinianism wisely recognizes something deep in the human experience—namely, *alienation*. In some profound sense, this world isn't our home; we're strangers in a strange land, and we know it. Gnosticism not only speaks to our rage at human evil; it also speaks to our rage at *natural* evil: ignorance and loss, deformity and disease, predation and destruction—all the forms of physical and mental anguish endlessly churned out by nature. And it encourages us to find fulfillment in a higher plane, where there is no change, no suffering, and no death.

But if this world can be traced back along an unbroken chain to the divine realm, how did we get such a disconnect between God's place and ours? Where is the rupture between light and darkness, eternity and finitude, good and evil? Irenaeus posed this same challenge to the Valentinians: If this world is a kind of shadow of the world above, it has to be continuous with it, since shadows rise or fall with whatever they shadow. Thus, ultimately, either that "higher" world has to be as broken as ours, or our world has to be as unbroken as God's.[2]

The narrative of escape also draws us toward a dangerous indifference regarding life in this world. If this place is just the off-sloughing of fallen powers and will eventually go up in flames—if it's as alien to us as we are to it—why bother? God wants nothing to do with this world, so why should we? Why spend time and energy fussing over education, medicine, agriculture, commerce, engineering, technology, or politics? The vertical gaze may give us

2. Irenaeus, *Against the Heresies* 2.8.1.

hope, but it's an icy hope with no heart. We have no reason to improve and extend life in this world, and every reason to shrug it off and leave it to fester. The universe, bled of its strangeness by our familiarity, is simply "a hat trick in a medicine show, a fevered dream, a trance bepopulate with chimeras having neither analogue nor precedent, an itinerant carnival, a migratory tentshow."[3] The best we can hope for is to be airlifted out of it.

—

The earthward way is man's place at the expense of God's place.

We see a prime example of this earthward tendency in modern utopianism, which seeks to turn earth itself into paradise. And no modern utopian has been more influential than one of Feuerbach's disciples: Karl Marx. The Feuerbachian influence is clear: "The more man puts into God," Marx declares, "the less he retains in himself."[4] Man has found "only his own reflection in the fantastic reality of heaven." Religion is not only the "opium of the people"; it's the "illusory sun about which man revolves so long as he does not revolve about himself."[5] A similar dynamic obtains between God's place and our own: "It is the task of history, once the other-world of truth has vanished, to establish the truth of this world. . . . The critique of heaven is thus transformed into the critique of earth."[6]

3. Cormac McCarthy, *Blood Meridian* (New York: Vintage Books, 1985), 245.

4. Karl Marx, "Estranged Labor," *Economic and Philosophical Manuscripts of 1844*, https://www.marxists.org/archive/marx/works/1844/manuscripts/labour.htm.

5. Karl Marx, "A Contribution to the Critique of Hegel's Philosophy of Right: Introduction," in *Early Political Writings*, ed. and trans. Joseph O'Malley (Cambridge: Cambridge University Press, 1994), 57–58.

6. Marx, 58.

The problem was still alienation—though not from God's world above, but from the fruits of our labor below. And the answer was a revolution to bring about the end of history. Man has to abandon his obsession with heaven and transform the world he has. This is the animating principle behind the last line of the *Communist Manifesto*: "The proletarians have nothing to lose but their chains. They have a world to win."[7] In the Catholic thinker Pierre Teilhard de Chardin's assessment, "The true name of communism should be earthism [*terrénism*]."[8]

This earthward dream continues to echo throughout the culture through John Lennon's "Imagine," which Lennon himself said is "virtually the *Communist Manifesto*, even though I'm not particularly a communist":[9]

> Imagine there's no heaven
> It's easy if you try
> No hell below us
> Above us, only sky
>
> Imagine all the people
> Living for today
>
> Imagine there's no countries
> It isn't hard to do

7. Karl Marx and Friedrich Engels, *The Communist Manifesto* (London: Penguin Books, 2002), 258.

8. Pierre Teilhard de Chardin, "La Crise présente," in *Études*, October 20, 1937; quoted in Henri de Lubac, *The Drama of Atheist Humanism* (San Francisco: Ignatius, 1995), 422–423.

9. John Blaney, *John Lennon: Listen to This Book* (Great Britain: Paper Jukebox, 2005), 83.

Nothing to kill or die for
And no religion too

Marxist utopians go right where religious escapists go wrong. Yes, the world can be a horror show, one filled with great suffering and pain, but it also has profound potential. Rather than casting this place aside as hopeless or worthless and rushing away to higher ground, they strive to use the time available to make the world—from the natural world up through the social world—healthier, happier, and more humane.

But with God and his paradise out of the picture, we're left with a great puzzle: Why does this world exist in the first place? Why is there something rather than nothing at all? The customary response, once given by Bertrand Russell—at one time a supporter of communism—is that the universe is *just there*. It's a "brute fact," and that's as far as we'll ever get in explaining it; our best hope is just to set the question aside and get on with the business of reforming it. But the mystery of the world's presence can't be set aside so nonchalantly; neither the human mind nor the human heart will allow it.

Dreamers of heaven on earth have also yielded earth's most hellish nightmares. Like the heavenward, they know that the world is broken, but in trying to fix it once and for all, they make it that much worse. We find an archetype of this rhythm in the story of the Tower of Babel (Gen. 11:1–9). A unified humanity strives to build a city "and a tower with its top in the heavens" to "make a name" for themselves. Though the tower rises vertically, it's ultimately a great horizontal project: what matters for them—what really grips their minds and hearts—is perfecting life here and now, bringing the greatness of God's place down to man's place. What results is confused languages, scattered peoples, and deserted ruins.

Even a cursory glance at the twentieth century is sufficient proof of the grave dangers of the Marxist Babel. Communism led to chaos wherever it took hold, from the gulags of Russia to the killing fields of Cambodia—each of which alone claimed over a million lives. Reflecting on all the death and destruction in Russia, the dissident Solzhenitsyn repeated a line that he had heard uttered by older men: "Men have forgotten God; that's why all this has happened."[10] Forgotten God—and imagined away his heaven. This earthward way has heart, but snuffs out all hope. The towers are ever new, but they always end in destruction. Utopia remains as its name signals in the Greek: "no place."

The Way is both God's place and man's place.

In the Our Father, the great prayer that Jesus taught his disciples, he doesn't encourage them to escape earth for heaven, which is what we would expect from a Gnostic prophet; nor does he encourage them to turn earth into heaven, which is what we would expect from a utopian dreamer. Instead, he encourages them to pray for God's will to be done "on earth as it is in heaven" (Matt. 6:10). The Christian mission is neither flight nor fight; it's *forge*—stubbornly calling heaven down to earth and lifting earth up to heaven, but

10. Templeton Prize, "Acceptance Address by Mr. Aleksandr Solzhenitsyn," May 10, 1983, https://www.templetonprize.org/laureate-sub/solzhenitsyn-acceptance-speech/.

without ever confusing the two. It holds promise "both for the present life and the life to come" (1 Tim. 4:8). God's place and man's place are mysteriously *about* and *for* one another—through, with, and in the Son.

Scripture goes even further. The Incarnation is the beginning of the Way—the coming together of heaven and earth—but it will only reach its fulfillment when, through Christ and in Christ, this world in every nook and cranny becomes one with heaven. At that time, St. Paul writes, all things will be subjected to the Son, "so that God may be all in all" (1 Cor. 15:24–25, 28). God will make "all things new"—"a new heaven and a new earth" united with paradise, all of it illuminated by the Lamb of God (Rev. 21:5, 1, 23). And we won't float *up* to this New Jerusalem; on the contrary, it will *come down* (Rev. 3:12, 21:2), just as the Son came down from heaven.

Though Christians often speak of "going to heaven" as the end goal of the journey—and, in saying that, imagine being in a purely spiritual heaven forever—this isn't what the Bible teaches. Instead, it teaches that the "eschaton" (end) is God's place and man's place again becoming one. The darkness of the world isn't the darkness of a tomb but the darkness of a womb: it's "groaning in labor pains" as it awaits the birth of the new creation (Rom. 8:22). What this transfigured cosmos will be like, "no eye has seen, nor ear heard, nor the human heart conceived" (1 Cor. 2:9). But it's what "eternal life" will be: a new world without end. And it's the consummation, in Christ, of the Way. He's the Alpha and the Omega, "the first and the last, the beginning and the end" (Rev. 22:13).

The Way, therefore, casts off heavenward escapism. This world isn't a cosmic fluke or a launching pad to rocket us into a spiritual paradise; it's *good*: "For you love all things that exist, and detest none of the things that you have made" (Wis. 11:24). This is precisely why God sent his only Son: because he "loved the world" (John 3:16). As God loves the world, so we should love the world—not the false world of sin (1 John 2:15–17), but the true world of God's good creation. Thus, with the earthward, those on the Way alleviate the suffering of the poor, the imprisoned, the sick, and all the marginalized of society here below. They cultivate the land, the culture, and all the things that make life in this world wonderful. C.S. Lewis, in an echo of his teacher (Matt. 6:33), wrote that heaven has to take the priority: "Aim at Heaven and you will get earth 'thrown in': aim at earth and you will get neither."[11] But this doesn't mean turning our backs on the world; on the contrary, "the Christians who did most for the present world were just those who thought most of the next."[12] We can't be, as Johnny Cash sang, so heavenly minded we're no earthly good, precisely because earth itself is destined for heaven.

At the same time, the Way also casts off the other extreme of utopianism. The world is indeed fallen and incapable of saving itself; it needs help from outside. Christian hope, therefore, can't be aimed at this world—and when we get this wrong, we get everything wrong. Man remains a kind of spiritual castaway, a pilgrim on the way to a higher kingdom in God: "Life is your barque not your home!"[13] Utopias fail because we were never meant to look for heaven on earth or make ourselves too comfortable here.

Christ thus opens up an interplay between the light of God's place and the darkness of man's. It's a Way of both consolation and

11. C.S. Lewis, *Mere Christianity*, in the *Signature Classics* (New York: HarperOne, 2002), 112.

12. Lewis, 112.

13. Thérèse of Lisieux, *Story of a Soul* (Park Ridge, IL: Word on Fire Classics, 2022), 89.

desolation, both understanding and ignorance, both joy and suffering. When we share in Christ's sufferings, we rejoice (1 Pet. 4:13); even original sin, the source of all our trouble, is a *felix culpa*, a happy fault. We remain in this place, but its many shades of darkness—both literal and existential—bless the Lord (Dan. 3:72). Without that darkness below, we're left with a divine farce, and without the light of grace above, a human tragedy; both together yield the divine comedy.

The troubles of this world are ours, but we're not theirs. "Teach us to care and not to care," T.S. Eliot wrote—and this isn't a contradiction in terms, but a deeply Christian prayer on the Way.[14]

14. T.S. Eliot, "Ash Wednesday," in *Collected Poems (1909–1962)* (New York: Harcourt, Brace, 1962), 86, 95.

CHAPTER 4

Man's Place: The Spiritual or the Physical

When we zoom in on the world itself, we again see a heaven-earth dilemma. Man's place is not just earthly; it also contains glimmers of heavenly light. We experience not only physical realities, which ground us in this world below, but also higher spiritual ones, which speak of a world we can't touch or see.

Should we place our trust in the spiritual or the physical?

I

The heavenward way is the spiritual at the expense of the physical.

A heavenward dualism is the defining feature of all Gnosticism: the world, for the Gnostics, is a great tug-of-war between the spiritual and the material. And accompanying this dualism was a plunge into spirituality and a rejection of the physical as a kind of trap: the more we become entangled in physical things, the worse we become.

The Gnostics were especially alert to three dangers: meat, wine, and sex. Gnostic literature regularly treats the first two as images of worldly entrapment: "They mixed me drink with their cunning, and gave me to taste of their meat."[1] These themes persisted wherever Gnosticism latched onto Christianity: the Encratites (from the Greek *enkrateia*, meaning "self-control") refused to eat animal meat, and the Aquarians (from the Latin *aqua*, for "water") refused to drink wine on the altar. But sex—because of its natural orientation to new life—was, for the Gnostics, the very icon of spiritual death. A new baby wasn't a gift; it was a tragedy—yet another snare for the divine light in this darkness. In Genesis, God's first command to Adam and Eve is "be fruitful and multiply" (Gen. 1:28); in the *Poimandres*, a mystical text with ties to the Valentinian movement, the line is repeated with a kind of derision, and followed by a summons to do the exact opposite: "The cause of death is love. . . . [Anyone] who has cherished the body issued from the error of love, he remains in the darkness erring, suffering in his senses the dispensations of death."[2]

The Manichaeans systematized this rejection of the physical. For Mani, the great war between the Father of Greatness and the King of Darkness penetrated the whole world. Human beings were surrounded by these two warring principles—light and darkness, good and evil, spirit and matter, the pure and the impure—and it was incumbent upon them to take up with the right side and join the fight.

The ideal Manichaean—the one who maximally released the particles of divine light—disentangled himself from the physical as much as possible. This meant abstaining from animal flesh, wine,

1. *The Hymn of the Pearl*, in Hans Jonas, *The Gnostic Religion* (Boston: Beacon, 2001), 114.

2. *The Poimandres of Hermes Trismegistus* 17–18, in Jonas, 152.

and, of course, marriage and "the procreation of children," which would sink the divine light "deeper in matter."[3] But this was just the beginning. It also meant not having possessions, a trade, or a place to call home; it meant not killing animals or even plucking fruit, which might harm the light inside; it even meant being careful about the movement of one's feet on the ground and hands through the air, since divine light was trapped even in those basest of elements. One Manichaean confession manual took religious guilt to a whole new level: "We always and incessantly, in thought, word, and deed, and in seeing with our eyes, in hearing with our ears, in speaking with our mouths, in grasping with our hands, and in walking with our feet, torment the Light."[4]

Naturally, very few were able to live at such an intense level of spiritual separation. The holy war against the physical was thus reserved for a priestly caste: "the Elect" or "the Perfect." Common believers, hooked as they were on fleshly attachments, were instead given a bare-minimum regimen: avoid certain evils, commit to some prayer and fasting, and, above all, support the Elect. These "Hearers" brought fruits and vegetables on bended knee to their priests for them to set the light free by eating them, but they refused food and even water to non-Manichaean beggars, who would further trap it in this world.

Manichaeism nobly seeks the more essential reality of the spiritual life. Inwardness and prayer, self-denial and self-sacrifice, attentiveness and repentance—all these things tap into a higher plane, connecting us with the blessedness of the divine. The pleasures of the physical, on the other hand—rich meats, hearty wines,

3. Alexander of Lycopolis, *Of the Manicheans* 4.
4. *Chuastuanift*, chap. 15, in Jonas, 232.

passionate embraces—can so easily blunt the mind and heart, sinking us into the carnality of the animals.

But the problem isn't the Gnostic's caution with the physical; it's his rejection of it as inherently evil. Don't we have to take in physical things—air and water, food and drink—all the time? Indeed, don't we have to take them in for the spiritual life to get off the ground in the first place? How does the physical come into such regular contact with the spiritual without degrading it as evil? And how does the spiritual come into such regular contact with the physical without ennobling it as good? The more this dualist dreamscape faces the natural interconnectedness of life, the more incoherent it appears.

This extreme also tends toward enantiodromia—a vengeful eruption of the opposite extreme. The Gnostic disgust with meat and wine and sex, bottled up long enough, exploded into a frenzy of indulgence in all three. In some cases, this was secretive: Augustine, himself a former Manichaean, eviscerates the moral hypocrisy of the Elect, who "were not competent to abstain from the things they professed to abstain from, if they found an opportunity in secret or in the dark": many "were caught at wine and animal food"; others "seduced other men's wives"; and they were generally found to be "full of envy, full of covetousness, full of greed for costly foods, constantly at strife."[5] The worship of a god escaping the belly collapses into the worship of the belly as god (Phil. 3:19).

In other cases, it was out in the open: Gnostic spirituals became libertines freely indulging in physical pleasure, though with marriage and procreation still prohibited, or at least disparaged. Clement of

5. Augustine, *On the Morals of the Manichaeans* 19.71, 68.

Alexandria reports on the orgiastic feasts of the Carpocratians, who taught that everything, including spouses, should be common to all: "After they have stuffed themselves . . . they knock over the lamps, put out the light that would expose their fornicating 'righteousness,' and couple as they will with any woman they fancy."[6] Irenaeus also writes of the Cainites—named for their veneration of Cain, the first murderer—whose "perfect knowledge" involved a complete liberality with the body and a "rush into such actions as it is not lawful even to name."[7]

This libertinism wasn't a rejection of heavenward dualism; it was simply another way of living it out. As gold "submersed in filth" isn't harmed by the filth, they reasoned, so the spiritual is unharmed by submersion in the physical.[8] Like the patrons of *Westworld*, the Gnostic libertines were alien visitors in a kind of play-reality, free to break all the rules. In fact, they *had* to: the spirit is released up to God only after it has committed "every kind of action that can be practiced in this world."[9] The accusation of moral lawlessness would only be a compliment: the moral law is given by the cosmic tyrant enslaving humanity, and the enlightened *pneuma* is over and against the law.

The obsessive rejection of the physical and the compulsive abuse of it—a "purity culture" that abhors sensuality and an impurity culture that gorges on it—are within a hair's breadth of each other; both share in the same painful rift in the life of man on

6. Clement of Alexandria, *Stromateis* 3.10, trans. John Ferguson (Washington, DC: The Catholic University of America Press), 262.

7. Irenaeus, *Against the Heresies* 1.31.2.

8. *Against the Heresies* 1.6.2–3.

9. *Against the Heresies* 1.25.4.

earth. "Man is neither angel nor brute, and the unfortunate thing is that he who would act the angel acts the brute."[10] Even if we avoid this enantiodromia, we constantly experience our carnality as a source of anxiety and—especially for those who fail to maintain their purity—shame. It's not the light around us that we torment; it's the light of our own souls.

—

The earthward way is the physical at the expense of the spiritual.

Once again, the direct counterpoint to Gnosticism takes shape in the New Axial Age, where materialism—the view that only physical things exist—overturns the dualisms of the ancient world, and the refusal of spirituality becomes as zealous as the Manichaean refusal of physicality. Logical positivism, a philosophical movement in the early twentieth century, made the claim that only empirical science or pure logic can give us meaningful statements about the world. Everything else rattling around in our minds—whether in philosophy, poetry, or literature—isn't so much nonexistent as nonsensical. The analysis of physical facts, in short, is the gateway to reality, and anything that deviates from it will give us a distorted picture of the world.

One of the founders of logical positivism, A.J. Ayer, later abandoned the project, admitting that "nearly all of it was false."[11] But the doctrine took hold in the broader movement of "scientism,"

10. Blaise Pascal, *Pensées* 358, trans. W.F. Trotter, in *Pensées; The Provincial Letters* (New York: Modern Library, 1941), 118.

11. Philosophy Overdose, "Logical Positivism & its Legacy - A. J. Ayer & Bryan Magee (1977)," April 5, 2022, https://youtu.be/gBSUMC3CqGg, 34:08.

which popularized its one-sided emphasis on the physical. In scientism, the methodology of science becomes a mentality, and its framework of observation and testing becomes an entire worldview: only science can give us the truth about the world, and everything else is just a tangle of subjective impressions and spiritual "deepities"—deep-sounding but empty phrases.

Scientism has in its corner, of course, the resounding success of modern science. On a practical level, nothing has ever worked so well. Whenever we set foot on a plane or pick up a prescription at the pharmacy, we're placing our well-grounded trust in science to deliver us from point A to point B, from sickness to health. And science is not only a problem-solver; it's also a comfort-maker. So many conveniences of daily life, from dishwashers to cell phones, are impossible without it.

But can the spiritual, like worship, vanish so easily? Science itself presupposes a conscious mind, the intelligibility of the world, and a correspondence between the two; yet none of these things are physical; thus, scientism is stuck in a self-contradiction. And this hidden reliance on the spiritual, if not acknowledged, tends to erupt in dysfunctional ways—an enantiodromia running in the other direction. Auguste Comte, who inaugurated positivism in the nineteenth century—a vision of "order and progress" that inspired the motto and flag of Brazil (*Ordem e Progresso*)—divided human history into three stages: the theological (religion), the metaphysical (philosophy), and the positive (science). The positive stage, Comte dreamed, would culminate in a new religion run by a priesthood of scientists, who would administer no less than nine "social" sacraments and lead humanity in the worship of the true supreme being: humanity itself. The Manichaeans had spirituality down to a science; Comte made science a spirituality.

This earthward way, more importantly, leaves us with a world too cramped to satisfy the soul. Scientism may love what the heavenward lose, but it loses what they wisely loved. Christopher Hitchens admitted that one of the most compelling arguments for religion was the experience of "the numinous, or the transcendent, or at best I suppose the ecstatic," especially the spiritual experiences into which beautiful music can lift us.[12] Why? Because a reductionistic view of reality demands that we drain these experiences of all their ecstasy—the *ek-stasis* of standing outside oneself. Beauty, we have to admit, is in the eye, just as goodness is in our glands and truth in our gray matter. We can wax poetic about these physical experiences if we like, but the world is, at the end of the day, the churning mass that science tells us it is. The earthward world of mere physics is too dark and cold to really be habitable.

The Way is both the spiritual and the physical.

The Christian life isn't one long interlude between the Incarnation and the new creation. It's the drama of the Church, which is the extension of the Incarnation through space and time; it follows Christ as a body follows its head. Christ is the spiritual made physical: "the image of the invisible God, the firstborn of all creation; for in him all things in heaven and on earth were created, things visible and invisible, whether thrones or dominions or rulers or

12. TheMunkDebates, "Munk Debates Podcast Episode #10 - Religion," August 4, 2020, https://youtu.be/ENGLaFxRoG4, 27:38.

powers—all things have been created through him and for him" (Col. 1:15–16). And at the heart of the Church's life is Christ in disguise, still drawing together spiritual and physical reality: the Real Presence of Jesus in the Eucharist.

The Eucharist—like Christ himself, because it *is* Christ himself—is the Way. It's a continuation, here and now, of heaven on earth, and a fulfillment of Christ's promise that he would remain with his disciples: "I am with you always, to the end of the age" (Matt. 28:20). But what's so astonishing about this new presence is that the God-man now conceals himself under the appearance of ordinary bread and wine. These humble elements—fruit of the earth and the work of human hands—become, through the power of the Word, the Body, Blood, Soul, and Divinity of Jesus.

Thus, on the one hand, the Eucharist is the highest spiritual reality: God himself. C.S. Lewis once remarked that our neighbor is the holiest object presented to our senses, with one exception: the Eucharist.[13] When we look at it, we're looking through a kind of porthole into the ocean of the infinite. But, on the other hand, the Eucharist is also the lowest material reality: inanimate matter for consumption and digestion, subject not only to the body, but to all kinds of potential neglect and abuse in the world. Thus, in the Eucharist, the spiritual and the physical join at the most extreme limits, the most powerful and glorious reality touching down as the most helpless and humble, the "bread of angels" becoming manna for mortals (Ps. 78:24–25)—a convergence of all reality rightly called Holy Communion.

John 6 is often the flashpoint for this theme, but the Last

13. C.S. Lewis, *The Weight of Glory* (New York: HarperOne, 1980), 46.

Supper scenes in the synoptic Gospels have a deafening directness all their own: "While they were eating, Jesus took a loaf of bread, and after blessing it he broke it, gave it to the disciples, and said, 'Take, eat; this is my body.' Then he took a cup, and after giving thanks he gave it to them, saying, 'Drink from it, all of you; for this is my blood of the covenant, which is poured out for many for the forgiveness of sins'" (Matt. 26:26–29). The disciples were to eat his body and drink his blood—and not just that one time, but again and again: "Do this in remembrance of me" (Luke 22:19).

They couldn't have fully understood—Christians still don't—but they accepted the word of the Lord and did as they were told. The breaking of bread became the central act of the Way (Acts 2:46, 20:7, 20:11, 27:35). St. Paul, in a letter written even before the Gospels, recounts the institution of the Eucharist (1 Cor. 10:16–22, 11:23–30), and in the book of Revelation, we find a glimpse of the heavenly liturgy, culminating in the "marriage supper of the Lamb" (Rev. 19:9)—a distant reflection of the early Church's worship. From the Church Fathers down to the Reformation, we see an overwhelming consistency of this teaching with few exceptions.

The Eucharist is the most important of what would later be called the "sacraments," which, beginning with Baptism, all follow the same logic of spiritual and physical communion. A sacrament is, in Augustine's formula, a visible sign of an invisible grace, the lowliest physical things—bread and wine, water and oil—channeling the highest things of the Spirit.[14] The sacraments are not magic; human beings are still free to close their hearts to the Spirit, and even when they open them wide, transformation is often gradual

14. Augustine, *On the Catechizing of the Uninstructed* 26.50.

and painful. They are mysteries: the things of God have been veiled in the ordinary—including the ordinary struggle for holiness.

This sacramental quality of the Church rules out a Manichaean approach to the world. For the Manichaeans, the things of the flesh have to be rejected; there's no room for them in the spiritual life. But for the Way, the Word not only became flesh, but works through and even assumes the appearance of matter. The Gnostics despised meat, wine, and sex; but in the Eucharist, God offers his flesh and blood to us under the forms of bread and wine—all as a foretaste of the marriage supper of eternity. Hans Urs von Balthasar rightly calls the Eucharist "the culmination of the case against Gnosticism."[15]

The Church, of course, continued to make room for those who would deny themselves these things, but only insofar as they were denying themselves something good. St. Paul rejects the proto-Gnostics who "forbid marriage and demand abstinence from foods . . . for everything created by God is good" (1 Tim. 4:3–4). And St. Jude warns of proto-Gnostic "dreamers," those libertines who "defile the flesh" like "irrational animals"—"wandering stars, for whom the deepest darkness has been reserved forever" (Jude 10, 12–13). The message is clear: on the Way of heaven and earth, matter *matters*. It's not inherently evil any more than spiritual things are automatically holy. In fact, evil itself is a spiritual reality, not a material one, and the lowest pit of hell is reserved not for matter, but for pure spirit: the angel Lucifer (the "light-bearer"), the "morning star" that fell from heaven "like a flash of lightning" (Isa. 14:12; Luke 10:18).

15. Hans Urs von Balthasar, *The Glory of the Lord: A Theological Aesthetics*, vol. 2, *Studies in Theological Style: Clerical Styles*, trans. A. Louth, F. McDonagh, and B. McNeil (San Francisco: Ignatius, 1984), 55.

But sacramental Christianity also rules out a positivist or scientistic approach. Many of the pivotal figures of modern science—Bacon, Copernicus, Galileo, Descartes, Pascal, Mendel, Pasteur, Lemaître—were faithful Christians, because science, like matter itself, is inherently good. But it's also limited. If scientists were to put the Eucharist under a microscope in a lab, they would still not see anything but the chemical properties of bread. But this doesn't mean that the Eucharist is only bread; it simply means that the scientific study of matter isn't our only gateway to reality. "Spirit" is not just a pleasant illusion or a more poetic way of talking about the physical; it's real—and not only real, but the most real thing we'll experience this side of heaven. Angelic messengers, divine revelations, prophetic visions, amazing grace, the inrushing of the Holy Spirit—all of these heightened realities are integral to the human story. Science has thankfully purified us of all kinds of "magical" thinking, which rushes to supernatural explanations for natural phenomena. But scientism risks dragging us into a worse superstition: explaining even supernatural things naturally.

The sacramental approach of the Church—right from the beginning—honors both sides of the world.

CHAPTER 5

Man:
The Spirit or the Flesh

Man experiences himself as a kind of living centaur, a creature of both the spiritual and physical realms. Here, the dilemma between heaven and earth comes full circle: man's gaze, which first looks out and sees the vertical and the horizontal all around it, now turns back upon itself. *What are you?*

Are you an immortal spirit or mortal flesh?

I

The heavenward way is the spirit at the expense of the flesh.

All Gnostic hatreds—of man, of the world, and of the physical—converge on a hatred of the flesh: "Why have you carried me away from my place into captivity," cries one text, "and cast me into the stinking body?"[1] Even talk of a "soul" was, for the Gnostics, too earthly: our true identity, the inner sanctum of the self, is pure

1. *Ginza* 388, in Hans Jonas, *The Gnostic Religion* (Boston: Beacon, 2001), 88.

spirit, as alien to this world as God above; the soul, like the body, belongs here below. Our personalities, too, are costumes.

At the heart of this spirit-flesh dilemma is the question of death: What does it mean to die? Where will I go? For the Gnostics, the answer is clear: if we live entangled in the flesh, we'll go "the way of all the earth" (1 Kings 2:2), vanishing as dust in the wind. But if we come to know our identity as spirit, we'll rise to our spiritual home. The body is a prelude, a tune-up; the real show—as Norman Greenbaum later sang in a Gnostic register—is with the spirit in the sky.

The spirit's release in death is thus the culmination of all *gnosis*: "Arise Adam, put off thy stinking body, thy garment of clay, the fetter, the bond . . . for thy time is come, thy measure is full, to depart from this world."[2] We reach it like Truman at the edge of Seahaven, touching an artificial limit of an artificial world, rising to reclaim our true selves. The spirit ascends past the archons, who can no longer detain it, and is stripped, bit by bit, of all its earthly barnacles, leaving only a naked *pneuma*.

This divestiture of the flesh, a key theme of the Valentinians, is given a poetic presentation in the *Poimandres*. It begins with a clear movement away from the flesh: "My mind was mightily lifted up, while my bodily senses were curbed." And it culminates with a vision of the spirit ascending through the cosmos after death—the reversing of its calamitous slide down into earthly life. The body is the first thing to dissolve, and as the spirit ascends, everything else begins to fall away too: sensation, desire, and all of the many evils of both soul and body that plagued life in this world. The purified

2. *Ginza* 430, in Jonas, 85.

spirit is then welcomed into its spiritual fatherland: "This is the good end for those who have attained *gnosis*—to become God."[3]

Though Gnosticism has faded away, this identification of man with spirit, and eternity with immateriality, continues to crop up in religious consciousness. Bahá'u'lláh, the Persian founder of the modern Bahá'i faith, speaks of the human being in a way that—except for its embrace of the soul and more optimistic outlook—would be right at home among the ancient Gnostics: "Up from thy prison ascend unto the glorious meads above, and from thy mortal cage wing thy flight unto the paradise of the placeless. O my servant! Free thyself from the fetters of this world, and loose thy soul from the prison of self."[4] The actor Rainn Wilson, a Bahá'i and the founder of SoulPancake, has echoed his teacher: "I fully know—it goes beyond belief—I fully know that I am a soul, and that I am inhabiting or attached to or in connection with a bodily form; . . . that who I am and what I am is not my body, it's not even my personality; . . . that there is a little spark of the divine inside of me."[5]

A Gnostic dualism of man rightly acknowledges the higher dimension of our being and the deeper longing of our heart. It affirms that there's more to us than just our flesh, and that the death of the flesh is not the end. The body weakens and breaks and dies, but the spirit offers hope of an eternal life to come.

But its rejection of the flesh in all its facets leaves us to wonder: What on earth would it look like to leave the body behind forever?

3. *The Poimandres of Hermes Trismegistus* 1, 26, in Jonas, 153.

4. *Hidden Words of Bahá'u'lláh*, trans. Shoghi Effendi (New York: Baha'i Publishing Committee, 1924), 45.

5. Rich Roll, "We Need a Spiritual Revolution | Rainn Wilson x Rich Roll Podcast," April 17, 2023, https://youtu.be/6sYl2XLuX-s, 1:55:58.

Could we really do this while remaining, in any meaningful sense, ourselves? Irenaeus, examining the ascent of the spirit in Gnostic teaching—the shedding not only of the body but also of the soul—asked an insightful question: "What part of them, then, will still remain to enter into the *pleroma*?"[6] The spirit is soulful, and the soul is so full of the body; our very identity, rooted in all our thoughts and experiences, is shaped by the flesh. It would seem that either we need to take something of the body with us (if only in memory), thus never leaving it behind, or else fully leave the flesh behind, thus not really remaining ourselves.

Worse yet, until we die and experience release, life in the body, however meaningful, becomes an agonizing torture. Death may be a great prison break, but we pass our days in a kind of solitary confinement, sunken in the pit of the flesh and assailed daily by its darkness. Evil is not only outside of us, in meat, wine, and sex; it encases and encloses us through our own guts, gullets, and genitals. We're stuck in our carnality, and that carnality is a curse.

—

The earthward way is the flesh at the expense of the spirit.

If all heavenward projects converge on the hatred of the human body, all earthward projects converge on the denial of the human spirit. Here, we encounter the opposite approach to the riddle of death: the literal dead end of nihilism. For the nihilist, when the body dies, we die—and that's all there is to it. There's no divine presence above us, no heavenly realm beyond us, no spiritual reality

6. Irenaeus, *Against the Heresies* 2.29.3.

within us: "We fat ourselves for maggots. . . . That's the end."[7] We're not in a war against the archons but against entropy, and it's a war that we all lose. Even the universe itself is hurtling toward heat death.

Thus, we might be able to find meaning in a very truncated sense—the meaning of a friendship, an aspiration, a fleeting pleasure—but not in any ultimate sense. The judge in *Blood Meridian* spoke the bitter truth: "Your heart's desire is to be told some mystery. The mystery is that there is no mystery."[8] Life has no end goal, no inner meaning.

> It is a tale
> Told by an idiot, full of sound and fury,
> Signifying nothing.[9]

Nihilism at least holds on to what so many heavenward spirits despise. Even if the mortal body with its sensations and passions is all we have, and ultimately means nothing at all, it's a strange and wonderful thing to be alive. Our planet is teeming with death, and as far as we know, the rest of the universe is devoid of life. And we not only have the opportunity to sense and to feel like other animals, but also, as rational animals, to think, to speak, and to act. Those human beings who wake up and get out of bed each day are the incredibly lucky winners of a cosmic lottery.

7. William Shakespeare, *Hamlet*, act 4, scene 3, in *The Riverside Shakespeare*, 2nd ed. (Boston: Houghton Mifflin, 1997), 1219.

8. Cormac McCarthy, *Blood Meridian* (New York: Vintage, 1992), 263.

9. William Shakespeare, *Macbeth*, act 5, scene 5, in *The Riverside Shakespeare*, 1219.

But if we're just our flesh, we're left with the puzzle of explaining an experience shared by almost all human cultures in history: the presence of some immaterial and immortal principle within connecting us to a higher world. Can all of that really be a grand delusion—or at least, an honest mistake—from which we're just now waking up? Are we really more enlightened about man than all the great religious traditions combined? We're left in an intellectually arrogant, if not spiritually precarious, stance.

But above all—or below all—is the threat of despair. We try our best to stave it off, like Joshua Michael Tillman in his song "Pure Comedy." Tillman laughs sardonically at the absurd "horror show" of human life—religion, politics, evolution, and, at bottom, "random matter suspended in the dark"—yet tries to end this crushing nihilism on a hopeful note: "I hate to say it, but each other's all we've got." One viral video has even been so bold as to make the case for "optimistic nihilism."[10] A meaningless universe, it argues, may not be as scary as it sounds, since it frees us from the weight of our past—our own mistakes, humiliations, and evils—and liberates us to explore the present: "We might as well aim to be happy and build some kind of utopia in the stars."

But it's not for nothing that countless souls have fled into Gnosticism; it's precisely to elude the Nothing. Without the reality of the spirit, life below—this endless welter of ignorance and confusion, manipulation and injustice, illness and death—becomes unbearable. Life is not only meaningless; it's relentlessly vicious. The attempt to overcome or at least overlook the horror of it all and

10. Kurzgesagt – In a Nutshell, "Optimistic Nihilism," July 26, 2017, https://youtu.be/MBRquoYOH14.

whistle past the graveyard only distracts us from the truth, and only for so long; the silence of the tomb approaches.

Nihilism has led, naturally, to "antinatalism"—against-birth-ism. For antinatalists, what was said of Judas could be said of every person: "It would have been better for that one not to have been born" (Matt. 26:24). Rust Cohle in *True Detective*—inspired, in large part, by the antinatalist text *The Conspiracy Against the Human Race*—muses that the self is an illusion, and everybody's nobody. What follows? "The honorable thing for our species to do is deny our programming, stop reproducing, walk hand in hand into extinction—one last midnight, brothers and sisters opting out of a raw deal." Yet when Cohle speaks of the death of his daughter, his words take on a Gnostic hue: "The hubris it must take to yank a soul out of nonexistence into this meat, and to force a life into this thresher. As for my daughter, she spared me the sin of being a father." The nihilist and the Gnostic meet in their extremes: life, for both, becomes a curse to avoid at all costs.

+

The Way is both the spirit and the flesh.

The central claim of Christianity—without which "faith is futile"—is that, after the Crucifixion, Christ didn't stay dead, but "was raised on the third day in accordance with the scriptures," the "first fruits" of eternal life: "For as all die in Adam, so all will be made alive in Christ" (1 Cor. 15:17, 6, 20, 22).

This is the shocking doctrine of the Resurrection. Christ didn't rise as a resuscitated body, nor as an ethereal spirit; he rose as a "spiritual body" (1 Cor. 15:44). He passed through locked doors, but also asked his disciples to see and touch his hands—"for a ghost does not have flesh and bones as you see that I have" (Luke 24:39). He appeared and disappeared suddenly, but also consumed ordinary food in the ordinary way.

And he ascended to his Father in heaven after forty days, but also took his body—and even his bodily wounds (John 20:27; Rev. 5:6)—with him: "The mystery of our religion is great: He was revealed in flesh, vindicated in spirit, seen by angels, proclaimed among Gentiles, believed in throughout the world, taken up in glory" (1 Tim. 3:16). In the Incarnation, heaven enters the flesh, and in the Ascension, the flesh enters heaven; each is now implicated in the other. After descending to the lowest low, Christ carries earth into the highest heights. Paradise is no longer the purely "spiritual" place of the angels; it's the dwelling of the risen Way, who is both spirit and flesh: "He who descended is the same one who ascended far above all the heavens, so that he might fill all things" (Eph. 4:10).

All of this has radical implications for human life, because what happened in Christ—the "death of death"—will also happen in his followers.[11] We, too, through the power of Christ, are destined to rise again in the same way: "If the Spirit of him who raised Jesus from the dead dwells in you, he who raised Christ from the dead will give life to your mortal bodies also through his Spirit that dwells in you" (Rom. 8:11). We live for a time on earth with a mortal body; after death, we live for "a time" as pure spirit; then, at the end of time, the two will be reunited in the spiritual body, and

11. Augustine, *Sermons on the Liturgical Seasons*, trans. Mary Sarah Muldowney (Washington, DC: The Catholic University of America Press, 1959), 221–222.

in that state we'll remain forever. Our spiritual life in heaven is only an intermediate state; our eternal state will be a bodily life. This is the ultimate expression of Christian hope: not escape from the body as from a hell, nor an embrace of the body as our heaven, but an awaiting of the resurrection on the Way. The flesh has become the "hinge" of salvation;[12] the body is meant for the Lord, "and the Lord for the body" (1 Cor. 6:13).

But Christ not only reveals man's destiny; he also reveals man's very identity. We're "ensouled bodies" of both spirit and flesh, the image of God in the dust of the earth, a puzzle to angels and animals—and ourselves. We see this revelation beginning to bud in the Old Testament, where these two "sides" of man are almost indistinguishable: the "soul" or "breath of life," *nephesh*, is also translated as "throat" or "neck." And though the Hebrew Scriptures lay more emphasis on bodily death—we go down into "the pit," into Sheol, and that's the end—we also find hints of eternal life, as when the witch of Endor conjures Samuel, a "divine being coming up out of the ground," bodily yet also spiritual (1 Sam. 28:13). We even find a dream of resurrection beginning to form: "Many of those who sleep in the dust of the earth shall awake, some to everlasting life, and some to shame and everlasting contempt" (Dan. 12:2). By the first century, the Sadducees denied the immortality of the soul and the resurrection of the body (Matt. 22:23), while the Pharisees believed in both. But the rising of Christ reveals the fullness of truth: that he himself is "the resurrection and the life" (John 11:25), and has inaugurated the new creation within the old.

The Way is thus fiercely anti-Gnostic: the flesh is essential to

12. *Catechism of the Catholic Church* 1015; Tertullian, *De res.* 8.2 (PL 2, 852).

our identity, not accidental, and its death is a natural evil, not the ultimate liberation. The spiritual soul animates the body, which, though lower and weaker, is good—so good that God desires it to live forever. "All flesh is like grass" (1 Pet. 1:24; see Isa. 40:6–8), but this grass is precious; God himself has walked upon it. There is a spiritualist motto attributed to the priest and scientist Pierre Teilhard de Chardin: "We are not human beings having a spiritual experience. We are spiritual beings having a human experience." But Teilhard never said this—it traces back to spiritualist self-help author Wayne W. Dyer—and it's not the Way. We are human beings having a human experience, and that experience is both spiritual and bodily, and will be forever in the resurrection.

But the Way is also fiercely anti-nihilistic. Man can't be reduced to his body or desperately cling to it, good as it is. This way madness lies, and the *memento mori* tradition of the Church keeps death before our eyes, lest we forget to start letting go before it's too late to know how: "We must all die; we are like water spilled on the ground, which cannot be gathered up" (2 Sam. 14:14). But death—though a splitting of our nature—isn't the end, and for the Christian, its sadness is enveloped by a greater joy, since it moves us into a higher communion with God. For St. Paul, "dying is gain"; his desire was "to depart and be with Christ, for that is far better" (Phil. 1:21, 23). The Christian can savor this mortal body, but ultimately has to hope for what lies beyond it, crying, *Muero porque no muero*: "I die because I do not die."[13]

In *The Treasure of the Sierra Madre*, gold miners rush like mad for ten months to grow their stockpile, only to have it all, in a

13. Teresa of Avila, "Vivo sin vivir en mí . . ." in *The Complete Works*, vol. 3 (New York: Burns & Oates, 2002), 277.

great dust storm, blow right back to the earth. The younger miner reacts with pure horror, but the older and wiser miner draws him into his raucous laughter: "Oh laugh, Curtin, old boy! It's a great joke played on us by the Lord, or fate, or nature, whatever you prefer. But whoever or whatever played it certainly had a sense of humor! The gold has gone back to where we found it!" This is our human condition: the dust is death, the gold the body, the miner the spirit—and the ten months of mining our ten decades, at best, of life. We spend our time meticulously nurturing and protecting the body, only to commit it back to where it first came from. We are dust, and to dust we will return.

The earthward recoil from this loss with horror, scrambling to hold on to as much of the gold as they can for as long as they can. The heavenward, on the other hand, abandon the gold with disgust and leave it all behind. But the man on the Way gathers the gold patiently, but carries it loosely. He laughs at the divine comedy, bearing "this treasure in clay jars" (2 Cor. 4:7); he looks up and cries out, "In my flesh I shall see God" (Job 19:26).

PART II
The Dilemmas of Philosophy

CHAPTER 6

Philosophy: Essence or Existence

Midway through the Axial Age, Greece gave birth to philosophy, "the love of wisdom." For the philosophers, reason, not revelation, is our guiding light. B'ut the same great dilemmas of heaven and earth appear in philosophy in new forms.

The central obsession of philosophers has varied over time. For the ancients, it was being; for the medievals, God; for moderns, knowledge; today, language. But within this evolving history, William Barrett wisely observed a single tug-of-war: the pull between essence, or the universal and heavenly form of *what* a thing is, and existence, or the particular and earthly reality *that* a thing is.[1]

Do the wise turn toward essence or existence?

I

The heavenward way is essence at the expense of existence.

Western philosophy, Alfred North Whitehead wrote, "consists

1. William Barrett, *Irrational Man: A Study in Existential Philosophy* (New York: Anchor Books, 1990), 101–104.

of a series of footnotes to Plato."[2] And though Plato's dialogues feature his own teacher, Socrates, the latter often becomes a mouthpiece for Plato's metaphysics, at the center of which is his concept of essences. What are these "ideas" or "forms"? They're not thoughts or shapes, as the English suggests; instead, they're the unchanging realities above that define the changing things of the world below. We see lots of different trees in the world with all kinds of shapes and colors, all of them in states of growth or decay. But there's only one unchanging essence defining them *as* trees: the form of Tree.

With these two tiers of reality, Plato overcomes an earlier dilemma between Parmenides (who said that nothing changes) and Heraclitus (who said that everything changes). For Plato, they're both right: things change below, but the forms above don't. They belong to a higher, immaterial, eternal world—a noble world of reason and mathematics, of bliss and beauty, of being beyond all becoming. Philosophy trains us for death by bringing us face to face with the essences of our "pure home that is above."[3] With Plato, philosophical heaven is born.

Plato gives his famous illustration of the forms in the allegory of the cave.[4] In the allegory, people are chained in a dark cave, forced to watch passing shadows on its back wall. One prisoner breaks out and sees the truth: at the opening of the cave are people carrying statues, which are casting shadows from a fire behind them. As he

2. Alfred North Whitehead, *Process and Reality: An Essay in Cosmology*, ed. David Ray Griffin and Donald W. Sherburne (New York: Free Press, 1978), 39.

3. Plato, *Phaedo* 114. All excerpts from Plato's dialogues are taken from Benjamin Jowett's *Dialogues of Plato* translation (Oxford: Clarendon, 1871).

4. Plato, *Republic* 514–520.

gets used to the light, he sees actual things beyond the cave's entrance. Finally, he sees the sun itself, shining above. The prisoner goes back down into the cave to tell the others, but they laugh at him: they think the illusion is reality, and reality the illusion. In Plato's allegory, the cave stands for this world; the shadows for our warped perceptions; the statues for the things we experience; the fire for the sun; the real things for the essences; and the sun for the ultimate essence by which we're enlightened: what Plato calls the Good, which later Platonists would naturally connect to God, the "sun of righteousness" (Mal. 4:2).

Platonism has the same vertical orientation as Gnosticism—indeed, Plato was one of the key inspirations of the Gnostics—but it doesn't fall into the same deep pessimism. Plato looks upward to God—not only the divine Demiurge but also a mysterious "Father" above—but he doesn't despise man; instead, the philosopher, "conversing with the divine and immutable, becomes a part of that divine and immutable order, as far as nature allows."[5] He looks upward to a divine realm far from this "endless slough of mud" below,[6] but he doesn't abandon the world; on the contrary, the *Republic* lays out a vision for both the just man and the just state. He looks upward to spiritual things, but doesn't argue for a complete withdrawal from the physical; rather, the soul is like a charioteer (reason) guiding "a pair of winged horses," one pulling us up to heaven (the "spirited" passions) and one dragging us down to earth (the bodily desires).[7] And he looks upward to the winged souls of heaven—so much so

5. *Republic* 500.
6. Plato, *Phaedo* 110.
7. Plato, *Phaedrus* 246.

that philosophers are "enemies of the body,"[8] which is like an oyster shell, the bars of a prison, or even a tomb (*soma sema*)[9]—but he doesn't leave behind the body altogether; in fact, he teaches that departed souls "transmigrate" back to new bodies after death.

But is this heavenward way as steady as it sounds? The contrast between heaven and earth is there, but isn't there a problematic separation between them? Plato's greatest pupil, Aristotle—who was more preoccupied with natural subjects like physics and zoology than his teacher—saw the problem. He argued that the Platonic forms weren't sufficient to connect heaven and earth: "To say that they are patterns and the other things share in them is to use empty words and poetical metaphors."[10] Instead, he offered an alternative view: "The essence of each thing is what it is said to be in virtue of itself."[11] Forms are *in* things, like the power of sight in the eye; they're not abstract realities in some distant heaven, but earthly realties that the mind abstracts. Aristotle's solution raised new problems—when things perish, so do their forms, and the same appears to be true of the human soul, which is "the form of a natural body"[12]—but he saw that the Platonic path was a dead end.

Platonic essentialists face a further problem: that of suicide. Might suicide be a door to the heaven of Platonic essences? In the *Phaedo*, Socrates, who is awaiting his own execution, seems to discourage it: "A man should wait, and not take his own life until God

8. Plato, *Phaedo* 67.

9. Plato, *Phaedrus* 250; *Phaedo* 82; *Gorgias* 493.

10. Aristotle, *Metaphysics* 1.9, in *The Basic Works of Aristotle*, ed. Richard McKeon (New York: Modern Library, 2001), 708.

11. *Metaphysics* 7.4, 786.

12. Aristotle, *De Anima* 2.1, in *The Basic Works of Aristotle*, 555.

summons him, as he is now summoning me."[13] But the last part of the line is key: the prohibition permits of certain exceptions—including situations like the one in which Socrates finds himself. Indeed, the Stoic Roman Senator Cato the Younger, after reading and rereading the *Phaedo*, slew himself with his sword rather than suffer dishonor at Julius Caesar's hands, and was later lionized as a model philosopher and citizen for it. The Manichaeans, for all their hatred of existence, strictly prohibited suicide on religious grounds; but the Platonists, for all their attention to existence, struggle to convince "enemies of the body" to refuse it.

—

The earthward way is existence at the expense of essence.

Raphael beautifully captured the different emphases of Plato and Aristotle in his *School of Athens* fresco. At the center, walking toward us side by side, are master and student. On the left, Plato, holding his metaphysical *Timaeus*, points his finger up toward the heavens; on the right, Aristotle, holding his practical *Nicomachean Ethics*, stretches out his palm over the earth. For one, there's an emphasis on what's above, and for the other, a balancing emphasis on what's below. These dual emphases define the whole history of philosophy: "Every man is born an Aristotelian or a Platonist."[14]

Yet, ultimately, Plato and Aristotle were more alike than different: both were Athenians, both lovers of wisdom, and both essentialists. A more unilateral stress on existence emerges with the

13. Plato, *Phaedo* 62.

14. Samuel Taylor Coleridge, "Notes on Hooker," in *Notes on English Divines* (London: Edward Moxon, Dover Street, 1853), 14.

modern movement that bears the very name: existentialism. Unlike the Greeks, the existentialists weren't focused on physics, metaphysics, or even reason itself; rather, they were focused on the brute fact of concrete, individual life. They held as ultimate everything that the essentialists set aside as relative: desire and passion, finitude and anxiety, suffering and death.

The father of existentialism, the atheist Jean-Paul Sartre, gave the movement its famous definition: "Existence precedes essence."[15] But the formula misrepresents existentialism: if existence merely *preceded* essence, then some essence would remain in the picture, and for the existentialists, it doesn't. We find a better definition in Martin Heidegger: man, for Heidegger, is *Dasein* ("Being-there"), and "the 'essence' of Dasein lies in its existence."[16] We are *that* we are; we have no essence at all beyond our "being in the world." We're *thrown* into reality, coping with it before we conceptualize it; we experience our own frailty and mortality, "being-toward-death"; and we run into a fear deeper than any phobia: the dread of our own alien presence.

In the midst of all of this, we're "condemned to be free," possessing the dizzying power to shape our own lives.[17] The end result of the existential program is thus a quest for authenticity—of becoming what one truly is. In the film *I Heart Huckabees*, a couple of "existential detectives" shadow a business executive at work, showing him how he repeats a story about Shania Twain and her

15. Jean-Paul Sartre, "Existentialism and Humanism," in *Basic Writings*, ed. Stephen Priest (London: Routledge, 2001), 28, 29, 32.

16. Martin Heidegger, *Being and Time*, trans. Joan Stambaugh (Albany, NY: State University of New York Press, 2010), 41.

17. Sartre, "Existentialism and Humanism," 32.

hatred of mayonnaise over and over again—"propaganda" to prove his impressive connections and good humor. Can he be himself without it? "How am I not myself?" he fires back. He walks off, anxious, into his own charade, the question on a loop in his mind. He doesn't have the slightest idea who he is. When colleagues in a board room meeting beg him to "tell the Shania story"—to revert to the false self he's constructed for the world—he promptly vomits.

This is the great power of existentialism, and it's no mere flash in the philosophical pan; on the contrary, its roots run back through both medieval and ancient thought, and its embrace of existence remains a vital element of the love of wisdom. It rightly refuses either a pure being tucked away from the human drama or a pure superficiality "distracted from distraction by distraction."[18] Instead, it insists that man, to be fully human, has to inhabit his own flesh and blood, searching for the truth out of the concreteness of his own situation.

But existentialism's seemingly optimistic quest of self-discovery is, at bottom, pure self-creation; we can only ever discover what we ourselves ordain. The satisfaction of finding higher truths outside of ourselves and the hope of overcoming our own frailty both vanish, and we're inevitably drawn, in an enantiodromia, right back into the spiritual alienation and pessimism of the Gnostics. Only now, there's no higher place into which this alienation calls us, no paradise beyond our pessimism. There is, in a word, no exit.

Needless to say, suicide also remains an open question on this earthward way. In fact, the existentialist Albert Camus wrote that suicide is the "one truly serious philosophical problem."[19] If

18. T.S. Eliot, *Four Quartets* (New York: Harvest, 1971), 17.
19. Albert Camus, *The Myth of Sisyphus*, trans. Justin O'Brien (New York:

existence is depleted of any light of essence, isn't life just a bleak, empty absurdity? Why live at all? "Nothing, nothing mattered," Camus' Meursault admits after lashing out at a priest, "and I knew why. So did he. Throughout the whole absurd life I'd lived, a dark wind had been rising toward me from somewhere deep in my future."[20] Camus argued that the absurdity of existence was a summons to live valiantly. Like the mythological Sisyphus, we may be rolling a boulder up and down a hill until we die, but we must imagine ourselves happy doing it; we make our own meaning in the struggle of living. But the boulder is heavy and the journey long; existentialism, even more than essentialism, faces an uphill battle in assuring us that it's all worth it.

The Way is both essence and existence.

Christian philosophy takes the best of both Plato and Heidegger. Both of their virtues come together on the Way: essences are real, and higher, but existence is no separated shadow or unreality; the two remain intimately connected. And what draws them together is the Way of the Word made flesh.

We see this coming together of essence and existence again and again in the two greatest philosophers of the Church's history: St. Augustine and St. Thomas Aquinas. Neither is beyond critique for the Christian thinker, and there are, of course, countless other valuable philosophers in the tradition of the Way. But these two

Vintage Books, 1991), 3.

20. Albert Camus, *The Stranger*, trans. Matthew Ward (New York: Vintage Books, 1989), 121.

minds, taken together, are the touchstone for Christian reason: and in them, we see a communion of the immutable and the mutable, being and becoming, essence and existence.

Augustine, a former Manichaean, was converted to Christianity by way of Neoplatonic philosophy. Naturally, an affinity for Platonism carries over into his work: "There are none who come nearer to us than the Platonists."[21] But Augustine, with his eyes fixed on Jesus, embraced the earthly in ways a good Platonist never would. He refused a sharp dualism that would denigrate or separate existence, for "no existence is contrary to God."[22] He also emphasized concrete, passionate, individual experience, writing the first autobiography in the Western tradition: the *Confessions*. With good reason, he's often counted among the Christian forerunners of existentialism.

Aquinas, a Scholastic thinker, synthesized the faith with the writings of Aristotle, whom he reveres as simply "the Philosopher." Aristotle grounds Aquinas in existence, and Aquinas, too, has been called an existential thinker. Yet with his eyes fixed on the same Way, he also departs from the earthward in his upward gaze to heaven. He drew a sharp distinction between essence and existence, arguing that we can understand the former apart from the latter, and that the two are only identical in God himself, whose essence *is* his existence. He also elevated Aristotle's view of the soul as the "form" of the body, clearly affirming the separability and immortality of the soul. In fact, Aquinas frequently leans into Neoplatonic Christians,

21. Augustine, *City of God* 8.5. All quotations from *City of God* are from the Henry Bettenson translation (London: Penguin Books, 2003).

22. *City of God* 12.2.

including Augustine himself, whom he cites in the *Summa* more than Aristotle.

And whereas in philosophy, the Platonists and the Aristotelians drift ever further apart, in the Church, Augustinians and Thomists remain one in Christ. Every Christian philosopher tends to be either an Augustinian or a Thomist, gifted with a clearer sense of either the essential or the existential. And the debate at times becomes heated—as in the medieval problem of universals, another eruption of the essence-existence dilemma. But on the Way, the two paths constantly intersect and intertwine, and are drawn back together at one and the same altar. Appropriately, the *School of Athens* painting in the Vatican appears directly across from Raphael's *Disputation of the Holy Sacrament*, which shows the Eucharist joining heaven and earth.

On this Way of both essence and existence, suicide—whether it be from a heavenward flight from the world or an earthward despair of it—is out of the question. Existence is essential, but death isn't the end; essence precedes existence, but life isn't dispensable. Augustine spends much of the first book of *City of God* speaking boldly against suicide, including in the case of Cato the Younger. Job is a far greater hero than Cato, Augustine reasons, for Job "would rather suffer horrible bodily distresses than free himself from all those torments by self-inflicted death."[23] Aquinas cosigns Augustine on the matter: "It is altogether unlawful to kill oneself," and "the passage from this life to another and happier one is subject not to man's free will but to the power of God."[24]

23. *City of God* 1.24.

24. Thomas Aquinas, *Summa theologiae* 2-2.64.5. All quotations from the

Christian philosophy sees the great wisdom in both essentialism and existentialism: the divine and rational heights of being on one side, and the human and visceral experience of becoming on the other. But it also sees the great folly in what each denies. An essentialism at the expense of existence is separatism; an existentialism at the expense of essence is absurdism. The Church, following its Head, extends its hands both ever upward and ever outward.

Summa theologiae are from the Fathers of the English Dominican Province translation, available at newadvent.org.

CHAPTER 7

Being:
The One or the Many

Philosophy begins in wonder, and wonder began with the one. What most confounded the earliest philosophers about the world was the question of multiplicity: we experience reality as one unified stream, yet there are different objects all around us. How do we explain it? A dilemma came into focus corresponding to the dilemma between God's place and our own.

Does reality come down to one thing or many things?

I

The heavenward way is the one at the expense of the many.

At first, philosophers couldn't get off the ground in searching for the one; every proposed candidate was some kind of earthly reality. For Thales, the first philosopher, it was water; for Heraclitus, fire; for Anaximenes, air. Parmenides elevated the debate when he said that the only thing, and the truly *real* thing, was simply an unchanging "one" of pure being—which, though more abstract and mysterious, was still physical. It was Plato, once again, who set the heaven-earth terms of the debate: the one is the Good, the form of all forms, which illuminates the mind as the sun does the eyes. It wasn't material, but immaterial; not temporal, but eternal; not below, but above.

But it was Plotinus, the founder of Neoplatonism, who made the connection to the divine explicit: the One was God, and God was the One. What, then, of the many—all the particular beings we encounter in the world? Plotinus answered that all these things *emanate*, necessarily, from the One. The good is diffusive of itself; Being naturally overflows out of itself into the otherness of beings. The world isn't created by God like a great painting; instead, it flows out of him like a great exhale.

In the Neoplatonic system, the One first emanates the Nous, the divine Mind containing the essences; then, the Nous emanates the World-Soul, a kind of bridge between heaven and earth; finally, the World-Soul emanates this world, turning invisible forms into visible things. The low point of this outward and downward breath—the darkest distance from the light of the One—is matter, which, though not intrinsically evil, is at least the principle of evil. But this great departure (*exitus*) from God leads to a great return (*reditus*) to him: after death, the philosopher's soul ascends out of this material world and returns to the One—"a quittance from things alien and earthly, a life beyond earthly pleasure, a flight of the alone to the Alone."[1]

Once again, we find here a far more holistic and balanced position than Gnosticism; in fact, Plotinus himself wrote a treatise of his own against the Gnostics. Neoplatonism gathers into itself

1. Plotinus, *Enneads* 6.9.11, in *Select Passages Illustrating Neoplatonism*, trans. E.R. Dodds (London: Society for Promoting Christian Knowledge, 1923), 124.

all the practical advantages of a Gnostic view—a mystical longing for God above, a sense of alienation in the world below, a suspicion of physical things—while avoiding its pessimism. Matter and the splintering of being into the many is part of a bigger picture, and all things work together in a harmonious whole oriented toward the One.

But this heavenward way still locks us into the same Gnostic disdain for the earthly. Plotinus' student Porphyry—a contemporary of Mani and a fierce opponent of the Incarnation—wrote that his master "seemed ashamed of being in the body."[2] Porphyry, too, seemed ashamed: "I am in reality not this person who can be touched or perceived by any of the senses, but that which is farthest removed from the body."[3] The philosopher, he advised, should eat "a fleshless diet" and go "without wine"; as for sex, it "defiles the soul" when it leads to pregnancy, and still "pollutes" it when it doesn't.[4] Porphyry married a widow with seven children, but his letter to her clarifies the purely spiritual and intellectual nature of the relationship: "It was not for the sake of having children that I wedded thee," he assures her, but to "propitiate the gods" and to give her "a share in philosophy."[5] Porphyry even broke with the Platonic doctrine of transmigration, arguing that purified souls can leave the earth and never come back.

A metaphysics of the Alone also poses a problem for that other great "alone": the human soul. The whole spiritual-philosophical

2. Porphyry, *The Life of Plotinus*, in *Plotinus*, vol. 1, trans. Arthur Hilary Armstrong (Cambridge, MA: Harvard University Press, 1966), 3.

3. Porphyry, *The Philosopher to His Wife Marcella*, trans. Alice Zimmern (London: George Redway, 1896), 60.

4. Porphyry, *On Abstinence from Animal Food*, in *Select Works of Porphyry*, trans. Thomas Taylor (London: Thomas Rodd, 1823), 39, 19, 163.

5. Porphyry, *The Philosopher to His Wife Marcella*, 53, 54, 55.

project becomes a mystical, vertical flight inward and upward—not only away from the body but also away from others. It ascends toward a transcendent unity, but it's a purely spiritual unity removed from community in the here and now; we become like disparate vertical lines all running upward and converging at the highest point, with no hope of connection here below. Until we meet in the Alone, we're all alone.

—

The earthward way is the many at the expense of the one.

It was a pre-Socratic philosopher, Democritus, who set the stage for this earthward way. While Aristotle held Democritus in high regard, Plato never mentions him once and, legend has it, even wanted all of his books burned. Indeed, it would be difficult to find an ancient theory of reality more antithetical to Plato's essentialism than Democritus' atomism.

For Democritus, reality is an infinite plurality of tiny atoms of all different shapes and types that affect us through the senses. These atoms can be neither altered nor destroyed; they can only be moved—and move they do. In Aristotle's description, they endlessly "collide and intertwine" with each other, resulting in the objects we experience all around us, until "some stronger compulsion" breaks them apart.[6]

Thus, for Democritus, there's no mystical One exhaling and inhaling the world—only the many. Instead, engulfing this endless interplay of infinite atoms is a great void. And while we can

6. Simplicius, *On Aristotle "On the Heavens"* 1.10–12, trans. R.J. Hankinson (London: Bloomsbury, 2006), 6.

reasonably speak of a "soul," that soul is, like everything else, composed of atoms—the same atoms, Democritus argues, that constitute fire, which are like "the motes in the air that we see in shafts of light coming through windows."[7] The whole of reality is simply the endless motion of the many in space, and the highest good is "cheerfulness" in the eye of this atomic storm: "The best thing for a man is to live his life as cheerfully as possible, and with the least distress."[8] If we can free ourselves from brutish pain and attain moderate pleasure, we'll make our peace with the many and live in a state of tranquility, symmetry, and harmony.

Atomism wisely refuses to treat the multiplicity of the universe as a kind of mistake or a force of evil. And it correctly sees beneath this multiplicity the interaction of elementary particles, forming something of a precursor to modern science. Most importantly, it bears an admirable humility about our own finitude, holding off any delusions of spiritual grandeur: we're atoms, and to atoms we shall return.

But how does this atomic universe, which isn't only ceaseless but causeless, come to be in the first place? We're left, once again, with the dissatisfying "brute fact" explanation of the universe: it simply is what it is. But even if the universe were infinite, it would, as Aristotle argued, still seem to require a "First Cause," a non-contingent source of contingent things. A further problem, which we sense in Aristotle's description of these colliding and cracking

7. Aristotle, *De Anima* 1.2, in *The Basic Works of Aristotle*, ed. Richard McKeon (New York: Modern Library, 2001), 538.

8. Democritus, fragment 53, in *Ethics: Stobaeus*, in *The Atomists: Leucippus and Democritus (Fragments)*, trans. C.C.W. Taylor (Toronto: University of Toronto Press, 2010), 23.

bundles of atoms, is the disordered nature of reality. Atomism, in the end, also threatens science, because science presupposes patterns, whereas atomism demolishes all patterns—and thus any hope of comprehending the world. The universe isn't just a brute fact; it's also a brutal fact.

Like its heavenward counterpart, atomism also poses a serious problem for human relationships. Why shouldn't physical atomism also entail *social* atomism—human actions presumably being just as disconnected, random, and aimless as the atoms that guide them? How can cheerfulness—or anything at all—emerge as more laudable or even more comprehensible than any other interlocking of atoms we experience? The earthward way may keep the many intact and morally neutral, but without the guiding goodness of the One, we're left with the aimless machinations of matter in the darkness. Behind the gaping grin of the "laughing philosopher" is the unease of metaphysical chaos.

+

The Way is both the one and the many.

For philosophers on the Way, God created the universe *ex nihilo* (out of nothing). This dogma, so taken for granted by Christians today, doesn't actually appear, explicitly, in Scripture. God is affirmed as the Creator of all things, but the phrase "out of nothing" is nowhere to be found. The closest we come is a passage of the deuterocanonical 2 Maccabees: "Look at the heaven and the earth and see everything that is in them, and recognize that God did not make them out of things that existed" (2 Macc. 7:28).

Instead, the phrase began to take shape in the writings of the

Church Fathers toward the end of the second century, beginning with the *Shepherd of Hermas*, which declares that the God of heaven "made out of nothing the things that exist."[9] Augustine, building on the theme, writes, "God made all things . . . not of those things that already existed, but of those things that did not exist at all, that is, of nothing."[10] The tradition continues up through Aquinas, who affirms that God created all reality and, quoting a gloss on Genesis 1, that "to create is to make something from nothing."[11]

Though both Augustine and Aquinas were deeply influenced by Neoplatonism and the *exitus-reditus* scheme, this doctrine of creation *ex nihilo* clearly rules out any emanationism. The universe is not a necessary outpouring from God; instead, the One freely creates the many. At the same time, it also clearly rules out an atomism that would see the universe as random and causeless; instead, the many find their source in the One. The One of God and the many of the world—distinct yet united—commune in the doctrine of creation.

But there's an even deeper communion of the one and the many on the Way, a mystery intimately related to the Incarnation: the dogma of the Trinity. The startling claim of Christians is that there is one divine nature in three persons: the Father, the Son, and the Holy Spirit. None of these persons are identical with another (they are really three), but each is fully God (they are truly one). This dogma is beautifully expressed in the pinnacle of all biblical revelation: "God is love" (1 John 4:8, 16). If God is love, then he

9. *The Shepherd of Hermas* 1.1.
10. Augustine, *On the Nature of the Good* 26.
11. Thomas Aquinas, *Summa theologiae* 1.45.1.

can't be the Alone; there has to be a relationality of Lover (Father), Beloved (Son), and the Love between them (the Holy Spirit).

But, like "out of nothing," the word "Trinity" doesn't explicitly appear in the Bible at all; instead, the idea emerged out of philosophical and theological discussion about divine revelation. And it didn't emerge easily. On one side was the heavenward heresy of Sabellianism. God, for Sabellius, was a monarchy, a single king with three "modes": just as the sun has a shape, light, and warmth, so the same God can be called Father, Son, and Spirit. On the other side was the earthward heresy of Arianism. Arius, too, wanted to protect and defend the oneness of God, but instead of absorbing the Son into the Father, made the Son a creature—the highest creature, but still a creature. The Word is "God in name only," because—unlike God—"there was a time when he was not."[12] The Sabellians absorbed the Son into the One, while the Arians absorbed him into the many; the first lost the distinction of the divine persons, while the second lost their unity in the divine nature.

Both heresies were overcome in the Council of Nicaea. The Church acknowledged, with the Sabellians, the oneness of God, but refused to eliminate plurality within him. And it acknowledged, with the Arians, the distinctness of the Son, but refused to deny his equality with God. Thus, the Son is "God from God, Light from Light, true God from true God, begotten, not made, consubstantial with the Father." The Greek term behind "consubstantial," *homoousios*, was the flashpoint of the whole debate, and in a brilliant stroke of divine humor, this pillar of orthodoxy first entered the Christian lexicon through the Gnostics and the Sabellians. God

12. Hilary of Poitiers, *On the Trinity* 5.25; Athanasius, *The Deposition of Arius* 2–3.

made straight his Way with crooked lines: God is One, but never has been, and never will be, alone.

Augustine, born shortly after Nicaea, picked up the Trinitarian banner. He wrote an entire treatise defending the Trinity as "the one and only and true God,"[13] and offered a helpful analogy to make sense of what seems like a logical contradiction: that of the human mind. The mind thinks, but it also knows itself and loves itself. All three—thought, self-thought, and self-love—are distinct, yet we have one mind, not three: "When the mind knows itself and loves itself, there remains a trinity: mind, love, knowledge. . . . All are in all."[14]

The word "person" in God, Aquinas adds, signifies "a relation as subsisting"—a union of the substance of oneness in a relationality of threeness.[15] And, pivoting off of Augustine's authoritative definition, he notes that the mystery of the Trinity steers the Catholic balance between the "two opposite errors" of Sabellius and Arius. The first's mistake was "unity of person with the unity of essence," and the second's "a Trinity of substance with the Trinity of persons."[16] The Way was a unity of essence and Trinity of persons.

Christian philosophy thus affirms, with the heavenward, the oneness of ultimate reality. There is one God—the Lord, Maker, and Creator of heaven and earth—and there is no other god beside him. It sings with the people Israel the *shema* prayer drawn from Deuteronomy 6: "Shema Yisrael, Adonai Eloheinu, Adonai ehad" (Hear, O Israel: The Lord is our God, the Lord alone). Yet it also

13. Augustine, *On the Trinity* 1.2.
14. *On the Trinity* 9.4.
15. *Summa theologiae* 1.30.1.
16. *Summa theologiae* 1.31.2.

affirms, with the earthward, the plurality of ultimate reality. This plurality is not, of course, material—it's not like atoms, animals, or stars—but it *is* a real plurality.

The Trinity also profoundly shapes the Christian understanding of human life. In the first chapter of Genesis, God—in a striking use of the plural—says, "Let us make humankind in our image, according to our likeness." He then creates man in the image of God, not as one, but as two: "Male and female he created them" (Gen. 1:26–27). And the two don't remain two, but generate a third: "Be fruitful and multiply" (Gen. 1:28). This isn't just an image of the family, but of all human community. What prevails for God—unity in plurality—has to prevail for his image, on earth as it is in heaven: "It is not good that the man should be alone" (Gen. 2:18).

But the ultimate reflection of one-yet-many in the world is the Church, which is the very Body of Christ (1 Cor. 12:27). On the one hand, the Church is one as God is one: it dwells in "the unity of the Spirit" (Eph. 4:3). On the other hand, this universal Church is many as God is many: there's a great diversity of particular churches, people, and gifts within that spiritual unity (1 Cor. 12:14–26). This is why St. Paul's metaphor of "the Body," Aquinas argues, is so fitting: "As in the natural body the various members are held together in unity by the power of the quickening spirit, so too in the Church's body the peace of the various members is preserved by the power of the Holy Spirit."[17]

This unity-in-plurality—so impossible on a merely human level—is realized through Baptism and the Eucharist. The bread itself demonstrates these dynamics: "By that Bread," Augustine

17. *Summa theologiae* 2-2.183.2.

preaches, "you are taught how you must love unity. For is that bread made of but one grain of wheat? Were there not in fact many grains? But before they became bread, they were separate; by water they were joined together."[18] This bread becomes the Body of Christ, one in being with the Father in the unity of the Spirit—and the Church becomes what it eats: "The bread that we break, is it not a sharing in the body of Christ? Because there is one bread, we who are many are one body, for we all partake of the one bread" (1 Cor. 10:16–17).

18. Augustine, Sermon 227, in *The Faith of the Early Fathers*, vol. 3, ed. W.A. Jurgens (Collegeville, MN: Liturgical, 1979), 30.

CHAPTER 8

The Good Life: Discipline or Passion

Ancient philosophers were not only interested in the nature of reality; they were also intensely interested in what makes a life worth living. How should the wise person live? Here, philosophers have been split between two basic paths corresponding to the spiritual and the physical: on the one hand, a top-down movement of reason and duty, and on the other, a bottom-up movement of emotion and desire.

Is the good life a life of discipline or passion?

I

The heavenward way is discipline at the expense of passion.

We see a vivid example of the path of discipline in the Stoics. Though generally materialists, the Stoic philosophers thought and spoke in a Platonic register. In his *Meditations*, the Roman emperor Marcus Aurelius spurns "the filth of life on the ground," turning instead to the divine heights: "This is a fine saying of Plato: That he who is discoursing about men should look also at earthly things as if he viewed them from some higher place."[1] He quotes Epictetus' characterization of the human being as "a soul carrying a corpse."[2] And he regards death—"when the soul shall fall out of this envelope"—as a fate to be welcomed: "Come quickly, death."[3]

But the Platonic tone is most pronounced when Marcus turns to "the poor passions of the flesh."[4] The philosopher, he writes, should retreat to his own "clear sky and calm voyage" within, guided by the mind and the will.[5] He has to grit his teeth and set his face, regarding his emotional reactions, whether high or low, as false judgments: "Don't join in mourning, or in ecstasy."[6]

He especially has to see physical delight—"the body and its gross pleasures"—as a worthless distraction.[7] Though Marcus doesn't reject meat altogether like the Gnostics, he approaches it with a cold and clammy disgust: "How good it is, when you have roast meat or suchlike foods before you, to impress on your mind that this is the dead body of a fish, this the dead body of a bird or pig."[8] Likewise, he regards wine as just juice squeezed from grapes, sex as just a mechanical exchange between bodies, and even a purple-dyed robe as just "the hair of a sheep soaked in shell-fish blood."[9] The good life

1. Marcus Aurelius, *Meditations* 7.24, trans. Martin Hammond (London: Penguin Books, 2006).
2. *Meditations* 4.41, 9.24.
3. *Meditations* 9.3.
4. *Meditations* 7.66.
5. *Meditations* 9.41.
6. *Meditations* 7.43.
7. *Meditations* 11.19.
8. *Meditations* 6.13.
9. *Meditations* 6.13.

is in reason, duty, and the denigration of pleasure, because pleasure is "neither beneficial nor a good."[10]

Stoicism, so in line with Platonic impulses, offers a compelling image of the well-disciplined soul, one that wisely avoids a life of instant gratification. Has anyone ever attained to greatness—whether in music, sports, or even philosophy itself—without emotional and physical discipline? And how often has succumbing to some fleeting passion led to the unraveling of great souls? Stoic austerity and sobriety are powerful aids in the struggle for a life well lived.

But this heavenward path, once again, lands us in an inhuman disdain for earthly things, sharply separating the directing soul from the acting body. Stoicism not only denigrates the emotions; it also overestimates the degree to which they're in our control, as if grief or joy were as easy to pick up or put down as a glass of cabernet. And while a certain disciplining of pleasure is healthy, Stoicism's separation of the mind from the immediacy of those pleasures seems not only unhealthy but impossible. We can be our own vigilant guides, but not our own absolute masters; our feelings and desires pull us back down to earth, reminding us of our own creaturely limits.

The path of pure self-discipline also leads into an enantiodromatic trap: obsessing with the high of *spiritual* pleasure. This can take the form of a spiritual gluttony that delights in our own mental advances, but also—maybe even simultaneously—of a spiritual masochism that delights in our own physical hardship. Either path turns the whole program of discipline against itself: through the

10. *Meditations* 8.10.

mind's constant focus on its own rectitude, the pleasure principle secures a surreptitious victory.

—

The earthward way is passion at the expense of discipline.

For the earthward, reason, as Hume wrote, is "the slave of the passions."[11] These passions include our emotions, which are bound up with the body: the Greek word *splanchnon*, which translates as "compassion," "tenderness," or "heart," is also translated as "bowels." We feel things *viscerally*, as if in our very intestines.

But among the passions, the most visceral—and the most conspicuous for philosophers on this path—are pleasure and pain. Here, we see the direct counterpoint to Stoicism—namely, hedonism, which makes the pursuit of pleasure and avoidance of pain the organizing principle of life. The great hero of this tradition, Epicurus, argued that the good life isn't based on the disciplined pursuit of virtue or wisdom, but pleasure. Positive feeling is the *summum bonum*, the highest good we can aim for: "Pleasure is the beginning and end of living happily."[12]

For Epicurus, this didn't mean the wanton sensualism that "hedonism" calls to mind. A descent into brutish self-indulgence, he saw, will only multiply our pains in the long run. Instead, pleasure primarily consists of the absence of pain in the body and of fear in the soul. True gratification is a pain-free and stress-free life—nothing more and nothing less. Epicurus especially targeted the fear of

11. David Hume, *A Treatise of Human Nature* (Oxford: Clarendon, 1896), 415.

12. Epicurus, *Letter to Menoeceus*, in Diogenes Laërtius, *Lives and Opinions of Eminent Philosophers* (London: Henry G. Bohn, 1853), 470.

death and of the judgment of the gods after death. He agreed with Democritus that all things—even the soul itself—are atoms in the void, and that death, which is just extinction, has to be regarded as "nothing to us": "When we exist, death is not present to us; and when death is present, then we have no existence. It is no concern then either of the living or of the dead."[13] Having freed ourselves of pain and fear, we can then pursue the pleasures that, in moderation, lead to tranquility, serenity, and happiness.

Epicureanism has more in its favor than heavenward minds admit. Just think of how the promise of small, simple bodily pleasures—a favorite chair, a hot shower, a delicious meal, a quiet walk—can be enough to keep us trudging through a difficult day. Think, too, of the loftier pleasures that make life rich and wonderful: intellectual self-improvement, pleasant conversation, acts of generosity. Hedonism rests on the basic experiential truth that we pursue these physical, mental, and spiritual pleasures and avoid physical, mental, and spiritual pains. It affirms the goodness of the former, the badness of the latter, and the power of both in shaping who we are and what we do.

But this earthward way naturally raises two questions. First, why should our pleasure be modest? Is the avoidance of an abstract and uncertain pain in the long run enough? Amid the passionate love affair of Romeo and Juliet, Friar Laurence, the voice of reason, counsels Romeo to "love moderately": "These violent delights have violent ends, / and in their triumph die, like fire and powder, / Which as they kiss consume."[14] But if we die an untimely death, this

13. Epicurus, 469.

14. William Shakespeare, *Romeo and Juliet*, act 2, scene 6, in *The Riverside Shakespeare*, 2nd ed. (Boston: Houghton Mifflin, 1997), 1120.

takes long-term suffering off the table, and, after all, death remains "nothing." Why shouldn't we seek the triumph of violent delights?

This leads to a second question: Why shouldn't the pursuit of pleasure be all about the gratification of the body? Before Epicurus, Aristippus of Cyrene made precisely this argument: that *sensual* pleasure is the whole goal and meaning of human life. If life is simply bodies in the void, it's difficult to see why the higher intellectual and spiritual pleasures should ever take precedence over physical pleasures when the two come into conflict—or why the freedom from pain in another should take precedence over the presence of pleasure in the self.

These two difficulties are not mere abstractions; they manifest in the hedonistic tradition of libertinism. Two thousand years after Epicurus, one Frenchman would become the most notorious hedonist in modern history: the Marquis de Sade. It's well known that Sade's violent sexual exploits gave sadism its name; it's less well known that he understood his project as *la philosophie dans le boudoir* (philosophy in the bedroom), pushing a materialist hedonism to its logical limit. Doesn't the mere pursuit of pleasure—moving from boredom to experimentation and back again—tend toward increasingly depraved ways of finding it, including cruelty and violence? The absence of discipline not only flattens our sense of pleasure; it also desensitizes us to pain. In a world of atomized bodies, each pursuing its own gratification without restraint, we're haunted by the ethic of Flannery O'Connor's Misfit: "No pleasure but meanness."[15]

15. Flannery O'Connor, "A Good Man Is Hard to Find," in *Flannery O'Connor Collection*, ed. Matthew Becklo (Park Ridge, IL: Word on Fire Classics, 2019), 59.

+

The Way is both discipline and passion.

The heavenward way is a great temptation for religious minds, in philosophy as in religion—and perhaps on this dilemma more than any other. There's a clear overlap between Stoic discipline and many New Testament exhortations. St. Peter instructs readers to "discipline" themselves—not once, not twice, but three times (1 Pet. 1:13, 4:7, 5:8). And St. Paul encourages the Church to gird itself for spiritual combat (Eph. 6:10–17). Clearly, Christians are not called to yield to whatever physical urge or emotional surge happens to erupt from below; on the contrary, they have to practice self-mastery for the sake of the kingdom. Thus, the writings of the saints are filled with the themes of ascetic fasting, mortification of the flesh, and *apatheia* or "passionlessness"—a term borrowed directly from the Stoics.

But we notice a key difference in the New Testament: it's not the passions themselves that are problematic, but rather *sinful* passions. The Stoics tell us to avoid all grief; St. Paul tells us to avoid the *worldly* grief that produces death, but to embrace the *godly* grief that leads to repentance (2 Cor. 7:10). The passions are not any more inherently evil than the body; indeed, if "the hearts of the saints" are all one thing, it's passionate about God (Philem. 7).

This dual embrace of both discipline and passion marks the Way. In his *City of God*, Augustine analyzes Stoic discipline, arguing that, like Platonic discipline, it regards the passions as necessary evils, and spiritual resistance as the key: "Both sides champion the mind and the reason against the tyranny of the passions."[16] Against both traditions, Augustine champions a both/and: "In our discipline, the question is not *whether* the devout soul is angry, but *why*; not whether it is sad, but what causes its sadness; not whether it is afraid, but what is the object of its fear."[17] The passions can and should be restrained—not because they're evil, but so that they might become "instruments of justice."[18]

And it's Christ who shows Augustine the Way: "Human emotion was not illusory in him who had a truly human body and a truly human mind."[19] Jesus felt anger, gladness, yearning, and even mourning, weeping at his friend Lazarus' tomb. True, Augustine admits: he felt these feelings perfectly, whereas our passions routinely go haywire and overwhelm us. But the answer isn't in throwing out the earth; it's in lifting it up to heaven.

Aquinas follows Augustine's approach to the dilemma. In the *Summa*, he asks the question "whether every passion of the soul is evil morally." After quoting the *City of God*, he concludes that the "passions are not called 'diseases' or 'disturbances' of the soul, save when they are not controlled by reason."[20] Passions are an increase or decrease in the natural movement of the heart; if that movement is contrary to reason, it inclines us to sin, but if it isn't, it inclines us to virtue. Later in the *Summa*, he even argues that the *lack* of passions like anger or even playfulness can at times be sinful.[21]

None of this, of course, flips Christian philosophy toward

16. Augustine, *City of God* 9.5.
17. *City of God* 9.5.
18. *City of God* 9.5.
19. *City of God* 9.5.
20. Thomas Aquinas, *Summa theologiae* 1-2.24.2.
21. *Summa theologiae* 2-2.158.8, 2-2.168.4.

the opposite extreme of hedonism. Augustine has choice words in the *Confessions* about his own pre-Christian lifestyle of pleasure-seeking in the "region of unlikeness"—an image borrowed from Platonism. And Aquinas readily agrees with the Philosopher's assessment of a philosophy of pleasure as "suitable to beasts," not to men: "If the happiness of man would consist in this, dumb animals enjoying the pleasure of food and sexual intercourse would have to be called happy for the same reason. Assuming that happiness is a characteristically human good, it cannot possibly consist in these things."[22] The philosopher on the Way doesn't imitate the passionate Aristippus of Cyrene who went the way of pleasure, but rather the compassionate Simon of Cyrene who went the way of the cross.

Yet pleasure is still integral to the Way. In his *Screwtape Letters*, C.S. Lewis' demon remarks that God is a "hedonist at heart": "All those fasts and vigils and stakes and crosses are only a façade. Or only like foam on the seashore. Out at sea, out in His sea, there is pleasure, and more pleasure. He makes no secret of it."[23] This theme emerges in Augustine, who doesn't deny for a moment the good pleasure of the earth: "This life we live here below has its own attractiveness, grounded in the measure of beauty it has and its harmony with the beauty of all lesser things."[24] Indeed, it was his passionate search for happiness in this world—his restless heart—

22. Aristotle, *Nicomachean Ethics* 1.5, in *The Basic Works of Aristotle*, ed. Richard McKeon (New York: Modern Library, 2001), 938; Thomas Aquinas, *Commentary on the Nicomachean Ethics* 5.60, trans. C.I. Litzinger (Chicago: Henry Regnery, 1993), 21.

23. C.S. Lewis, *The Screwtape Letters*, in the *Signature Classics* (New York: HarperOne, 2002), 249.

24. Augustine, *Confessions* 2.5. All quotations from the *Confessions* are from the Frank J. Sheed translation (Park Ridge, IL: Word on Fire Classics, 2017).

that led him to find true happiness in God: "Where was I to find such pleasures save in You, O Lord?"[25]

Thomas Aquinas picks up this same theme and, drawing on Aristotle, arrives at a basic philosophical principle: all men desire happiness (*eudaimonia*), and they only find it in God. Happiness is the *summum bonum* (supreme good) that motivates all that we do, but it's found, in the end, only in our Creator. This ultimate happiness includes, Aquinas goes on to say, pleasure: thus, "a certain pleasure of man may be said to be the greatest among human goods." Aquinas cites the Psalms as proof: "In your presence there is fullness of joy; in your right hand are pleasures forevermore" (Ps. 16:11).[26]

We even see this same pattern in Christian love, which is the very heart of the Way. Love connects us to our final end and greatest good, for "God is love, and those who abide in love abide in God, and God abides in them" (1 John 4:16). But Joseph Ratzinger—a "decided Augustinian"[27]—saw that human life consists in the convergence of two forms of love. *Agape* is a disciplined love—a "descending" love of self-sacrifice and self-gift. But there is also the passionate love of *eros*—an "ascending" love of desire and possession. The great temptation is to set these two loves off in an antithesis, rejecting one or the other, but the Way is a way of one love: "*Eros* and *agape*—ascending love and descending love—can never be completely separated. The more the two, in their different

25. *Confessions* 2.2.

26. *Summa theologiae* 1-2.34.3.

27. Joseph Ratzinger, *Salt of the Earth: An Exclusive Interview on the State of the Church at the End of the Millennium* (San Francisco: Ignatius, 1993), 33.

aspects, find a proper unity in the one reality of love, the more the true nature of love in general is realized."[28]

For the Christian, the good life—whether in the littlest acts, the most momentous decisions, or the not uncommon convergence of the two—is neither in dispassion nor disorder, but in "love, joy, peace, patience, kindness, generosity, faithfulness, gentleness, and self-control" (Gal. 5:22–23).

28. Benedict XVI, *Deus Caritas Est* 7, encyclical letter, December 25, 2005, vatican.va.

CHAPTER 9

History: Divine Providence or Human Freedom

When philosophers turned their minds to God, they found themselves in an extension of the God-man dilemma: the pull between divine providence and human freedom. If God controls everything through his providence, then are we really free to act? If we're fully free to act, does God really control everything?

Is the director of human events God or man?

I

The heavenward way is divine providence at the expense of human freedom.

The Stoic tradition, once again, is an exemplary case of this heavenward way. The Stoics believed that all things were divine—a single, harmonious Whole of both God and Nature: "The works of the gods are full of providence," Marcus writes. "The works of Fortune are not independent of Nature or the spinning and weaving together of the threads governed by providence."[1] Everything that happens in our lives has been ordained for us by God through that great Whole, and our only response can be rationally consenting to it and acting in accordance with it: "Come to love your given lot."[2]

But how can we talk about consenting or acting if these, too, are ordained? Another Stoic, Chrysippus, saw the problem, and tried to make the needed room for freedom. Yes, everything we do is fated, he admitted, but we still have to *live*; we can't just sit back and let fate live for us. And in this sense, we're free, and because free, also responsible for what we do—even if, truth be told, we couldn't have done otherwise. Freedom becomes a kind of legal fiction within the grand scheme of providence.

Like atomism, Stoicism humbles us: we see our exceedingly small role in the grand scheme of things and how little we're in control of what happens. But, unlike atomism, it avoids the dangerous conclusion that our lives are simply chaotic and random; instead, everything that happens is part of a bigger plan soaring up into the mind of God. There's great order and beauty in the Stoic recognition of, and submission to, providence.

But for all of its emphasis on the grip of fate, Stoicism has to assume the fact of freedom—not only by making room for it theoretically, but also by relying on it practically. The Stoics can't help but appeal to the freedom to choose; otherwise, their various exhortations are drained of all their power. Indeed, so strong is the emphasis on freedom that "Stoicism" tends to be associated more

1. Marcus Aurelius, *Meditations* 2.3, trans. Martin Hammond (London: Penguin Books, 2006).

2. *Meditations* 12.1.

with rugged determination than a placid resignation. To live at all, we have to think of ourselves—or at least treat ourselves—as free.

But to the degree that Stoicism does deny freedom and affirm fatalism, it draws us into a cold indifference toward human suffering. Socrates had declared that "no evil can happen to a good man";[3] to live in virtue is necessarily to live securely. The Stoics picked up the idea and took it further: no evil can really happen at all. Things simply are as they have to be, and we shouldn't so much as frown at what the Whole ordains. When anything happens to you, Marcus writes, "your directing mind must not of itself add any judgment of good or bad."[4] Good and evil are not in life and death, pleasure and pain, wealth and poverty, joy and suffering—only in our reactions to them: "There is nothing either good or bad, but thinking makes it so."[5] With an aloof heartlessness, we place ourselves above and beyond the triumphs and travails of being human.

—

The earthward way is human freedom at the expense of divine providence.

Standing opposite the Stoic way of providence, we again find the figure of Epicurus. Though a hedonist, he was passionate about the pursuit of virtue, and saw that the whole ethical life hinged on freedom—and thus, the rejection of fate: "Our own will is free; and this freedom constitutes, in our case, a responsibility that makes us

3. Plato, *Apology* 41.

4. Marcus Aurelius, *Meditations* 5.26.

5. William Shakespeare, *Hamlet*, act 2, scene 2, in *The Riverside Shakespeare*, 2nd ed. (Boston: Houghton Mifflin, 1997), 1203.

encounter blame and praise."[6] If we're fated, we can't be responsible for what we do; but we *are* responsible for what we do; therefore, we can't be fated. As for the gods, Epicurus imagines them happily dwelling far away from the world with no thought of human affairs below. Thus, there's no prewritten plan for our lives; we're simply left to our own devices.

But Epicurus faced a new threat to human freedom—a fatalism not from above through God's providence, but from below through atomic motion. If, as Epicurus believed, all things are determined by the movement of atoms, including the soul, then how can we be free to act? His solution to this problem was the "swerve": atoms occasionally move in unexpected ways, leaving space for the soul to step in and act freely. These swerves "sunder the covenants of fate."[7] Thus, we're no more predetermined from below than we are from above: life remains a great choose-your-own-adventure.

Epicureanism rightly embraces our power to choose one thing rather than another. This autonomy secures the necessary latitude to live: the gods are not pulling our strings from above, and our lives are ours to direct. It also secures a deep sense of responsibility: we're accountable for the actions we take, because we're truly free.

But it's hard to see how the Epicurean "swerve" or anything like it can give us authentic freedom. At best, it would seem to make our decisions completely spontaneous and arbitrary; at worst, it plunges us right back into the fatalism we set out to avoid in the first place. The Epicurean is as haunted by fate as the Stoic is by freedom.

6. Epicurus, *Letter to Menoeceus*, in Diogenes Laërtius, *Lives and Opinions of Eminent Philosophers* (London: Henry G. Bohn, 1853), 470.

7. Lucretius, *On the Nature of Things*, book 2, trans. William Ellery Leonard (London: J.M. Dent & Sons, 1916), 55.

Indeed, Marcus Aurelius had a soft spot for Epicureanism—not because of its love for freedom, but precisely because of its fatalistic logic. Whether all things are governed by God or by atoms, Marcus often said, you have to do what you have to do, and that's all there is to it. The heavenward way of providence loses freedom; the earthward way of freedom loses both.

Even if we do accept the "swerve," the earthward way drains our freedom of any final *telos*—any end or purpose—beyond pleasure. For the Stoics, the trials and tragedies we inflict on each other may be preordained, but they are at least meaningful; for the Epicurean, they have no purpose at all beyond a clash of free wills in the void. The cold order of pure providence may be heartless, but it's a far less crushing view of the human story—certainly in the long run—than the fiery chaos of pure freedom.

+

The Way is both divine providence and human freedom.

In the film *Anything Else*, Woody Allen's character tells a joke—one, he says, with more insight "than most books on philosophy"—playing off this dilemma. There's a boxer getting clobbered in the ring, and his mother is in the audience watching. She says to a priest sitting next to her, "Father, father! Pray for him, pray for him!" The priest says, "I *will* pray for him. But, you know, if he could punch, it would help."

The priest's answer is funny—and true—because it's paradoxical: God's governance doesn't preclude punching, nor punching preclude prayer. In fact, the two things are, in the grand scheme of things, intimately connected to each other: God is "mighty in power and sees everything," but he also left human beings "in the power of their own free choice" (Sir. 15:18, 14).

We can consider the dilemma in two different ways. The first focuses on divine foreknowledge. God is all-knowing, and therefore he knows everything that we're going to do before we do it. The script of our lives—all the dialogue and action, the story from beginning to end—is already written in his mind. In his *City of God*, Augustine acknowledges that this seems to put us in a bind: "Either there is some scope for our will, or there is foreknowledge." On the one hand, we can deny that we have free will: but the consequences of this are not only "discreditable and absurd" but also "perilous to human life."[8] On the other, we can deny that God has foreknowledge: this was the path taken by Cicero, but it was no less a dead end.

What was the solution? It was to recognize the dilemma as false: "The religious mind chooses both, foreknowledge as well as liberty; it acknowledges both, and supports both in pious faith."[9] But how? First, we have to purify "foreknowledge" of any implication of "destiny" or "fate," which would suggest that the script of life is written in the stars. There's "a causal order where the will of God prevails," but no fatalism. Then, we have to see the interaction of God's knowledge and our own freedom aright: "Our wills themselves are in the order of causes, which is, for God, fixed, and is contained in his foreknowledge."[10]

Other Christian philosophers, of course, have proposed other solutions to the problem. Boethius argues that God "discerns all

8. Augustine, *City of God* 5.9.
9. *City of God* 5.9.
10. *City of God* 5.9.

things in his eternal present";[11] thus, there is no "foreknowledge," properly speaking, because there's neither past nor future for God—only the eternal now. Luis de Molina later argues for God's "middle knowledge": between his knowledge of what *could* happen and his knowledge of what *will* happen is his knowledge of what *would* happen—and it's in this "middle" space that providence and freedom are reconciled. Whatever the approach, neither God's omniscence nor man's freedom can be denied on the Way.

The second way to consider the problem is in terms of divine power. In his *Summa*, Aquinas considers the following argument against human freedom: "What is moved by another is not free. But God moves the will. . . . Therefore man has not free will." This argument, one very much in line with Stoicism, seems persuasive. If God is the cause of all things, and we're one of those causes, then how can we be truly free?

Aquinas' eloquent resolution brings incarnational logic to bear on the problem: God is indeed "the first cause" of all things, but this includes secondary causes, "both natural and voluntary." He's the heavenly cause of all things according to his providence, but he also operates through earthly causes—and that includes our free will. He moves our will on a higher level, but doesn't compete with it on the lower level: "Rather is he the cause of this very thing in them; for he operates in each thing according to its own nature."[12] Thus, Aquinas retains both the power of God and the freedom of man, and draws them together.

11. Boethius, *The Consolation of Philosophy*, book 5, trans. Scott Goins and Barbara H. Wyman (San Francisco: Ignatius, 2012), 169.

12. Thomas Aquinas, *Summa theologiae* 1.83.1.

From whatever vantage point, and whatever the solution, philosophers on the Way refuse to jettison either one or the other: both divine providence and human freedom govern our stories.

CHAPTER 10

The Self: The Soul or the Body

The spirit-flesh dilemma haunts philosophy as it does religion. But here, in the life of the mind, the focus isn't man's ultimate fate in death so much as his intrinsic nature in life—not on his immortality or mortality but on his immateriality or materiality.

Is man a soul or a body?

I

The heavenward way is the soul at the expense of the body.

If all of philosophy is a footnote to Plato, all of modern philosophy is a footnote to René Descartes. And both thinkers are connected by the same sharp divide between soul and body. The philosopher Antoine Arnauld—who would later become convinced of Descartes' views—noted that his *Meditations* seemed to bring readers "back to the Platonic view . . . that man is nothing but a soul, and the body, in fact, is nothing but the vehicle of the soul."[1]

1. Antoine Arnauld, Fourth Objections, in René Descartes, *Meditations on*

But with Descartes, the focus shifts, and the picture sharpens: we're no longer spirits or even souls reaching upward, but *minds* looking inward; the flesh isn't a prison to escape, but a *machine* like the rest of nature; and it isn't death that defines our inner divide, but *thought*.

Descartes' picture of the self hinges on a simple idea with profound implications: the mind and the body are two different substances. The mind is a *res cogitans*, a "thinking thing," while the body is a *res extensa*, an "extended thing." An old philosophical joke captures the sharp contrast of this substance dualism: "What is mind? No matter. What is matter? Never mind." The immaterial self is no longer the "form" of the body, but something entirely separate; indeed, Descartes candidly admits in a letter that his ideas "destroy the principles of Aristotle."[2]

In his defense, Descartes—a brilliant philosopher and a faithful Catholic—wanted to keep mind and body united as one rather than leave them separated. Given the experience of sensation, he reasons, we're clearly not present in the body "as a pilot is present in a ship." Instead, the mind is "very closely conjoined" to the body so as to "form a single entity with it."[3] Man, he concludes, is "a composite of mind and body."[4] Descartes famously pointed to one part of the brain as being the "seat" of the mind: the pineal gland.

First Philosophy, trans. Michael Moriarty (Oxford: Oxford University Press, 2008), 130.

2. René Descartes to Mersenne, January 28, 1641, in *The Philosophical Writings of Descartes*, vol. 3, *The Correspondence*, trans. John Cottingham, Robert Stoothoff, Dugald Murdoch, Anthony Kenny (Cambridge: Cambridge University Press, 1997), 173.

3. Descartes, *Meditations*, 57.

4. Descartes, 62.

But his proposed reconnection of mind and body didn't satisfy either philosophers or scientists, and from then on, rationalists fell into talking of the two as utterly separate, and Cartesian dualism was born. It has proven to be one of the most alluring and intractable ideas in all of modern philosophy, and indeed all of modern culture. The whole "body swap" genre of storytelling, from *Freaky Friday* to *Being John Malkovich*, is one of many cultural offshoots of the Cartesian conception of the self.

Cartesian dualism, like Gnostic dualism, has its positive elements. It wisely acknowledges a higher dimension of human experience beyond the bodily. It especially defends human reason, refusing to collapse abstract thought into a stream of sense experience. And it nobly attempts to marry the idea of an immaterial self—with all that this implies for religion and morality—with the mechanistic trajectory of modern science.

But the Cartesian path has found itself mired in the "mind-body problem" or "interaction problem": How does the mind influence the body? Where and how exactly does this thinking thing touch down and make contact with this extended thing? The challenge, as for Plato, is somehow reconnecting what's been so sharply separated. Some philosophers proposed "occasionalism": human life is the "occasion" for God's dual causation of mental and bodily events. Others opted for "pre-established harmony": mind and body are like two pendula swinging in perfect harmony according to natural laws established by God. But these resolutions never took off, leaving dualists stuck in the problem.

The Cartesian reduction of the soul to the mind also leads to an artificial shrinking of the self in philosophical discourse. Today, rather than "the soul," it's fashionable for philosophers of mind instead to obsess over "consciousness," which essentially means sentience or awareness. How do we make sense of the "hard problem of consciousness"—the fact that we have raw inner experiences at all? Might there be "philosophical zombies"—human beings who mimic human life, but without any conscious awareness? Such conversations don't do much to move the needle on the mind-body problem, but they do restrict our view of the human person: "the soul," like "the spirit," ceases to be of interest to either side of the dilemma.

—

The earthward way is the body at the expense of the soul.

Running parallel to the rise of Cartesian dualism was the earthward rise of materialism. For the materialists, everything that exists is material, including the human being. Descartes' contemporary Thomas Hobbes agreed with the mechanistic side of his theory—"life is but a motion of limbs"[5]—but saw the idea of a spiritual or mental substance as a kind of legacy system, a last domino of medieval thought to be knocked over by reason and science. In his critique of the *Meditations*, Hobbes acknowledges that man is indeed a thinking thing, but adds that "a thinking thing is material rather than immaterial."[6] We speak coherently of bodies and their qualities, but to say "incorporeal substance" is little better than "round quadrangle"; it "signifies nothing, but is a mere sound."[7] Behind this argument was the same ancient pull between essence

5. Thomas Hobbes, *Leviathan* (New York: Touchstone, 2008), 3.
6. Thomas Hobbes, Third Objections, in Descartes, *Meditations*, 109.
7. Hobbes, *Leviathan*, 26–27.

and existence animating philosophy, and Hobbes had no patience with the former: "Essence, in so far as it is distinguished from existence, is nothing other than a coupling of names by the word 'is.' Thus essence without existence is a fiction of our own creation."[8]

Dualism was once dogma for philosophers, and materialism the heresy: Hobbes himself, who professed to remain a believer in God, narrowly escaped being formally condemned as a heretic in England. Today, the situation is almost completely reversed: dualism is heterodoxy, and materialism is orthodoxy. Some philosophers try to stake out positions between the two; others try to evade the dilemma altogether with "panpsychism," arguing that reality is mind all the way down. But the general trend has been along Hobbesian lines: rejecting the Cartesian mind as a "ghost in the machine," and reducing man to the body and the mind to the brain. The contemporary successors of Hobbes are the "eliminative materialists," who, as their name suggests, want to eliminate all traces of an immaterial mind completely: thoughts and beliefs, desires and choices, and all of the "folk" ideas traditionally associated with a Cartesian self.

Materialism rightly insists on the unity of the human being and the close connection between mind and body—a connection that substance dualism severs. The mind-body problem, on materialism, effectively disappears; it's no problem at all because there isn't any "mind" to speak of. It also leans into the great victories of modern science and encourages the study of the body and the brain, yielding important insights into human behavior.

But this earthward way, like scientism, faces the snare of a self-refuting definition. For materialists, all beliefs are illusions; but

8. Hobbes, Third Objections, in Descartes, *Meditations*, 122.

materialism itself is a belief; therefore, materialism is an illusion. This isn't just a clever rhetorical move; it shows that the self, even as it arcs fully toward the material, has to occupy some kind of immaterial space. The only alternative is to cease being the kind of selves that we naturally are.

Even if we manage to work our way around this self-contradiction, or at least ignore it, the cost of snuffing out the soul and mind like smoldering wicks is astronomically high. The integrity of human thought, the mystery of human freedom, the objectivity of moral value—all of these aspects of human life become fictions we tell ourselves in order to live. We're not even *rational* animals at all, because rationality presumes a mind with which to reason. But these experiences of the self—so integral to the history of philosophy—are too immediate and basic to be wiped away. And this is far from a religious talking point: such gaping holes in the reigning materialist worldview led the atheist philosopher Thomas Nagel to conclude that it's "almost certainly false," and that some metaphysical alternative has to be on the horizon.[9]

+

The Way is both the soul and the body.

"What a piece of work is a man, how noble in reason, how infinite in faculties, in form and moving, how express and admirable in action, how like an angel in apprehension, how like a god! The beauty of the world; the paragon of animals; and yet to me what is

9. Thomas Nagel, *Mind and Cosmos: Why the Materialist Neo-Darwinian Conception of Nature Is Almost Certainly False* (Oxford: Oxford University Press, 2012).

this quintessence of dust?"[10] These lines of Shakespeare, penned just a few years after Descartes' birth, reflect an understanding of man through philosophy on the Way: we're a microcosm of both heaven and earth, a living tension of the spiritual and physical—and therefore, a creature of both soul and body, both angelic apprehension and crumbling dust.

In his earlier writings, Augustine tilts in the direction of a Platonic soul, using the language of "the prison of the body" and defining man as "a rational soul with a mortal and earthly body in its service."[11] But by the time of his *City of God*, he gives a full-throated endorsement of the Way, rebalancing his earlier lean: "Man is not merely a body or merely a soul, but a being constituted by body and soul together. . . . It is the conjunction of the two parts that is entitled to the name of 'man.'"[12] The image of God is primarily in the soul, but the body participates in that reality in a unified human nature. We are, in short, "a kind of mean between angels and beasts."[13]

Aquinas aligns with the Augustinian approach: the human soul is the "boundary line" between the spiritual and the physical, dwelling on "the horizon of eternity and time"; "it approaches the highest by receding from the lowest."[14] He agrees with Aristotle that the soul is the substantial "form" of the body, the two intimately united

10. William Shakespeare, *Hamlet*, act 2, scene 2, in *The Riverside Shakespeare*, 2nd ed. (Boston: Houghton Mifflin, 1997), 1204.

11. Augustine, *Soliloquies* 1.24, in *The Happy Life; Answer to Skeptics; Divine Providence and the Problem of Evil; Soliloquies*, trans. Thomas F. Gilligan et al. (New York: CIMA Publishing, 1948), 375; *Of the Morals of the Catholic Church* 27.

12. Augustine, *City of God* 13.24.

13. *City of God* 12.22.

14. Thomas Aquinas, *Of God and His Creatures* 2.80–81, trans. Joseph Rickaby (London: Burns and Oates, 1905), 158.

in one human nature, but he also agrees with Plato that the soul is immortal, leaning on the authority of the Neoplatonic Pseudo-Dionysius: "Human souls owe to divine goodness that they are 'intellectual,' and that they have 'an incorruptible substantial life.'"[15]

How does Aquinas reconcile these two sides of the soul—its contrast of immortality on the one hand, and connection to the body on the other? He concedes that, after death, the separated soul lacks its bodily powers; it will be *more* complete in one sense, having been found in God, but *less* complete in another sense, having been divided from its body.[16] It remains a whole soul but "not wholly at rest"—not until the resurrection of the dead.[17]

For both philosophers, this union of soul and body has its corresponding union in the sacraments, which engage the whole person. Augustine famously defines the sacraments as "sacred signs," "things visible" that honor "invisible things."[18] Aquinas leans into Augustine's authority, as well as Aristotelian categories: "In the sacraments, words and things, like form and matter, combine in the formation of one thing."[19] Thus, in Baptism, the matter is water, and the form is "I baptize you in the Name of the Father, and of the Son, and of the Holy Spirit." To tinker with either of these is to lose the sacrament. This logic of union, for Aquinas, only intensifies with the Eucharist: the form is the prayer of consecration, and the matter is the bread and wine. But after that prayer, the *substance* of the bread and wine becomes Christ (trans-substantiates); only the *accidents* of the bread and wine—whiteness, roundness, etc.—remain.

15. Thomas Aquinas, *Summa theologiae* 1.75.6.
16. *Summa theologiae* Suppl. 70.1.
17. *Summa theologiae* 1-2.4.5.
18. *City of God* 10.5; *On the Catechizing of the Uninstructed* 26.
19. *Summa theologiae* 3.60.6.

Aquinas lived and wrote before Descartes and Hobbes, of course, but Jacques Maritain and Étienne Gilson, who spearheaded an "existential Thomism" in the twentieth century, bring the Way to bear on modern philosophy in powerful ways. For both men, Cartesianism—which simultaneously radicalized the way of the soul and the way of the body—was where modern philosophy's trouble began, and a return to the holistic dualism of "hylomorphism" (literally, "matter-form-ism") was where hope was found. "St. Thomas brings together," Maritain writes. "Descartes cleaves and separates."[20] "Man is not a mind that thinks," Gilson adds, "but a being who knows other beings as true, who loves them as good, and who enjoys them as beautiful."[21]

Philosophers on the Way agree, in part, with the heavenward: the rational soul exists, and is higher and nobler than the body. But they also agree, again in part, with the earthward: the material body is integral to human nature, and its mechanisms can and should be studied. We can't be reduced to mere matter any more than we can be reduced to mere mind. The Way honors both sides of the human being as it honors both sides of all being: as one.

20. Jacques Maritain, *The Dream of Descartes*, trans. Mabelle L. Andison (New York: Philosophical Library, 1944), 166.

21. Étienne Gilson, *The Unity of Philosophical Experience* (San Francisco: Ignatius, 1999), 255.

CHAPTER 11

Knowledge: Thought or Experience

The New Testament defines faith as "the assurance of things hoped for, the conviction of things not seen" (Heb. 11:1). What, then, is reason? We might define it, broadly, as the assurance of things *intelligible*, and the conviction of things *sensible*. The intelligible we access through logic and reason, and the sensible through intuition and instinct. But at the birth of modern philosophy, we also see a splintering of these two modes of reasoning, the spiritual and the physical parting ways on the path of knowledge.

Does human knowledge come from angelic thought or animal experience?

I

The heavenward way is thought at the expense of experience.

Here again, there's no better example than Descartes, the consummate modern rationalist. In fact, Descartes' whole program rises out of his desire to overcome the creeping influence of skepticism. What is truth? Can we really *know* anything at all? Descartes was convinced we could; in fact, he had an epiphany that he would be the one to lead the way. On November 10, 1619, the young philosopher—then serving as a soldier—locked himself in a small room with a stove, and there had a mystical vision of the unification of all of the sciences into a single rational and mathematical system. Pure thought would be the unshakeable foundation on which to ground all knowledge, from physics up through metaphysics—a realm of distinct ideas "like the very heaven for clearness" (Exod. 24:10). This was the birth of Descartes' philosophy, of modern philosophy itself—even of the whole modern world.

Descartes knew that he first had to beat the skeptics at their own game. He begins the *Meditations* with a systematic doubt of the existence of everything: God, the world, even his own body. He imagines that he has "no hands, no eyes, no flesh, no blood, and no senses,"[1] and that, instead, reality is a great web of lies spun by a "malicious demon" that makes all these things seem real. In a more recent image tossed around by philosophers, the self is like a brain in a vat, experiencing reality as a kind of dream. The world is like the virtual reality of the Matrix, but there's only one participant, and it's you. Descartes likens this radical skepticism to the delusions of the insane, but by it, he means to gain back a secure foundation for reason.

Because even as everything else can be doubted, there's one thing that can't: thought itself. To be deceived at all, some thinking subject needs to be there in the first place. Descartes draws the inevitable conclusion: "I am therefore, speaking precisely, only a thinking thing, that is, a mind, or a soul, or an intellect, or a

1. René Descartes, *Meditations on First Philosophy*, trans. Michael Moriarty (Oxford: Oxford University Press, 2008), 16.

reason."[2] This is the famous *Cogito ergo sum*—"I think, therefore I am."[3] At the bottom of the most exaggerated skepticism, we find a new, unshakeable foundation for knowledge.

The whole tradition of modern idealism, which approaches the world through the mind, flows out from the *cogito*. It's also the source of the distinctively modern attitude of individualism and self-reliance; indeed, Americans, in Alexis de Tocqueville's assessment, are all unconscious Cartesians: "America is therefore the one country in the world where the precepts of Descartes are least studied and best followed. . . . Each therefore withdraws narrowly into himself and claims to judge the world from there."[4]

Cartesian rationalism is right to affirm and defend our capacity for thought and to strive to elevate philosophy through "clear and distinct" ideas. And it wisely sees that philosophy, which accesses higher realities and nobler truths, remains vitally important; it has to be in close dialogue with math and science, and taken with great seriousness in its own right.

But without some grounding in experience, it leaves us marooned in the *cogito*. Descartes—again, to give him his due—didn't want to leave us there. He tried to reconnect thought and experience, and the link for him was God, who, unlike a malicious demon, isn't a deceiver. But how can we show, with pure thought alone, that God exists? Descartes leaned into Anselm's ontological argument, which reasons from the mere *concept* of God to God's

2. Descartes, 19.

3. René Descartes, *Discourse on Method*, trans. Desmond M. Clarke (London: Penguin Books, 2003), 25.

4. Alexis de Tocqueville, *Democracy in America*, trans. Harvey C. Mansfield and Delba Winthrop (Chicago: The University of Chicago Press, 2000), 403–404.

actual existence. But Thomas Aquinas himself had challenged the soundness of this argument centuries before: the concept "God" could very well just be an empty concept.[5] The joint connecting thought and experience was wobbly at best.

And if God's existence can't be proven from within the *cogito*, we're not only left with the unbridgeable chasm between subject and object; we're also left with the awful possibility of solipsism: the only thing that exists, or that we can reliably say exists, is our own stream of consciousness. The *cogito* is not only the foundation; it's also the walls, the roof, and the locked door separating it from anything outside of itself. Descartes' victory against the skeptics was Pyrrhic: we gain the *cogito* but lose the whole world. "We think of the key, each in his prison," wrote T.S. Eliot. "Thinking of the key, each confirms a prison." In the poet's notes for these lines, he quotes Dante's *Inferno*—"And I heard them below locking the door / of the horrible tower"—and the idealist F.H. Bradley: "The whole world for each is peculiar and private to that soul."[6]

Recent philosophers have proposed that the whole world might be a computer simulation, and commentators have naturally drawn comparisons to Descartes. But there's no comparison: a computer simulation at least gets us out of our own head and into a shared experience, artificial though it may be. The way of thought alone culminates in a hellishness of utter loneliness.

5. Thomas Aquinas, *Summa theologiae* 1.2.1.

6. T.S. Eliot, *The Waste Land*, in *Anthology of Modern American Poetry*, ed. Cary Nelson (Oxford: Oxford University Press, 2000), 300–301.

—

The earthward way is experience at the expense of thought.

Many philosophers, of course, have rejected rationalism altogether, refusing to set foot into the labyrinth of the mind; instead, they've gone this opposite way of empiricism, rooting knowledge in experience. And if Descartes was the consummate rationalist, we find the consummate empiricist in David Hume. Like Descartes, Hume applied the rigor of science to philosophy, but in the opposite direction. The Scotsman argues that our thoughts (or "ideas") are faint copies of more immediate sense data (or "impressions"), and that the mind is just a "bundle" of these impressions. When we reason, we deal with two distinct realities: relations of ideas (like one plus one is two) and matters of fact (like the sun rising in the morning). Relations of ideas are purely logical and thus certain, whereas matters of fact are purely experiential and thus uncertain.

Hume thus introduces a radical new skepticism into philosophy. Facts that we take for granted as true—like the sun rising every morning—are simply old habits of the mind. As a matter of fact, we don't really *know* that the sun will rise tomorrow. We don't even know for sure that one thing causes another at all; "causation" is just our familiarity with event B following event A over and over again. All we really have, at the end of the day, is the act of "compounding, transposing, augmenting, or diminishing the materials afforded us by the senses and experience."[7]

Empiricism is right to affirm the elemental truth of our experience of the world through the five senses. These impressions

7. David Hume, *An Enquiry Concerning Human Understanding* (Indianapolis: Hackett, 1993), 11.

overwhelm us from birth; long before we form memories, exercise thought, or articulate ideas, we're drinking from a firehose of sights, sounds, textures, tastes, and smells from the world around us. There's something not only eminently practical but also deeply human in empiricism's refusal to let experience be stripped away from us.

But is a world of pure experience without thought any more livable than a world of pure thought without experience? Rationalism evaporates the outer world into ideas, but empiricism condenses the inner world into the senses. The implications are disorienting: life is just one thing after the other, an interminable sequence of disconnected perceptions, a raging Heraclitan river of mere appearances. Hume himself had difficulty settling into his own worldview: at the end of his treatise on human nature, he admits, "Where am I, or what? . . . What beings surround me? . . . I am confounded with all these questions, and begin to fancy myself in the most deplorable condition imaginable, environed with the deepest darkness." It was only through diversions—"I dine, I play a game of backgammon, I converse, and am merry with my friends"—that he found relief from his "philosophical melancholy."[8]

The way of pure experience also harbors an enantiodromatic whiplash back into the way of pure thought. There's clearly an earthward affinity between empiricism and materialism, but one of Hume's fellow empiricists, George Berkeley, pushed empiricism into a new extreme: *to be is to be perceived.* All we have is impressions from the senses, yes, but these impressions themselves are *mental* impressions. We can't appeal to anything outside of them;

8. David Hume, *A Treatise of Human Nature* (Oxford: Clarendon, 1896), 269.

therefore, we can't really speak of matter existing at all. Samuel Johnson famously kicked a stone in a desperate attempt to refute Berkeley, but it was, of course, no use: empiricism, like rationalism, lodges us in our own heads and away from the land of the living.

+

The Way is both thought and experience.

Étienne Gilson saw the whole history of philosophy as an alternating push and pull between the dogmatism of pure thought and the skepticism of pure experience. As soon as one side triumphantly reaches the end of either certainty or doubt, the other breaks through and reasserts itself: "Philosophy always buries its undertakers."[9] But in the writings of both Augustine and Aquinas, we find a union of thought and experience that evades the extremes of both sides. Where thought drifts up and away, they draw it back down to earth; where experience collapses in on itself, they lift it back up to heaven.

Augustine, pivoting off the Platonic tradition, instinctively stresses thought on the Way. He argues that the intellect arrives at truth apart from experience; in fact, it's granted through divine illumination from above. In his early *Soliloquies*, he writes that God's kingdom is "unknown to sense" and that "these things of sense must be forsaken entirely."[10] And in the *City of God*, he even offers a

9. Étienne Gilson, *The Unity of Philosophical Experience* (San Francisco: Ignatius, 1999), 246.

10. Augustine, *Soliloquies* 1.3, 1.24, in *The Happy Life; Answer to Skeptics; Divine Providence and the Problem of Evil; Soliloquies*, trans. Thomas F. Gilligan et al. (New York: CIMA Publishing, 1948), 345, 375.

kind of proto-*cogito*: "They say, 'Suppose you are mistaken?' I reply, 'If I am mistaken, I exist.'"[11]

Nevertheless, Augustine holds off a one-sided rationalism. Divine illumination doesn't wash out our senses, nor does the proto-*cogito* lodge us in the mind. And in his *Retractions* toward the end of his life, Augustine revises his statements from the *Soliloquies*, which sold physical experience too short: it's not that God's kingdom is unknown to sense itself, he corrects himself, but to "the sense *of the mortal body*"; and "the things of sense of 'the new heaven and the new earth'" we need not forsake.[12]

Aquinas finds his balance in Aristotle's more natural theory of knowledge. In the *Summa*, he modifies Augustine's theory of divine illumination: man "needs divine help" from God as first cause to know anything, but he "does not need a new light added to his natural light" to know natural things.[13] And he praises the Philosopher's "middle course" between two extremes: on the one side was Democritus, who grounded knowledge in sense impressions, and on the other, Plato, who grounded knowledge in the forms. For Aristotle, knowledge is grounded in both: intellect and sense are contrasted but connected.[14]

In the Philosopher's account of knowledge, which Aquinas takes up, physical objects impress themselves upon the mind (as "phantasms") through sense experience: "Nothing is in the intellect that was not first in the senses."[15] But knowledge isn't simply a

11. Augustine, *City of God* 11.26.

12. Augustine, *Retractions* 4.2–3, trans. M. Inez Bogan (Washington, DC: The Catholic University of America Press, 1968), 17–18.

13. Thomas Aquinas, *Summa theologiae* 1-2.109.1.

14. *Summa theologiae* 1.84.6.

15. Thomas Aquinas, *De veritate* 2.3.19.

passive reception of impressions, which would leave us stuck in the snare of skepticism; instead, thought then enters the picture and takes the lead. After the mind receives the phantasm, the intellect then *abstracts* and receives the form of the object, becoming, in a way, one with it. Aquinas thus offers us, as G.K. Chesterton later put it, both "the appeal to Reason and the Authority of the Senses," refusing to sacrifice one to the other.[16]

Man is neither a thinking thing nor a sensing thing but—here and now, and in the life of the world to come—both.

16. G.K. Chesterton, *St. Thomas Aquinas*, in *St. Thomas Aquinas; St. Francis of Assisi* (San Francisco: Ignatius, 2002), 29.

CHAPTER 12

Action: Subjective Freedom or Objective Causation

When turning to human action—even if we bracket the question of God's providence—we face another dilemma of freedom and necessity. The dilemma shifts from God and man to the spirit and the flesh, but the main question—the integrity of human freedom—remains the same. Epicurus first hit on the problem, but it only intensifies with modern science, which shows that the universe operates according to fundamental physical laws.

Are human actions determined by subjective freedom or objective causation?

I

The heavenward way is subjective freedom at the expense of objective causation.

On this "libertarian" path (from the Latin *libertas*, meaning "freedom"), our decisions finally come down to our own inner free choice. Take the decision of what to do for dinner tonight. Naturally, you might consider any number of enticing options based on what's in the fridge, in your bank account, or on your schedule. But for libertarians, the decision—say, to stay home and cook some slightly expired pasta—ultimately rests with a kind of "command center" above the body. Whatever you choose was entirely your choice, meaning you could have easily chosen otherwise if you desired. You're the master of your fate and the captain of your soul.

Though Descartes is best known as a philosopher of thought, he's also—in fact, far more fundamentally—a philosopher of freedom. The will, he writes in the *Meditations*, is "unbounded by any limits."[1] It's the primary source of the *imago Dei* in us: "It is chiefly on account of the will that I understand that I bear a certain image and likeness of God."[2] The will is even greater than the intellect: "There is no other property in me, apart from this one, that is so perfect or so great that I cannot understand how it could be more perfect or greater."[3]

This passion for free will stands behind Descartes' oft-quoted line that human beings, through reason and science, should become "the lords and masters of nature."[4] The relationship between subject and object has become one of pure antagonism, and man—a thinking thing orbiting the earth and liberated from its constraints—manipulates nature from above. Indeed, the *cogito* itself is made possible by a defiant act of the will that precedes it. To

1. René Descartes, *Meditations on First Philosophy*, trans. Michael Moriarty (Oxford: Oxford University Press, 2008), 41.

2. Descartes, 41.

3. Descartes, 41.

4. René Descartes, *Discourse on Method*, trans. Desmond M. Clarke (London: Penguin Books, 2003), 35.

arrive at pure thought, Descartes first *refuses* experience, saying no to the whole of external reality.

Philosophical libertarianism honors our commonsense understanding of ourselves as free agents with the ability to choose one thing rather than another. And in honoring this power of choice, it also protects our responsibility for what we choose—and, therefore, the entire edifice of law and punishment that informs both religion and society. Neuroscience itself even bears witness to this "top-down" causation: certain habits of mind can literally remap the brain's physical structure out of OCD and other disorders, a "neuroplasticity" best explained by free will.

But on top of bringing us back to the interaction problem—How does free will operate in and through a completely separated body?—a "top-down" spiritual freedom against nature also ends up blending with that other totalizing of the will: a "bottom-up" human freedom against God. Divine laws, like physical laws, become just another constraint on our own lordship, and the divine nature, like physical nature, just another external object to master. A will "unbounded by any limits" has no inclination to bind itself—whether from above or below.

We see this play out in the strange affinity of two thinkers—otherwise diametrically opposed to each other—on the subject of freedom: Descartes and Sartre. Descartes was a firm believer in God, spirit, reason, and values; the existentialist Sartre casts all four aside. God doesn't exist, Sartre writes, and "there disappears with him all possibility of finding values in an intelligible heaven" or even in "the heaven of intelligence."[5] Yet Sartre praises Descartes' absolu-

5. Jean-Paul Sartre, "Existentialism and Humanism," in *Basic Writings*, ed. Stephen Priest (London: Routledge, 2001), 32, 29.

tizing of human freedom: the *cogito* opens the way to a "translucent refusal of everything."[6] In fact, for Sartre, the problem wasn't that Descartes went too far; it was that he didn't go far enough. He made man "only nominally free" by still depending on God and reason.[7] Sartre completes the project of self-creation begun in the *cogito* by refusing both: "Man is a freedom," he concludes, and that freedom is "total."[8] Sartre even presents man in dualistic terms that call Descartes to mind: man is "being-for-itself" opposed to "being-in-itself," a pure subjectivity in a sea of objects.[9]

Sartre's own fiction shows where this struggle between the free subject and everything surrounding it leads us. In the play *No Exit*, one character famously remarks, "L'enfer, c'est les autres!" (Hell is other people!).[10] And in his first novel, he describes the external world with the image of "nausea": "It was there . . . all soft, sticky, soiling everything, all thick, a jelly . . . filling everything with its gelatinous slither. . . . I choked with rage at this gross, absurd being. . . . I shouted, 'Filth! What rotten filth!'"[11] Absolute freedom ends not in mastery over nature but in an impotent frenzy.

6. Jean-Paul Sartre, *Literary and Philosophical Essays*, trans. Annette Michelson (New York: Collier Books), 190.

7. Sartre, 193.

8. Sartre, 183, 184.

9. Jean-Paul Sartre, *Being and Nothingness: A Phenomenological Essay on Ontology*, trans. Hazel E. Barnes (New York: Washington Square Press, 1975), 25.

10. Jean-Paul Sartre, *No Exit*, in *"No Exit" and Three Other Plays* (New York: Vintage, 1989), 45.

11. Jean-Paul Sartre, *Nausea*, trans. Lloyd Alexander (New York: New Directions, 1964), 134.

—

The earthward way is objective causation at the expense of subjective freedom.

Standing opposite libertarianism is the path of determinism—the view that all of our choices are in fact illusory. Thus, your "free choice" to cook that expired pasta for dinner—as well as all your reasons for choosing that instead of something else—was decided for you from the moment of the Big Bang. Every "choice" we make is nothing but the necessary result of a long chain of physical causes preceding it. There is, in the end, nothing free about us at all: you are not the master but the mastered.

In the century after Descartes, Julien Offray de La Mettrie stepped boldly into this earthward way. La Mettrie was a materialist and hedonist in the tradition of Epicurus: "We shall be Anti-Stoics!" he writes. "Those philosophers are sad, strict, and unyielding; we shall be cheerful, sweet-natured, and indulgent. They are all soul and ignore their bodies; we shall be all body and ignore our souls."[12] His own life bears witness to the risk of hedonistic excess: he died at just forty-one—apparently from a gastric illness after devouring a large helping of pheasant and truffle pâté.

But La Mettrie is best known not for his hedonism but for his determinism. In *Machine Man*, he defends a mechanistic view of the human being: the mind is, as for Hobbes, simply part of its mechanisms, and the will is subjected, like everything else in us, to the necessity of the body: "For every order it gives, it is forced a

12. Julien Offray de La Mettrie, *Anti-Seneca or the Sovereign Good*, in *"Machine Man" and Other Writings*, ed. and trans. Ann Thomson (Cambridge: Cambridge University Press, 1996), 119.

hundred times to obey."[13] Thus, free will is an illusion. There's no invisible agent calling the shots from within, no inner self pulling the strings from above. La Mettrie's view of man is the inverse of Sartre's: we're condemned to be unfree. "Man is a machine despotically governed by absolute fatalism."[14]

Determinism rightly embraces the "bottom-up" impact of the brain on the mind—a truth revealed not only by common sense but also by neuroscience. Our choices are deeply rooted in the soil of physical processes beyond our control: the heart beats without our permission, and the brain's hundred billion neurons fire without our direction. And this is just the body: there's also the whole expanse of environmental factors pushing and pulling on us all the time.

But in jettisoning free will entirely, determinism also ends in grave dangers, chief of which, as Epicurus saw, is the loss of moral responsibility. This has clear social implications: If we aren't free to choose what we choose, what sense is there in the criminal justice system with its juries and judges, its punishments and prisons? Isn't it all predicated on a mistake, and manifestly unfair? La Mettrie admits as much: criminals are guilty in an "arbitrary" sense of social relations, but not in any *real* sense. The criminal is just the "slave of the blood galloping in his veins, as the hand of a watch is the slave of the works which make it move"; therefore, he "only deserves compassion."[15]

13. Julien Offray de La Mettrie, *Machine Man*, in *"Machine Man" and Other Writings*, 30.

14. Julien Offray de La Mettrie, *Preliminary Discourse*, in *"Machine Man" and Other Writings*, 155.

15. La Mettrie, *Machine Man*, 143.

This loss of moral responsibility has led many earthward minds to shy away from determinism. But where is a good materialist to go, if libertarianism is no longer an option? The conventional answer has been "compatibilism": the view that subjective freedom and causal determinism are compatible. But the resolution isn't as balanced as it might appear: compatibilism simply redefines freedom as a freedom *from* external restraint, rather than a freedom *for* choosing this instead of that. With good reason, William James called it "a *soft* determinism that abhors harsh words."[16]

Sam Harris and Daniel Dennett—both atheists—exposed these respective weaknesses in each other's positions in a public clash on free will. Harris, a determinist, argued that since free will is an illusion, "even the most terrifying predators are, in a very real sense, unlucky to be who they are."[17] Compatibilists who cling to freedom, he adds, are little better than theologians: they just can't let their "cherished illusion" die.[18] Dennett, a compatibilist, shot back that Harris is "throwing out the baby with the bathwater," and that freedom remains "a reliable part of the foundations of morality." Without it, "there really is no morally relevant difference between the raving psychopath and us."[19]

But determinism is not only socially destabilizing; it's also intellectually dissatisfying. As with the narrow Stoic lens of providence, the narrow scientific lens of determinism leaves us in a conundrum: to live at all, we can't help but think and speak of

16. William James, "The Dilemma of Determinism," in *"The Will to Believe" and Other Essays in Popular Philosophy* (Mineola, NY: Dover, 1956), 149.

17. Sam Harris, *Free Will* (New York: Free Press, 2012), 53.

18. Harris, 18.

19. Daniel Dennett, "Reflections on 'Free Will,'" Naturalism.org, January 24, 2014, https://naturalism.org/resources/book-reviews/reflections-on-free-will.

ourselves as free to choose. Determinists, in practical and political contexts, sometimes even extol a radical Sartrean freedom, assuming as indispensable what they've already denied as impossible. But we can't have our cake and eat it too: either authentic human freedom is the fundamental fact we take it to be, or we are stuck in a self-contradictory incoherence—one that we can ignore but not overcome.

+

The Way is both subjective freedom and objective causation.

To treat man as either manipulating the body from above as its master or being manipulated by it from below as its slave are equal and opposite mistakes. In accordance with the union of spirit and flesh, freedom and causation commune on the Way.

That man has a spiritual soul capable of choosing good or evil, and that he's responsible for his choices, is a bedrock presupposition of Christianity. The whole story of salvation hinges on it, and it all falls apart without it. At the same time, if the soul is the *form* of the body, forming a unit with it, there has to be a certain bottom-up conditioning of the human person too. Our identity is a result not just of what we decide but also of what's been decided for us. The primacy of subjective freedom and its close connection with objective causation both have to be honored.

Augustine was a passionate defender of free will throughout his career, but was primarily concerned with overcoming the dilemma between providence and freedom, and resisting those who choose one side at the expense of the other. The union of spiritual freedom and physical causality comes into sharper focus with Aquinas. In the *Summa*, he considers the following argument against freedom: we choose in accord with what we are, as Aristotle argued; "but it is not in our power to be of one quality or another, for this comes to us from nature"; therefore, we're not really free to choose.[20] In answering the argument, Aquinas does admit that the body and its powers push and pull on us against our will: we often have a certain "temperament or disposition" due to "corporeal causes."[21] But ultimately, "these inclinations are subject to the judgment of reason, which the lower appetite obeys."[22] The soul isn't determined any more than the body is autonomous.

But Aquinas also considers a second, more formidable objection to freedom, one that cuts against his own thinking more directly: the will can't desire evil, but only what it perceives as good; this means that the will "tends of necessity to the good which is proposed to it"; thus, the will isn't free.[23] Aquinas, following Aristotle, accepts the first premise. We don't always choose what is, in fact, good, but we do always choose what we *perceive* as good: "The will can tend to nothing except under the aspect of good."[24] Yet he denies that this requires a deterministic necessity: "Because good is of many kinds, for this reason the will is not of necessity determined to one."[25] The will can also freely intervene, weighing and evaluating various goods and their implications: "What causes us to will need not compel us to will, since will itself can interfere

20. Thomas Aquinas, *Summa theologiae* 1.83.1.
21. *Summa theologiae* 1.83.1.
22. *Summa theologiae* 1.83.1.
23. *Summa theologiae* 1.82.2.
24. *Summa theologiae* 1.82.2.
25. *Summa theologiae* 1.82.2.

with the process."[26] Thus, the will is both compelled to choose the good and free to recalibrate itself.

Very few philosophers have had libertarians, determinists, and compatibilists all claiming them as one of their own, but St. Thomas Aquinas is one of them, and it's because he thought with the Way of heaven and earth. A Christian approach to human action is, in a sense, libertarian: it honors the reality and primacy of the freedom of the spirit, which rises above the body. But it's also, in a sense, determinist: it honors the causality of the physical world, including in our bodies and brains, and its impact on—and intimate connection with—our freedom. In a word, it aspires to a true compatibilism.

26. Thomas Aquinas, *Quaestiones Disputatae de Malo* (*Opera Omnia*, Leonine ed., vol. 23), in *Selected Philosophical Writings*, ed. Timothy McDermott (Oxford: Oxford University Press, 1993), 182.

CHAPTER 13

The Good: Values or Facts

Behind the philosophical debates about the good life and free will is a more fundamental debate: the nature of goodness itself. Here, another extension of the spiritual-physical dilemma appears. On the one hand, we find absolute and universal laws of right and wrong; on the other, we find the shifting and particular circumstances in which we have to make choices.

Is the good defined by values or facts?

I

The heavenward way is values at the expense of facts.

This way is rooted in Socrates, who was primarily an ethical thinker. Against the Sophists, who defined values like justice according to various facts below—the will of the state, the obedience to laws, the strength of the powerful—Socrates searched for a universal standard above that applied to all. But we find the modern exemplar of the way of values in Immanuel Kant and his deontological ethics.

Though he was only five feet fall, Kant was a titan of heavenward ideas. He was a man of discipline, whose strict daily walking routines had neighbors nicknaming him "the Königsberg clock"; a man of thought, who contributed massively to the Enlightenment, modern philosophy, and philosophical idealism; a man of spirit, who took seriously the reality of an immortal soul; and a man of faith, even as he circumscribed religion "within the limits of reason alone." Kant, in a word, was a stargazer; indeed, he famously said that two things fill the mind with awe: "the starry heavens above me and the moral law within me."[1]

And the impetus for his project was David Hume, who awoke him from a "dogmatic slumber."[2] How can matters of fact give us structures of reason? How can an "is" possibly give us an "ought"? In the face of Hume's skepticism, Kant rose to the defense of traditional religion and morality, essentially reducing the former to the latter in a bid to protect both: "Even the Holy One of the gospel must first be compared with our ideal of moral perfection before he is recognized as such."[3]

At the heart of Kant's ethical program was what he called the "categorical imperative": "Act only according to that maxim whereby you can at the same time will that it should become a universal law."[4] What's right is right for all, everywhere and always. This duty doesn't spring from God or from the forms, but from the

1. Immanuel Kant, *Critique of Practical Reason*, ed. and trans. Mary Gregor (Cambridge: Cambridge University Press, 2003), 133.

2. Immanuel Kant, *Prolegomena to Any Future Metaphysics*, ed. and trans. Paul Carus, 3rd ed. (Chicago: Open Court, 1912), 7.

3. Immanuel Kant, *Grounding for the Metaphysics of Morals*, trans. James W. Ellington (Indianapolis: Hackett, 1993), 21.

4. Kant, 30.

rational mind itself: we're autonomous "self-legislators." The categorical imperative is categorical because it's unconditional, and it's an imperative because it's unavoidable. We can't doubt it, and we have to follow it. We also have to honor the self-legislating power of other rational beings, leading to Kant's second formulation of the principle: treat other people "as an end and never simply as a means."[5]

One writer challenged Kant on the following thought experiment: Suppose a murderer is hunting down your friend, who is hiding in your home, and the murderer shows up on your doorstep and asks if your friend is inside. Would lying to him be wrong? Kant—not putting too fine a point on it—titled his response "On a Supposed Right to Lie because of Philanthropic Concerns." Lying, he argued—even in this dramatic situation—is wrong: "To be truthful (honest) in all declaration is, therefore, a sacred and unconditionally commanding law of reason that admits of no expediency whatsoever."[6] What if your friend secretly slips out the back? If you tell the truth (as you know it), then the murderer will search the house, but your friend will live. If you lie, the murderer will leave, but perhaps see your friend on the way out. Then you will not only have a lie still on your lips; you will have blood on your hands. We can't predict the future, but we can always act in accordance with our duty.

Deontology rightly affirms the dignity of human life and the objectivity of moral values and duties. How often do we accuse another but make excuses for ourselves? In how many countless ways do we use other people as a means to an end? How often do we use

5. Kant, 36.
6. Kant, 65.

rationalization and circumlocution to call what's wrong permissible—even good? The way of value challenges us to stand upright, to admit what has to be done, and to do it.

But without due attention to concrete facts, it leaves us with a detached and ruthless consistency. Kant builds on the great tradition of the Golden Rule—do unto others as you would have them do unto you—but the gold becomes heavy and unwieldy. It's a path of absolute law that draws us toward legalism, and of absolute duty that draws us toward rigorism. By abstracting values from all the particular conditions in which moral decision-making happens, including multiple values coming into conflict, it cuts them off from the messy reality of human existence. It's an ethical drone: metallic, inscrutable, and hovering between the sky and the ground.

—

The earthward way is facts at the expense of values.

Deontology is typically set off against consequentialism—in particular, utilitarianism—which makes the consequence of an action the measure of its rightness or wrongness. But the true polar opposite of Immanuel Kant is Friedrich Nietzsche, the earthward nemesis of all stargazing. Nietzsche was a passionate thinker whose words blaze across the page; an existentialist who reviled both Socrates (a "decadent"[7]) and Plato ("a coward in the face of reality" who "escapes into the ideal"[8]) and undercut Enlightenment rational-

7. Friedrich Nietzsche, *Ecce Homo*, in *"The Anti-Christ" and Other Writings*, ed. Aaron Ridley, trans. Judith Norman (Cambridge: Cambridge University Press, 2005), 108.

8. Friedrich Nietzsche, *Twilight of the Idols*, in *"The Anti-Christ" and Other Writings*, 226.

ism ("Why not untruth instead?"[9]); a physicalist who reviled the spiritual ("Pure spirit is a pure lie"[10]) and denied the soul ("The knowing one says: body am I through and through, and nothing besides"[11]); and an atheist who shook the religious world to its core (Christianity is "the one great curse," "the one immortal blot on humanity"[12]). Across the whole range of philosophical dilemmas, his cry was resounding and consistent: "*Remain faithful to the earth* and do not believe those who speak to you of extraterrestrial hopes!"[13]

Nietzsche is often regarded as a nihilist, but he saw himself as a *prophet* of nihilism—the one warning about its immanent arrival. The West is hurtling, he argued, toward "the Last Men": a race of blinking, unfeeling beetles with small minds, small hearts, and small stomachs. The way out of this nihilistic fate is a "transvaluation of values," beginning with the overcoming of traditional morality. Thus, Nietzsche throws out Kant and the "mortal danger" of his categorical imperative.[14] More fundamentally, he throws out the "slave morality" of Judaism and Christianity that gave us Kant—a value system that, for Nietzsche, is based on weakness, pity, and resentment. Man has to go "beyond good and evil." There are no objective values—only facts. In fact, there aren't even really

9. Friedrich Nietzsche, *Beyond Good and Evil*, ed. Rolf-Peter Horstmann and Judith Norman, trans. Judith Norman (Cambridge: Cambridge University Press, 2002), 5.

10. Friedrich Nietzsche, *The Anti-Christ*, in *"The Anti-Christ" and Other Writings*, 8.

11. Friedrich Nietzsche, *Thus Spoke Zarathustra*, ed. Adrian Del Caro and Robert B. Pippin, trans. Adrian Del Caro (Cambridge: Cambridge University Press, 2006), 23.

12. Nietzsche, *Anti-Christ*, 66.

13. Nietzsche, *Thus Spoke Zarathustra*, 6.

14. Nietzsche, *Anti-Christ*, 10.

facts—"only interpretations."[15] "Everyone should invent his *own* virtues, his *own* categorical imperatives."[16]

But from within this apparently relativistic "perspectivism," Nietzsche dreams of a new value system emerging, one rooted in the "master morality" of Greek heroism. It would be a moral system of strength instead of weakness, power instead of pity, daring instead of resentment. And it would emerge through the *Ubermensch*, the "Overman" or "Superman," who would rescue humanity from the jaws of nihilism with life-affirming vigor: "Let your will say: the overman *shall be* the meaning of the earth!"[17]

Nietzsche's transvaluation of values bears within it an important defense of the earthly: life in all its energy and vitality, man in all his power and potential, and the gritty facts that condition both. He rightly rejects the wrongheaded detachment of the idealist who seals himself off from life's messy realities and thinks that "these sorts of things are *beneath* him."[18] He calls on man to escape his own abstractions and instead plant his feet firmly in the ground again.

But Nietzsche's transvaluation collapses in on itself: his moral relativism undercuts his heroic morality—and vice versa. And despite his vicious attack on traditional values, he was haunted by the longing for an absolute, fixed, heavenly good—not only in his dream of the Overman but also in his dream of the "eternal recurrence," wherein "time itself is a circle" and life repeats again and again on a loop forever.[19] "I seek an eternity for everything—ought

15. Friedrich Nietzsche, *Writings from the Late Notebooks*, ed. Rüdiger Bittner, trans. Kate Sturge (Cambridge: Cambridge University Press, 2003), 139.

16. Nietzsche, *Anti-Christ*, 10.

17. Nietzsche, *Thus Spoke Zarathustra*, 6.

18. Nietzsche, *Anti-Christ*, 8.

19. Nietzsche, *Thus Spoke Zarathustra*, 178, 125.

one to pour the costliest balms and wines into the sea?—and my consolation is that everything that has been is eternal: the sea washes it up again."[20]

This earthward way also paved the way for some of the twentieth century's most heinous evils. In his last book, Nietzsche distances himself from both German nationalism ("Wherever Germany extends it spoils culture") and Darwinism ("Scholarly cattle have suspected me of Darwinism").[21] Nevertheless, his moral program would go on to inspire both Nazi Germany and social Darwinism, sowing devastation and death around the world. The way of facts without value leads us to the abyss of cruelty; "and when you stare for a long time into an abyss, the abyss stares back into you."[22]

The Way is both values and facts.

Augustine and Aquinas extend to humanity a way through both Kant and Nietzsche, elevating a path begun in their Greek predecessors: the way of *virtue*. The virtues are values made fact, norms in action—firm and fixed moral principles incarnated in human life as habits. They belong to the "natural law"—universal moral principles that are written on the heart of man and participate in the law of God.[23] This theme was picked up in a brighter moral spot in the century after Nietzsche: Martin Luther King Jr.'s

20. Nietzsche, *Writings from the Late Notebooks*, 216.
21. Nietzsche, *Ecce Homo*, 93, 101.
22. Nietzsche, *Beyond Good and Evil*, 69.
23. Thomas Aquinas, *Summa theologiae* 1-2.94.4, 6; 1-2.91.2.

"Letter from Birmingham Jail," which references both Augustine and Aquinas in connection with natural law.

This Christian way of virtue refuses both the Kantian way of duty and the Nietzschean way of power. We can't have a heart of stone: to act rightly, we have to be attentive to the facts of the matter. But we also can't "do evil so that good may come" (Rom. 3:8) or arrogate to ourselves, as Adam did, the right to determine good and evil in the first place. Instead—inhabiting a tension of absolute values and relative facts—we have to build character by habitually choosing the good.

What are the specific virtues? The ancients focused on what Christians call the four "cardinal" virtues: prudence, fortitude, temperance, and justice. Augustine picks up all four, but situates them under what are called the three "theological" virtues: faith, hope, and love, which are given to us as gifts from God. Without these theological virtues, Augustine insists, the ancient struggle to find happiness through virtue is doomed to failure: this life, "weighed down by such great and grievous ills," is just too overwhelming.[24] Thus, faith, hope, and love—especially love, "the greatest of these" (1 Cor. 13:13)—have to lead the Way. All virtue ultimately comes down to the virtue of love: love of God and love of neighbor. Virtue is, in Augustine's definition, just "rightly ordered love."[25]

Aquinas, for his part, dedicates the entire *Secunda Secundae* part of the *Summa* to the theological and cardinal virtues. And his metaphysics resists the sharp separation of values and facts even more. Aquinas defines virtue as "a good habit, productive of good works," and—citing the authority of Augustine—"a good quality of

24. Augustine, *City of God* 19.4.
25. *City of God* 15.22.

the mind" of which "no one can make bad use."[26] But what does it mean to be good? It means to be rationally ordered to our natural end: goodness "implies the idea of a final cause."[27] Thus, goodness and being, value and fact, ought and is—they all come together as one: "Goodness and being are really the same, and differ only in idea."[28] Virtue is man's living out of this convergence.

This balance of value and fact yields a more fruitful and sane engagement with moral questions. Augustine develops the just war theory—the notion that war is, under certain strict conditions, morally permissible. And Aquinas articulates the principle of double effect—the idea that a good or neutral action resulting in an unintended negative consequence is, again under certain conditions, also permissible. The way of virtue is at once stabilizing and sympathetic. It recognizes, with the deontologists, that certain actions are intrinsically evil, and that we're duty-bound to avoid them; but it also includes motives, contexts, and consequences in its moral calculus.

The long stand-off between heavenward and earthward ethics in modern philosophy led, unsurprisingly, to a revival in "virtue ethics" in the twentieth century. Catholic thinkers like Elizabeth Anscombe and Alasdair MacIntyre reintroduced the way of virtue in Aristotle and Aquinas to the modern world. Instead of obsessing over an abstract "formula" for ethical action or throwing out the idea of value completely, they asked a different question: What kind of person should we become? The answer is, of course, a good one—that is, a virtuous one.

26. *Summa theologiae* 1-2.55.3–4.
27. *Summa theologiae* 1.5.2.
28. *Summa theologiae* 1.5.1.

The precise shape of incarnated virtues has always been debated, and always will be. But keeping their eyes on Christ, philosophers of the Way remember both the eternal values that never change and the fresh circumstances that never stop changing, aspiring toward their communion in a life well lived.

CHAPTER 14

The Soul Power: The Intellect or the Will

In the soul itself—down where, as Lucinda Williams sang, "the spirit meets the bone"—we arrive at the strangest philosophical dilemma of all. Man has an intellect, symbolized by the head—his body part closest to the heavens. But he also has a will, symbolized by the heart—his center of gravity beating with the rhythms of the earth. We're torn between the head and the heart, the speculative and the practical—another extension of the spirit-flesh dilemma.

Is the intellect or the will the defining power of the soul?

I

The heavenward way is the intellect at the expense of the will.

Besides the categorical imperative, Kant is best known for his "transcendental idealism": the notion that the world doesn't, through *a posteriori* experience, structure thought, but rather that thought, with *a priori* categories, structures the world—a "Copernican revolution" that changed the landscape of philosophy for centuries. Indeed, while Kant also emphasized practical ethics and the exercise of the will, it was under the aegis of reason: "Since the derivation of actions from laws requires reason, the will is nothing but practical reason. . . . Reason infallibly determines the will."[1] He was, above all, a man of intellect.

We see this dynamic in his popular essay "An Answer to the Question: What Is Enlightenment?" Kant's answer is "the human being's emancipation from its self-incurred immaturity," a childish dependence on others to do our thinking for us. Thus Kant's proposed motto of the Enlightenment: "Have the courage to make use of your own intellect!"[2] Independent thinkers have to rise up and freely exercise their reason, promoting "the calling of every human being to think for himself."[3] The will plays a role in the essay, but more as a function of the intellect. In fact, the only freedom that "may be properly called freedom," Kant writes, is "to make *public use* of one's reason in all matters."[4] Enlightenment is only possible through freedom, but freedom is only truly free when it serves as an extension of reason.

This intellectualism honors the centrality of the life of the mind for philosophy—an intuition stretching all the way back to Plato and his charioteer. Man is most fundamentally a *rational* animal, not a willful animal, and to live a good life, the charioteer of reason has to rein in and tame the will and desires of the soul. When we

1. Immanuel Kant, *Grounding for the Metaphysics of Morals*, trans. James W. Ellington (Indianapolis: Hackett, 1993), 23.

2. Immanuel Kant, "An Answer to the Question: What Is Enlightenment?" in *"Toward Perpetual Peace" and Other Writings on Politics, Peace, and History*, ed. Pauline Kleingeld, trans. David L. Colclasure (New Haven, CT: Yale University Press, 2006), 17.

3. Kant, 18.

4. Kant, 18.

let those two horses take over and govern the intellect, disaster follows—both for the individual and those around him.

But this way of intellect, like the way of value, again cuts us off from the earthly. The will—with its intimate connection with the heart, the passions, and the body—binds us in a more immediate and visceral way to the world. But Kant's idealism, which chains the will to the intellect, leaves us hermetically sealed up in the mind. We can't know "things-in-themselves" (*noumena*) outside of the intellect; we can only how they appear to us (*phenomena*) through it. The world itself remains alien to us, and we to the world.

This earthward path also leads us to a narrowing of reason in philosophy. For Kant, classical metaphysics is a confused tug-of-war of contradictions, and the intellect has to withdraw into a more limited but well-lighted space. We see this tendency in the early champions of the analytic tradition, who reduced the life of the mind to the airtight formulas of mathematics, language, and logic, and looked down contemptuously on the existentialists grappling with desire, freedom, and finitude. On this way, we rationalize the mystery of being and bracket its more ambiguous and shadowy dimensions as unworthy of good philosophy. The head ceases to rationally interrogate the heart, and the heart ceases to intuitively condition the head—and both head and heart are worse off for it.

—

The earthward way is the will at the expense of the intellect.

No philosopher has followed the path of the will with the same relentless force as Friedrich Nietzsche. He is a philosopher of "the inward cave, the labyrinth of the heart."[5]

In his first book, *The Birth of Tragedy*, the young philologist articulates the dilemma of head and heart in terms of two gods of Greek mythology: Apollo and Dionysus. Apollo is the heavenly god of the sun, associated with reason, light, logic, purity, poetry, and order. Dionysus, on the other hand, is the more earthly god of wine, associated with passion, darkness, emotion, pleasure, music, and chaos. Surprisingly enough, Nietzsche—though he targets the logical Socrates, who received his philosophical mission from the oracle of Apollo—argues for the mutual necessity and harmonizing balance of the two sides in Greek art. We need both the splendor of Apollo and the vigor of Dionysus.

But by the end of his life, a very different Nietzsche had emerged. The pages of his last book, *Ecce Homo*, explode with Dionysian energy: "I am a disciple of the philosopher Dionysus; I would rather be a satyr than a saint."[6] Nietzsche longs for "a surplus of life on earth that will necessarily regenerate the Dionysian state."[7] What was once a kind of both/and has become a stark either/or. And the ultimate counterpoint to Dionysus is no longer Apollo, or even Socrates, but Jesus. The last words of this last book are "Dionysus versus the crucified."[8]

Toward the end of his lucid years, Nietzsche was planning a

5. Friedrich Nietzsche, *Untimely Meditations*, ed. Daniel Breazeale, trans. R.J. Hollingdale (Cambridge: Cambridge University Press, 1997), 139.

6. Friedrich Nietzsche, *Ecce Homo*, in *"The Anti-Christ" and Other Writings*, ed. Aaron Ridley, trans. Judith Norman (Cambridge: Cambridge University Press, 2005), 71.

7. Nietzsche, 110.

8. Nietzsche, 151.

four-volume series called *The Will to Power*. His penultimate book, *The Anti-Christ*, was meant to be the first volume in the series, and the fourth and final volume was to be titled *Dionysus*. Thus, in Nietzsche, the rejection of Christian morality and the rejection of Apollonian reason culminate in the will to power, a voluntarism that casts off the heavenly weights of both God and the intellect. Nietzsche's will to power cuts Kant's categorical imperative down to size: act only according to that maxim whereby *you will it*: "This world is the will to power—and nothing besides! And you yourselves too are this will to power—and nothing besides!"[9] Nietzsche would never complete the series: upon seeing a horse being viciously lashed in the streets of Turin, he rushed over to it, wrapped his arms around its neck, and collapsed—a nervous breakdown from which he never recovered. His last gesture was one not of willpower, but of the very pity—for an animal, no less—that he exhausted himself against.

Nietzsche's voluntarism rightly saw that the Dionysian—the life of the will, with all of its earthly associations—could not, and should not, be neglected. And it had been: his attacks on the hollow abstractions of rationalists and the smug moralism of Christians had behind them the noble aim of recapturing the vitality of the will and rescuing it from the ongoing decay of the Western mind, which was turning against itself.

But pushing against these threats, he fell into the opposite extreme, as far beyond reason as beyond good and evil. Some have traced Nietzsche's madness to the thoughts that racked his mind, others to the syphilis that racked his brain; it's not unreasonable

9. Friedrich Nietzsche, *Writings from the Late Notebooks*, ed. Rüdiger Bittner, trans. Kate Sturge (Cambridge: Cambridge University Press, 2003), 39.

to speculate that it was both. Yet whatever the case with Nietzsche himself, it's difficult to see how a philosophy of pure will doesn't, in the end, lead to a loss of the mind. At the hands of voluntarism, the love of wisdom itself is strangled. If philosophy is to endure, it can't follow Nietzsche down the dark road of pure will.

The stress on the will apart from the intellect also, like its heavenward opposite, leads to a dysfunction in philosophy. We detect it in the mainline of postmodernism—part of the continental tradition standing opposite the analytic—which builds on Nietzsche's perspectivism and will to power. For these thinkers, all is perspective and endless interpretation; there is no objective meaning above a given context, no universal truth outside of history—only the games of power governing discourse. Philosophers of the heart pluck our desires and play with words, but absent the guiding light of the intellect, they drag us into a bedlam of conflicting wills.

+

The Way is both the intellect and the will.

In the *Euthyphro*, Socrates poses one of the most famous dilemmas in philosophy: Is the good loved by God because he knows it as good, or is it good because it's loved by God? The first option would privilege the divine intellect at the expense of the divine will, the second the divine will at the expense of the divine intellect. "Intellectualist" Christians have taken the first option, dissolving God's heart into an intellectual mist; the God of the Bible becomes a kind of mythical picture of a higher intellectual reality. "Voluntarist" Christians, by contrast, have taken the second option, stupefying

God's head through the dictates of his will; if God wills it, one plus one can equal three, and blasphemy can be righteous.

But this is a false dilemma: intellect and will, truth and goodness, are one in God. He doesn't align with a standard of goodness outside of himself, nor does he arbitrarily decide the standard of goodness from within. God *is* goodness. "There is will in God, as there is intellect," Aquinas writes, "since will follows upon intellect. . . . And as his intellect is his own existence, so is his will."[10]

And the Son of God mirrors the Father. Christ, St. John tells us, is the *Logos* of God. This concept of Greek philosophy, stretching back to Heraclitus, translates not only as "Word" but also as "Reason." The Christian God is the God of reason: the Logos was with God, and "was God" (John 1:1). Yet the very food of this Logos "is to do the will of him who sent me" (John 4:34). Christ's descent to the cross is also one great display of loving obedience to the Father out of love for humanity. On the Way, the divine Mind leads to the piercing of the Sacred Heart.

Augustine follows this union of intellect and will in his *Confessions*. Throughout much of the book, he recounts his search for truth, reasoning his way through various philosophers, sages, and poets. Along the way, he encounters the Scriptures, but disregards them as childish and unserious. Later, with the help of St. Ambrose, he realizes that the Scriptures are far deeper and more sophisticated than he thought; they have a "twofold quality" of both lofty authority and "holy lowliness," both intellectual profundity and plain speech.[11] Later still, the writings of the Platonists clear up his

10. Thomas Aquinas, *Summa theologiae* 1.19.1.
11. Augustine, *Confessions* 6.5.

Manichaean misunderstanding of God as somehow bodily. These breakthroughs of the mind paved the way for his conversion.

At the same time, Augustine sees that it's impossible "to discover the truth by pure reason,"[12] and that what finally overcame his obstinate mind was God's action on his will. Indeed, Augustine is, in the end, more a philosopher of the heart than of the mind: "Thou hast made us for thyself and our hearts are restless till they rest in thee."[13] The gravity of the soul, either upward or downward, is "its love," and love is an act of the will.[14]

Intellect and will clearly flow together, but we're left with a nagging question: Which is higher? Aquinas brings Scholastic clarity to the question. In an absolute sense, the intellect is higher because ideation is a simpler and more spiritual activity than wanting. But in a relative sense, the will can also be higher: if the thing desired is *lower* than the soul (like a hamburger), knowing a thing is higher, since the thing is conformed to our mind; but if the thing desired is *higher* than the soul (like God), willing it is higher, since the will is conformed to the thing. Intellect and will belong together, and each moves the other in different ways, but intellect ultimately has an inherent primacy.

The same dynamic holds, for Aquinas, in the corresponding relationship of truth and goodness: the two coinhere, but "the true is prior to good"; "truth signifies something more absolute, and extends to the idea of good itself."[15] It even holds in the relationship of truth and love. When it comes to approaching God, Aquinas

12. *Confessions* 6.5.
13. *Confessions* 1.1.
14. Augustine, *City of God* 11.28.
15. *Summa theologiae* 1.16.4, 1.82.3.

acknowledges, the person who understands "all mysteries and all knowledge" but has no love is nothing (1 Cor. 13:2), and therefore, "the love of God is better than the knowledge of God."[16] Nevertheless, authentic love is enveloped—on both ends of the journey of faith—by a primacy of truth: "Knowledge precedes love in attaining, for 'nothing is loved save what is known,' as Augustine says"; and when we reach God in the end, the essence of that happiness, though it includes perfect love and joy, is the contemplation of truth.[17] Thus, on the Way, truth and love are inseparable—the Church speaks "the truth in love," and true love "rejoices in the truth" (Eph. 4:15; 1 Cor. 13:6)—but the former guides the latter to the heights.

The analytic and continental traditions have been caught on the horns of this intellect-will dilemma—the psychological side of the essence-existence dilemma—for decades. In 1971, Noam Chomsky, an analytic linguist, and Michel Foucault, a giant of postmodernism, debated this question: "Is there such a thing as 'innate' human nature independent of our experiences and external influences?" Chomsky, guardian of the intellect, argued yes; Foucault, the vanguard of the will, argued no. Nearly forty years later, Sam Harris and Jordan Peterson revisited the same dynamics in a similar debate: "What is true?" Harris, despite his skepticism of religion, cleaved to the heavenly way of the head, and Peterson, despite his skepticism of postmodernism, to the earthly way of the heart. Again and again, philosophers find themselves in stalemates that are impossible to overcome from either side of the divide.

Philosophers on the Way fall in both the analytic and con-

16. *Summa theologiae* 1.82.3.
17. *Summa theologiae* 1-2.3.4–5.

tinental camps, but, in the footsteps of Augustine and Aquinas, are always drawing together heaven and earth in the soul, even as they stress one or the other. They embrace reason and reject the will to power, but they also embrace the will and reject the reign of pure reason; they look to theory but also to practice, to metaphysics but also to history, to the head but also to the heart.

CHAPTER 15

Society: Order or Openness

Two other branches of philosophy, politics and aesthetics, meet in the question of society, from the microsociety of the family up through the macrosociety of the world stage. And beneath the classic social dilemma of "conservative" and "liberal" is a more telling psychological dilemma, one embedded in the pull between the spiritual and the physical: order and openness. Those who score high in the trait of conscientiousness (or orderliness) are more likely to identify as conservative, whereas those high in the trait of openness are more likely to call themselves liberal. We're torn between a blessed rage for order and an earthy openness to change, between vertical prescription and horizontal revolution.

Is the way of social sanity in order or openness?

I

The heavenward way is order at the expense of openness.

This path first crystallizes with Plato's *Republic*, an ideal state grounded in hierarchy, authority, and stability. But its modern champion, and the father of contemporary conservatism, is Edmund Burke, the Irish-born Englishman best known for speaking out against the French Revolution before its descent into "the Terror" of the guillotine.

And Burke's central preoccupation is social order: "Good order is the foundation of all good things."[1] Burke championed the hereditary monarchy, an aristocratic leisure class of elites, the duties of citizens, common customs, family and generational ties, moral values and sentiments, traditional religion—in short, all the time-tested and top-down structures that order society: "We fear God; we look up with awe to kings, with affection to parliaments, with duty to magistrates, with reverence to priests, and with respect to nobility."[2]

Burke was open to social reform—he lent qualified support to the American Revolution, and was one of the early defenders of the abolition of slavery—but balked at radical new talk of the "natural rights" of man. Social change, he argued, had to be gradual, careful, and in keeping with a given society's history and culture. It wasn't like bulldozing an empty building, but more like performing a high-risk surgery. It's very difficult to create order; it's very easy to destroy it. Therefore, the more prudent decision is often to let things be, conserving what works. The conservative "stands athwart history, yelling Stop."[3]

This Burkean path of order ties together those themes that—

1. Edmund Burke, *Reflections on the Revolution in France* (Indianapolis: Hackett, 1987), 215.

2. Burke, 76.

3. William F. Buckley Jr., "Our Mission Statement," November 19, 1955, https://www.nationalreview.com/1955/11/our-mission-statement-william-f-buckley-jr/.

generally speaking—unite conservatives. Regarding faith, they stand for religion—the patrimony of Judeo-Christian tradition—but stand athwart "spirituality." Regarding sexuality, they stand for the stability of sexual norms—the binary of the sexes, the complementarity of men and women, the procreative end of sex—and stand athwart the variables of sexual experience. Regarding art and culture, they stand for the highest achievements—those finer things historically associated with the leisure class—and stand athwart the low. Regarding technology, they stand for old customs—a more immediate, familiar, and natural experience of the world—and stand athwart new innovations. And regarding politics, they stand for the local—the individual, the family, the community, the business, the nation, and the duties and loyalties between them—and stand athwart the global. From chants of "law and order" to the jurisprudence of "originalism," order is the way of the conservative mind.

This heavenward way puts first things first: religion, values, family, culture, and the local community. It also recognizes and curbs the deep limitations of the earthly. We live in a broken world filled with broken people, and it's pure hubris to think that it can be perfected over time. Every society also has a complex network of unwritten rules with a complex history of interwoven events behind it, and it's the height of folly to think that it can be revolutionized overnight.

But when this instinct for order takes over, cut off from a balancing openness, it hardens into the same old Gnostic pattern: a revulsion at the physical. In fact, those who call themselves "conservative" tend to have a higher disgust sensitivity: when shown the same set of revolting images—cockroaches, vomit, mutilation—

they consistently register a more visceral reaction than those who identify as liberals. The orderly instinctively gravitate toward purity and structure, and instinctively recoil from the frothy, fleshy unpredictability of the world.

This knee-jerk disgust tends toward three great threats: a reactionary resistance to the new, an authoritarian control of the unsettling, and a utilitarian manipulation of the traditional. We see all three emerge together, and with full force, at the extreme right: the fascist state of Nazi Germany. Hitler himself had a Gnostic disgust with the physical: he swore off meat and alcohol, presented himself as a celibate, and was obsessed with good hygiene, sometimes bathing multiple times a day.

This same obsession with purity—and its corresponding dangers—permeated Nazi ideology. The Nazis were reactionaries: they resisted women's rights, "degenerate" modern art, and even food processing, popularizing a movement of all-natural eating first started by far-left radicals in Germany. They were authoritarians: they targeted people with same-sex attraction, people with disabilities, and especially the Jewish people, implementing a program of ethnic cleansing through forced sterilization, which was imported from the Eugenics Record Office in New York, and the elimination of "life unworthy of life," including six million Jews in the Holocaust. And in all of this, they were utilitarians: they used traditional religion and family life as tools to serve this "orderly" state.

Without any openness, the way of order is in danger of devouring itself, like the Gnostic *ouroboros* swallowing its own tail. It swallows even the religious and moral order at the foundation of all good things.

—

The earthward way is openness at the expense of order.

We find a modern champion of this way in the intellectual inspiration for the French Revolution: Jean-Jacques Rousseau. In the orderly Burke's assessment, this erratic and occasionally paranoid philosopher—who left his five children born out of wedlock to an orphanage and applauded himself for it—was "a wild, ferocious, low-minded, hard-hearted father, of fine general feelings; a lover of his kind, but a hater of his kindred."[4] But his social and political theory shaped much of modern liberalism—not only in Europe but also in the United States.

Raised in Geneva as a Calvinist, Rousseau eventually flipped from one extreme to the other: from man's total depravity to man's total innocence. The inflection point was a sudden epiphany—accompanied by "a dizziness that resembled intoxication"—that made him sink under a tree in tears. Though the incident resembled Augustine's own conversion, and Rousseau would go on to pen his own *Confessions*, the epiphany was the opposite of Augustinian. What Rousseau saw is that "man is naturally good, and has only become bad because of [our] institutions."[5] Wretchedness was a social disease, and the cure for it wasn't in religion; in fact, after a dalliance with Catholicism, he ended up regarding Christianity as a heavenward corruption: "Christianity is a completely spiritual

4. Edmund Burke, *A Letter from Mr. Burke to a Member of the National Assembly*, 3rd ed. (Paris: J. Dodsley, 1791), 37.

5. Jean-Jacques Rousseau, "The Encyclopaedist," in Maurice Cranston, *The Early Life and Work of Jean-Jacques Rousseau (1712–1754)* (Chicago: The University of Chicago Press, 1982), 228.

religion, concerned exclusively with things heavenly. The homeland of the Christian is not of this world. . . . So long as he has nothing to reproach himself for, it matters little to him whether anything is going well or poorly down here."[6]

Instead, the answer was a new society centered on "the social contract." Rousseau longed to cultivate a civil freedom reflecting the "state of nature"—a creative life of passion, emotion, and self-expression—and overcome the scourge of inequality bred by private property. This new state of liberty, fraternity, and equality would arrive through the "general will" of the people—the self-government of all aimed at the common good of all. In short, the answer to our social ills wasn't the order of religion and tradition, but an openness to man and a new future.

Here, too, this way of openness is what undergirds those themes that—again, in general terms—unite liberals. Regarding faith, they embrace spirituality—tolerance, exploration, and the rise of the "spiritual but not religious"—but shrug at religion. Regarding sexuality, they embrace sexual experience—individual diversity, social equality, bodily autonomy—and shrug at traditional sexual norms. Regarding art and culture, they embrace the "low"—pop art produced by and for the people—and shrug at the high. Regarding technology, they embrace innovation—new tech that pushes the boundaries of what's familiar and acceptable—and shrug at custom. And regarding politics, they embrace the global—the expansion of human rights and social justice—and shrug at the local. They answer shouts of "law and order" with "coexist" bumper

6. Jean-Jacques Rousseau, *On the Social Contract*, ed. and trans. Donald A. Cress (Indianapolis: Hackett, 1987), 100.

stickers, originalism with a "living constitution," and every demand for order with a cry for greater openness.

This way of openness, too, recognizes a vital principle of human society: that we can work to change the inherited order for the better. Small is beautiful, but if you're needlessly suffering, it's suffocating; stability is valuable, but if you're oppressed, it's the last thing you want or need. The open-minded tap into the goodness of our common humanity and common home, dream of a better and brighter future, and reach out with compassion to the marginalized. And it's undeniable that they've been a force for positive social changes now taken for granted—changes that, if it were up to the orderly, might have been far slower in arriving, or even never arrived at all.

But without the balancing structures of order, we fall into the opposite trap: the old utopian drive to "immanentize the eschaton,"[7] turning the world into a heaven of our own making. This fantasy inevitably leaves the open-minded in a state of unease. Indeed, liberals tend to register higher levels of neuroticism and anxiety—and lower levels of happiness—than conservatives. This earth will never be paradise, and without the structure and continuity of top-down order, we're left to internalize the ups and downs of a topsy-turvy world.

This open anxiety, like orderly disgust, leads to three great threats: an aimless refusal of tradition, a restless transgression of authority, and a violent rebellion against our given nature. And once again, all three threats come to life, in a kind of fever pitch, at the opposite extreme on the left: the regimes inspired by Marx and his

7. William F. Buckley's paraphrase of Eric Voegelin, *The New Science of Politics: An Introduction* (Chicago: The University of Chicago Press, 1952), 120.

vision of a more total emancipation of humanity beyond liberalism. The extremes of order and openness meet in totalitarian brutality.

The same trends of aimlessness, transgression, and violence have played out as Marxist philosophers turned their sights from economics to sexuality, and from the abolition of capitalism to the "abolition of the family."[8] Three successive social revolutions spearheaded by Marxist sympathizers—the sexual revolution, second-wave feminist revolution, and transgender revolution—have yielded a collapse in marriage numbers amid its ever-loosening definition; the health risks and "population implosion" associated with contraceptives; the ending of over sixty million lives through legal abortion; the promotion of sexual use and abuse through pornography; the hidden scourge of sex trafficking; the digitally mediated explosion in transgender identification and "transition," with its enantiodromatic return to Gnostic language; and the widespread sexualization of children. This social chaos is symbolically captured in the history of the rainbow flag: it originally lacked the order of all seven colors, and now endlessly changes, the social revolutions it symbolizes fragmenting and turning against one another. Order, at its limit, becomes engorged with itself; openness, at the opposite limit, disintegrates through itself.

The Way is both order and openness.

In Christ's public ministry, we see a daring balance between these two instincts, one that constantly sets his listeners—both

8. Karl Marx and Friedrich Engels, *The Communist Manifesto* (London: Penguin Books, 2002), 239

followers and skeptics alike—back on their heels. He was, on the one hand, an observant Jew steeped in tradition and attentive to authority. Yet he was also a revolutionary teacher who knew when ossified customs had to cede to the kingdom. He decried lawless hearts, but also championed open tables. He celebrated what perdures, but didn't shrink from novelty: "Every scribe who has been trained for the kingdom of heaven is like the master of a household who brings out of his treasure what is new and what is old" (Matt. 13:52).

The same balance is on display in the writings of St. Paul. On the one hand, Paul famously draws on the Greco-Roman "household codes" and counsels prudent submission to social authority. On the other hand, he was also a man of profound openness—an openness rooted in heaven, not earth—and penned easily the most socially radical line in all of ancient literature: "There is no longer Jew or Greek, there is no longer slave or free, there is no longer male and female; for all of you are one in Christ Jesus" (Gal. 3:28).

This communion of order and openness is at the heart of Catholic social teaching, which is rooted not only in Scripture but also in the philosophy of Augustine and Aquinas. This body of teaching, beginning with Pope Leo XIII's 1891 *Rerum Novarum*—an encyclical that references Aquinas multiple times—has four main pillars.[9] The first, the foundation of the other three, is the dignity of human life revealed by Christ—a principle of order. The second is "the common good," which is "the sum total of social conditions" that allow people to find fulfillment—a principle of openness.[10] The third principle, subsidiarity, shifts back to order: only where

9. *Compendium of the Social Doctrine of the Church* 160.
10. *Compendium* 164.

"individuals and intermediate groups" are overwhelmed—such as a "serious social imbalance or injustice"—is a global intervention warranted.[11] The fourth and final principle, solidarity, again balances back to openness: serious injustices do abound, and thus, we have to secure "equality of all in dignity and rights" and overcome "structures of sin" in society.[12]

This bilateral embrace of both of order and openness informs the Catholic Church's approach to social and political questions. Regarding faith, it stands for the one true religion of Christ and his Church, but also embraces an openness to spirituality—those of other denominations, other religions, and even no religion at all. Regarding sexuality, it stands for the stabilizing norms of the binary of male and female, their complementarity, and the ordering of sex toward a permanent marriage that's both unitive and procreative, but also embraces the varieties of experience: the wide range of individual qualities exemplified in the saints, the equality of women not only spiritually but also socially, and the goodness of sex itself, "a source of joy and pleasure" that's even "noble and honorable."[13] Regarding art and culture, it stands for what's highest, from Dante to Michelangelo, but also embraces what's "low," from folk singing to Catholic kitsch, and even finds "seeds" of the Word in secular culture.[14] Regarding technology, it stands for custom, warning of the dangers in new tech and setting clear limits on its use, but also embraces innovations, placing them "at the service of man" and

11. *Compendium* 185, 188.

12. *Compendium* 192.

13. *Catechism of the Catholic Church* 2362.

14. Justin Martyr, *The Second Apology* 13, in *Early Church Fathers Collection*, ed. David Augustine (Elk Grove Village, IL: Word on Fire Classics, 2024), 194–195.

his "true and integral good."[15] Regarding politics, it stands for the local, honoring personal duties and resisting socialism and communism, but also embraces the global, honoring universal rights and resisting "unbridled capitalism"—and even calling for the just distribution of property "as common to all," to be shared "when others are in need."[16]

It's tempting to see all these philosophical principles as mere abstractions—a way of skirting our social divide by not getting too specific. How *exactly* does one strike this balance? What movements and parties should we support? Catholic social teaching has been a guiding light for anarchists, distributists, and neoconservatives alike. Might a teaching with such a wide variety of expressions just be too ambiguous?

But Catholic social teaching isn't an alternative ideology; it's an anti-ideology. As with Augustine and Aquinas themselves, what unites its more conservative and more liberal adherents—a love for God and neighbor, and a resistance to both heavenward and earthward extremes—is deeper than what could ever divide them. And the words of Isaiah ring out prophetically to the faithful being pulled apart between the two sides: "And when you turn to the right or when you turn to the left, your ears shall hear a word behind you, saying, 'This is the way; walk in it'" (Isa. 30:21).

15. *Catechism* 2293–2294.

16. Leo XIII, *Rerum Novarum* 22, encyclical letter, May 15, 1891, vatican.va; see Thomas Aquinas, *Summa theologiae* 2-2.66.2.

PART III
The Dilemmas of Christianity

CHAPTER 16

Christianity: The Not Here and Not Yet or the Here and Now

On the Way, the heaven-earth dilemma doesn't disappear; on the contrary, it becomes more subtle and refined, more concentrated and explosive—precisely because the meaning of the Way itself is at stake. Vicious arguments erupt over a single word or a movement of just an inch, because "an inch is everything when you are balancing."[1]

The Christian dilemmas are less about cutting one side loose—there can be no complete turn away from either heaven or earth without ceasing to be a Christian—and more about distorting the proper relationship between them: heavenward Christians tend to overlook the earthly as sullied, while earthward Christians tend to undercut the heavenly as secondary.

This begins with the overarching dilemma for Christians: the dilemma between the "not here" of our heavenly citizenship and the

1. G.K. Chesterton, *Orthodoxy* (Park Ridge, IL: Word on Fire Classics, 2017), 99.

"here" of our earthly sojourn, and between the "not yet" of what's to come and the "now" of what already is. Here—and in all the Christian dilemmas—Scripture passages can be found to support either side, but the question remains how they fit together and where we put the emphasis.

Is the Way in the not here and not yet or the here and now?

I

The heavenward way is the not here and not yet at the expense of the here and now.

We see these heavenward impulses in one of the earliest factions of the Church—namely, Montanism. Montanus, a preacher flanked by two prophetesses, emerged in the streets of second-century Phrygia announcing new visions and messages from God. The three seers encouraged greater spiritual discipline to draw a sharper contrast with the world: more intense fasting, more fervent chastity, and a refusal of second marriages after the death of a spouse. And they claimed that the end was nigh: the new Jerusalem would soon be descending on the village of Pepuza.

The whole region had been a hotbed of mystical activity; indeed, the Montanist movement was inspired, in part, by the Revelation of John on the island of Patmos, due west of Pepuza. But whereas John's vision would gradually come to be seen as inspired, Montanism quickly drew suspicion from the Church. Tertullian defended the movement, arguing that the Montanists were being opposed by carnal minds that wanted to set up "boundary posts" to the work of the Spirit: "Shall human volition have more license than divine power?"[2]

But it wasn't the content of the Montanist message that drew concern so much as its medium—which wasn't unlike that of mediums. Their visions came rushing in through ecstatic frenzies and trances—an alternating terror and tranquility—and they spoke with presumptuous authority, as if their visions were higher than Scripture and Tradition. Montanus even spoke in the first person as God, claiming to be the mouthpiece of the Holy Spirit, the Paraclete. Aquinas, citing Augustine, wrote that these supposed prophets pretended that the promise of the Spirit was fulfilled "not in the Apostles, but in themselves."[3]

Montanism rightly champions the not here and not yet, which resounds throughout the New Testament. The night before he dies, Jesus lifts his eyes to heaven and prays his "High Priestly Prayer" to the Father, saying of his disciples, "They do not belong to the world, just as I do not belong to the world" (John 17:16). St. Paul builds on the theme in his letters: "Do not be conformed to this world," and "set your minds on things that are above," for "our citizenship is in heaven" (Rom. 12:2; Col. 3:2; Phil. 3:20). The "not yet" rings out just as clearly in Paul's preaching: adoption, redemption, sanctification, salvation—all these await their fullness in the eschaton, when "the dead will be raised imperishable," Christ will put all his enemies under his feet, and the Church will attain the "full stature of Christ" (1 Cor. 15:52, 25; Eph. 4:13). In the meantime, as sin and death continue to wreak their havoc, Christians wait and watch for his arrival with Advent expectation: "Come, Lord Jesus!"

2. Tertullian, *On Fasting* 11, 13.

3. Thomas Aquinas, *Summa theologiae* 1-2.106.4.

(Rev. 22:20). The heavenward rightly center the Christian's life on the holy—in Hebrew, *kadosh*, meaning "set apart"—and focus his mind on the ultimate.

But following this path, we run afoul of the Gospel and lose sight of the Way incarnate, who was born, died, and rose again in space and time. Overlooking the "here," we become infected with a spiritual escapism that resists what's good in man, the world, and the flesh, and overlooking the "now," we become infected with an apocalyptic pessimism that resists what's good in the present age.

In both cases, we detect the return of Gnostic pessimism: the earth becomes shrouded in darkness and desolation, and the only way out is to separate ourselves from our environing time and place. We have a clear sense of identity, but no desire to reach out to and relate to the world around us; we build tall and imposing walls, but demolish the bridges on which the world might enter into the kingdom; we have sharp contrast, but at the cost of true connection.

—

The earthward way is the here and now at the expense of the not here and not yet.

If we see the heavenward way in one of the earliest factions of the Church, we see the earthward way in one of the latest—namely, Modernism. The Modernists emerged out of the broader current of liberal theology, which, moved by a spirit of freedom and openness, attempted to reconcile Christian tradition with Enlightenment reason. In keeping with their name—from the Latin *modo* for "just now"—they leaned into this embrace of the here and now, accommodating the faith to the currents of contemporary life.

The Modernists proposed a double-sided reductionism: on the one hand, they reduced religion to internal spiritual experience, and on the other, they reduced reason to external scientific and historical facts. Gradually, this dual reduction threw the Church's teachings into question: since, on these new definitions, those teachings are neither religious nor rational, they could only be awkward and provisional attempts at articulating the faith. It also threw into question the Church's mission of evangelization: proclaiming the Gospel is a public act, but since religion is about private experience, also a secondary one. Thus, Christianity was recast as a more evolving and tentative journey of man in the world.

At the heart of the Modernist error is the noble aim of being present to the world—a theme that, like the not here, also echoes throughout the New Testament. In fact, immediately after he declares that Christians don't belong to the world, Christ adds that they still remain "in the world" (John 17:11, 15)—and not only that, but are also sent further out into it: "As you have sent me into the world, so I have sent them into the world" (John 17:18). And for St. Paul, the Christian life is not just not yet; in a real sense, we already possess, right now, those things we wait for. Christ is risen, and God has "raised us up with him and seated us with him in the heavenly places" (Eph. 2:6); he has "begun to reign" with "all authority in heaven and on earth" (Rev. 11:17; Matt. 28:18). The earthward are right that the Christian therefore can't just retreat to the above and beyond. We have to dwell, unashamed, in our own place, and live, unafraid, in our own time, because these belong to Christ too: "I have conquered the world!" (John 16:33).

But an overemphasis on the here and now throws off the balance of the Way. We don't deny altogether the heavenly elements of

Christianity—how could we and still call ourselves Christians?—but we neglect the *primacy* of those elements, or even treat them as mere afterthoughts. We still speak of heavenly things—the kingdom of God, the reality of the soul, unity in the Spirit—but more and more as metaphors for building up the earthly city. If the heavenward kick their feet against the here and now, the earthward shrug their shoulders at the above and beyond.

This earthward path leads us to a foolish optimism, one so fixated on the relevance of Christianity to the world that it forgets our deepest identity. We so focus on building bridges to the kingdom that we forget to fortify it with walls; we're all connection, but little contrast. At the limit, earthward Christians begin to make common cause with utopian dreamers, drifting into a de facto atheism and the loss of supernatural faith. Like the heavenward, the earthward turn their backs on the Word made flesh—not on his flesh, but on the very truth of his Word.

+

The Way is both the not here and not yet and the here and now.

The Church of the Way incarnate has to reflect both of these themes running through the Scriptures. It has to be both the light of the world shining on it from above and the salt of the earth flavoring it from below. It has to be a Church of both identity and relevance, both walls and bridges—in short, both contrast and connection, and in that order. It has to be both distinctively not of the world and also thoroughly in it, and both awaiting the kingdom to come and embracing the kingdom already present on earth.

Is the Catholic Church this Church? Countless arguments and counterarguments have been rehearsed down the centuries to defend—or debunk—this claim. But here, the test is this: How well does Catholicism walk the Way? If the Catholic Church is the Church Christ founded and intended all the world to join, then it has to build on his communion of heaven and earth. In both its formal teachings and inner life—especially in the witness of the saints—it has to occupy the great tension of being a Christian, a reflection of the tensions of Scripture itself.

And the sure test of the Church's commitment to living in this tension is its refusal of heresy—a *hairesis* or choice of one aspect of the faith at the expense of another. To be a heretic is to either choose the above and beyond, overlooking the here and now, or the here and now, undercutting the above and beyond. With St. Paul, the Church has to resist all such false teachers who distort the faith and divide the faithful: "I appeal to you, brothers and sisters, by the name of our Lord Jesus Christ, that all of you be in agreement and that there be no divisions among you. . . . Has Christ been divided?" (1 Cor. 1:10, 13). And when admonitions prove ineffective, and people prefer "their own desires" to "sound doctrine," the Church will "have nothing more to do with anyone who causes divisions" (2 Tim. 4:3; Titus 3:9–10).

And the Catholic Church did refuse the heresies of both Montanism and Modernism. Heaven didn't descend on Pepuza, but excommunication did descend on the Montanists around 177, though Tertullian's own sect of Montanists were later reconciled to the Church by Augustine. Likewise, Pope Pius X condemned

Modernism with its "blind and unchecked passion for novelty" in 1907, going so far as to call it "the synthesis of all heresies."[4]

From its earliest centuries up to the present age, the Catholic Church refuses those paths that overlook the here and now or undercut the not here and not yet. It insists on living out the fullness of the Way.

4. Pius X, *Pascendi Dominici Gregis* 13, 39, encyclical letter, September 8, 1907, vatican.va.

CHAPTER 17

The Light: Faith or Reason

Matthew Arnold wrote that the whole world is moved by two forces: Hebraism and Hellenism.[1] The struggle between the two paths is as old as their collision in the early Church. Hebraism, rooted in the Jewish tradition, is the way of conscience and conduct, religion and spirituality—in short, of divine faith or trust (*pistis*). Hellenism, rooted in the Greek tradition, is the way of logic and observation, philosophy and science—in short, of human reason. The first relies on God's law to fight sin, the second on man's mind to fight ignorance.

Should we follow the light of faith or the light of reason?

I

The heavenward way is faith at the expense of reason.

"What indeed has Athens to do with Jerusalem?" Tertullian asked. "What concord is there between the Academy and the

1. Matthew Arnold, *Culture and Anarchy: An Essay in Political and Social Criticism* (New York: Macmillan, 1896), 109–127.

Church?"[2] This heavenward line of thought ends in fideism—literally, faith-ism—which rejects any kind of "natural theology" demonstrating the truths of faith through reason. For the fideist, reason is a swamp of arrogance and error, and while the Christian can carefully wade through it, the assent of faith is a separate ascent.

The fideistic motto *Credo quia absurdum est*—"I believe it because it is absurd"[3]—would eventually be picked up by the Christian most often associated with this heavenward way: Søren Kierkegaard. For the melancholy Dane, the Christian faith is the paradox, and "the paradox is the absurd."[4] Kierkegaard wasn't against reason itself—he was a brilliant philosopher, and Socrates was his philosophical north star—but he *was* against natural theology: God is the great unknown, and "if he does exist, then it is foolishness to want to demonstrate it, since I, in the very moment the demonstration commences, would presuppose it not as doubtful."[5] Christianity, for Kierkegaard, wasn't a mere "leap of faith" from the rational to the religious—a phrase that he never actually used—but something far more radical.

In *Fear and Trembling*, Kierkegaard offers his great parable of the passion of faith: the *akedah*, the episode in Genesis 22 in which Abraham is commanded by God to sacrifice Isaac. The moral horror of that story—Abraham has to kill his only beloved son—is, for Kierkegaard, only the surface horror. The deeper horror is

2. Tertullian, *The Prescription Against Heretics* 7.

3. A paraphrase of Tertullian, *On the Flesh of Christ* 5: "The Son of God died; it is by all means to be believed, because it is absurd. And he was buried, and rose again; the fact is certain, because it is impossible."

4. Søren Kierkegaard, *Philosophical Fragments*, ed. and trans. Howard V. Hong and Edna H. Hong (Princeton: Princeton University Press, 1985), 52.

5. Kierkegaard, 39.

spiritual: Isaac is the symbol of God's own promise to Abraham of countless descendants (Gen. 15:5), and if he dies, the promise dies with him. So was it all just a cruel joke? "Everything was lost, even more appallingly than if it had never happened!"[6] Yet—and he repeats it again and again to make us see how absurd it is—"Abraham had faith."[7] And at the last moment, the angel of God intervenes to stay Abraham's hand, and the promise of the descendants is fulfilled: every Christian can now claim Abraham as their father in faith (Rom. 4:16).

For Kierkegaard, this supreme paradox—the collision of an utter loss of trust and a complete submission in trust—is faith. It's not the respectable moralizing of bourgeois society. It's not a journey that we can begin with rational evidence and arguments. On Mount Moriah, we stand poised between two abysses: dread and madness on one side, and faith and salvation on the other. And Abraham is the exemplar of "the knight of faith"—the one who passes heroically through logical absurdity into religious truth. As Kierkegaard puts it in one essay, this is "the difference between a genius and an apostle": a genius is born into the world, but an apostle is sent on a mission into it; the first wields a natural aptitude, the second a divine authority; the former belongs to the immanent sphere of thought, the latter to the transcendent sphere of the "paradoxical-religious."[8]

Fideism honors both the primacy of faith and the pitfalls of

6. Søren Kierkegaard, *Fear and Trembling*, ed. and trans. Howard V. Hong and Edna H. Hong (Princeton: Princeton University Press, 1983), 19.

7. Kierkegaard, 20–21.

8. Søren Kierkegaard, "The Difference between a Genius and an Apostle," in *The Book on Adler*, ed. and trans. Howard V. Hong and Edna H. Hong (Princeton: Princeton University Press, 1998), 173.

reason—both prominent themes in the Scriptures. Tertullian, like many Christians since, leaned into the words of St. Paul: "See to it that no one takes you captive through philosophy and empty deceit, according to human tradition" (Col. 2:8).[9] "We walk by faith," he tells the Corinthians, "not by sight" (2 Cor. 5:7), and Christ crucified is "foolishness" to the Greeks who desire wisdom (1 Cor. 1:22–23). Indeed, St. Paul's only explicit encounter with philosophers in the New Testament isn't a productive one: in Athens, "Epicurean and Stoic philosophers debated with him," and the two camps—usually busy disagreeing with each another—suddenly found a common enemy: "What does this babbler want to say?" (Acts 17:18). The Christian faith can't be found in the "calm light of mild philosophy,"[10] but only in personal trust and submission to the great Paradox of the Way incarnate. This emphasis also makes Kierkegaard, like Augustine, one of the great Christian existentialists: faith is above reason, but it also grips the individual in his concreteness; it's a dizzying relation to the absolute running from the heavens down into man's bones.

But fideistic verticality takes us right into the open jaws of irrationality. In throwing the baby of rationality out with the bathwater of rationalism, we become tempted toward a credulity that rushes to supernatural explanations; toward a superstition that treats faith as a form of magic; and toward an absolutism that can so easily turn to fanaticism—with all the abuse, cruelty, and violence that this can entail. The pure light of faith, without the robust presence of reason, can so easily darken the mind.

9. Tertullian, *Prescription Against Heretics* 7.
10. Joseph Addison, *Cato: A Tragedy*, act 1, scene 1 (London: 1734), 19.

—

The earthward way is reason at the expense of faith.

The opposite error of rationalism cropped up on occasion in the ancient and medieval worlds: the Origenists, inspired by Plato, argued that human souls preexist their bodies (a view Augustine rejected), and the Latin Averroists, inspired by Aristotle, argued that all men share one intellect (a view Aquinas rejected). But it really begins to take hold in the modern rationalism running from Descartes through Kant—a tradition that reaches a high point in Kierkegaard's great philosophical nemesis: Georg Wilhelm Friedrich Hegel.

Hegel trots out the same heavenward language running back to Plato: the one, the idea, the spirit, the eternal, the infinite, the absolute. He was also, at least nominally, a Lutheran. But for Hegel, reason is the bellwether of religion; in fact, reason, in a sense, is everything: "What is rational is actual; and what is actual is rational."[11] Reason "governs the world"; it's the very "substance of the universe," its "infinite energy."[12]

In Hegel's understanding, all of human history moves toward human thought, and all of human thought toward one universal self-thinking Thought, also called the Absolute, Reason, or Spirit. This self-thinking Thought—Aristotle's definition of God—is not above and beyond the world; on the contrary, it unfolds "in the phenomena of the world's existence."[13] As man marches down

11. G.W.F. Hegel, *Elements of the Philosophy of Right*, ed. Allen W. Wood, trans. H.B. Nisbet (Cambridge: Cambridge University Press, 1991), 20.

12. G.W.F. Hegel, *Philosophy of History*, trans. J. Sibree (New York: American Dome Library, 1902), 55, 52.

13. Hegel, 54.

through the centuries toward ever greater freedom, God gradually manifests himself in and through history.

And the engine of this process isn't supernatural revelation, but a rational dialectic. Though Hegel never actually used the terms, this dialectic essentially involves three steps: a thesis, an antithesis, and a synthesis. We begin with the thesis, which then turns into its opposite, the antithesis. Each reflects and moves toward the other, until finally, they converge on a synthesis, which "sublates" both to a higher level. Even human history, for Hegel, follows this same pattern: the first age, the thesis, is consciousness; the second age, the antithesis, is self-consciousness; and the third and final age—the synthesis, beginning with Christ, the "axis" of history—is the age of the Spirit.[14] In Hegel, the Way of Christ becomes the way of Thought, and the kingdom of God becomes the kingdom of Reason.

Reason, like faith, resounds in the New Testament. St. Paul was himself a learned man—so learned that some thought he had driven himself insane (Acts 26:24)—and in Athens, he does have a more fruitful dialogue on the Areopagus. St. Peter counsels us to always be ready to give an *apologia* (a rational defense) of the hope that's in us (1 Pet. 3:15). And the *Logos* himself commands us to love the Lord with all our minds (Matt. 22:37; Mark 12:30; Luke 10:27). Rationalists rightly embrace this scriptural heritage of reason, and Hegel, with his theory of contrasting opposites drawn together, has inspired many Christians on the Way, just like Plato before him.

But although rationalism draws the mind upward, it also draws

14. Hegel, 408.

heaven down to earth. For Hegel, there were no longer two worlds of heaven and earth at all; there was only this world. False religion, he writes, imagines God as "Lord of Heaven and Earth, living in a remote region far from human actualities";[15] a "heaven above" is just an invention of a more primitive human consciousness, and biblical religion a kind of visual aid to reason.

A second temptation follows from this immanentizing of heaven—namely, the deification of the state. For Hegel, the Spirit manifests as "the World-Spirit" in the political will of the state, which is the guarantor of human value and "the Divine Idea as it exists on earth."[16] The great "slaughter-bench" of history thus becomes part of the unfolding of God in the world.[17] There's some truth, in Hegel, to the judge's chilling proclamation in *Blood Meridian*: "War is god."[18] Hegel's exaltation of the state also entails an overly optimistic social progressivism: man changes, but gradually changes "for the better," harnessing his "impulse of perfectibility" through history. This principle, Hegel notes in passing, "has met with an unfavorable reception from religions—such as the Catholic."[19] The totalitarian horrors in the century after Hegel would vindicate the skepticism of religious minds.

This subordination of faith to philosophy and history tends, inevitably, toward its destruction. Indeed, Hegel was the primary inspiration—through Feuerbach, himself a Hegelian—for Karl Marx. But whereas Hegel reduced reality to the dialectics of Spirit,

15. Hegel, 100.
16. Hegel, 87.
17. Hegel, 66.
18. Cormac McCarthy, *Blood Meridian* (New York: Vintage, 1985), 249.
19. Hegel, *Philosophy of History*, 104.

Marx—who wrote his doctoral dissertation on Democritus and Epicurus—transformed it into a dialectical *materialism*. He kept the basic Hegelian frame, but praxis, not theory, is what filled it: "The philosophers have only *interpreted* the world in various ways; the point is, to *change* it."[20] Hegel drew God and Thought down into history; there, Marx extinguished them both.

+

The Way is both faith and reason.

Christ teaches his disciples to be both "wise as serpents and innocent as doves" (Matt. 10:16). They have to trust with childlike faith but also discern with cunning wisdom, both "call on the name of the Lord" and "argue it out" (Ps. 116:4, 13; Isa. 1:18). Thus, faith and reason come together on the Way. Faith is higher and far more important than reason, but not against it.

The Church thus opposed fideism, which was condemned throughout the nineteenth century. But it also opposed rationalism; several rationalistic propositions were condemned in Pope Pius IX's 1864 *Syllabus of Errors*. Instead, from St. Justin Martyr up through Pope St. John Paul II, the Church has embraced the Way of both revelation and reason, both religion and science, both *mythos* and *logos*, both salvation history and secular history, both the book of Scripture and the book of nature. It's even well within the Way to speak of a confluence of faith and involuntary doubt, a dramatic tension that ultimately strengthens one's trust in God: "I believe; help my unbelief!" (Mark 9:24).

20. Karl Marx, "Theses on Feuerbach," in *Selected Writings*, ed. Lawrence H. Simon (Indianapolis: Hackett, 1994), 101.

The Church agrees with fideists about the primacy of faith. In fact, the word "fideist" was first coined in French theology as an epithet to attack Catholics. St. Paul's warning isn't about philosophy itself but more about the "empty deceit" that can lurk there—a futile, prideful thinking that forgets our creaturely limits. And it's a warning that has to be taken seriously: "There are more things in heaven and earth, Horatio / Than are dreamt of in your philosophy."[21] In St. Anselm's formula, faith becomes *fides quaerens intellectum*: "faith seeking understanding."[22] But philosophy and science have to be circumscribed by religious and moral truth, and a living faith—a faith that can't be had through mental and spiritual effort—has to come first, because a living faith is what saves us (Eph. 2:8–9).

But the Church also agrees with rationalists about the indispensability of reason. Theology is the "queen of the sciences," but philosophy is the "handmaiden of theology." Thus, natural theology has an important role to play in the faith of Christians; in fact, the Church has formally declared, in keeping with Romans 1:20, that God "can be known with certainty from the created world by the natural light of human reason."[23] Even the truths of science and mathematics, entirely apart from the questions of religion, come from and point to the same source: "God cannot deny Himself, nor ever contradict truth with truth."[24]

We see this communion of faith and reason in Mary, the mother of the Way. This daughter of Israel is an image of pure faithfulness:

21. William Shakespeare, *Hamlet*, act 1, scene 5, in *The Riverside Shakespeare*, 2nd ed. (Boston: Houghton Mifflin, 1997), 1199.

22. Anselm, *Proslogion*, trans. Thomas Williams (Indianapolis: Hackett, 2001), 2.

23. *Catechism of the Catholic Church* 36; *Dei Filius* 2.

24. *Catechism* 159.

her *fiat* to the angel Gabriel, who invites her to become the Mother of God—"let it be with me according to your word" (Luke 1:38)—is a profound moment of Hebraic faith. And her canticle of praise (Luke 1:46–55) echoes similar canticles of faithful Israelites in the Old Testament. But she's also a woman of rational analysis: we're told twice that she "pondered" what she heard (Luke 1:29, 2:19)—a Greek term also translated as "questioned" or even "argued." The Church's insistence on a Marian dimension is, in part, a living out of this tension.

The unity of faith and reason is also on display throughout the Church's philosophical tradition, especially in Thomas Aquinas and his "five ways" of rationally demonstrating God's existence.[25] Even Aquinas' definition of faith itself is a beautiful testimony of the Way, one that draws together head and heart, faith and reason, and grace and freedom in one fell swoop: faith, he writes, is "an act of the intellect assenting to the divine truth at the command of the will moved by the grace of God."[26] Aquinas' adaptation of Aristotle was, in his day, met with great suspicion, and was even implicated in a series of condemnations issued by the Archbishop of Paris, but the Common Doctor's synthesis of faith and philosophy is now a touchstone for Catholic theology. The same communion also unfolds in science and technology, where many saintly Catholics, from Blessed Nicholas Steno through Venerable Jérôme Lejeune, have made key discoveries.

Arnold was right: Hebraism and Hellenism are the two points on which history turns. And it's the way of the world that they're always at war. But Christ is their peace, breaking down "the dividing wall" between them (Eph. 2:14).

25. Thomas Aquinas, *Summa theologiae* 1.2.3.

26. *Summa theologiae* 2-2.2.9.

CHAPTER 18

Christ: The Word or the Flesh

The Church was marked, from the start, by the scourge of division. Western and Eastern leaders fought as bitterly with themselves as with each other; bishops deposed each other and sent each other into exile to die; and priests and monks were swept up in alliances and betrayals, bribery and corruption.

And the theological debates involved were hardly trivial; on the contrary, in the first five centuries of its life, the Church almost completely spun out of control over the question of whether or not Jesus was truly God. The Word became flesh—on this all Christians agreed. But what did that mean? How exactly did divinity and humanity become one in him? In the figure at the center of Christianity, the great God-man dilemma exploded again, pushing the Church to the breaking point.

Was Christ defined by the Word of a divine nature or the flesh of a human nature?

I

The heavenward way is the Word at the expense of the flesh.

In the fifth century, there emerged a monk called Eutyches, who firmly resisted any talk of "two natures" after the Incarnation. "I worship one nature," he declared, "that of God made flesh and become man."[1] Christ's humanity was absorbed, as it were, into the divine. This was an improvement on Docetism—Eutyches, at least, acknowledged the real, full humanity of Jesus—but it was still captive to a fear of pulling heaven too close to the earth. The Eutychians worried that talk of Christ having a second nature was tantamount to acknowledging a second person, thus splitting Christ in two—thus compromising his divinity. Against their opponents, the Eutychians roared, "Cut him in two who divides Christ!"[2]

Eutyches' denial of Christ's human nature wasn't an isolated incident. Christians leaning in Eutyches' direction would come to be called Monophysites (from the Greek for "one nature"); before the Monophysites, there were also the Apollinarians, who denied that Christ had a human mind; and after the Monophysites, there were the Monothelites, who denied that Christ had a human will.

Whatever the stance, heavenward Christians agreed on the essential point: the Word became flesh—but not all the way. God became human—but not *that* human. The alternative seemed to be drawing God into the multiplicity of the earthly. Augustine, reflecting on his Manichaean past, captured a common sentiment of

1. Leo Donald Davis, *The First Seven Ecumenical Councils (325–787): Their History and Theology* (Collegeville, MN: Liturgical, 1990), 171.

2. Davis, 177.

the ancient world: "I feared to believe the Word made flesh lest I be forced to believe the Word defiled by flesh."[3]

This emphasis on Christ's divinity rings out in the Gospels, especially the Gospel of John, whom tradition symbolizes as an eagle. In his prologue, especially, John speaks powerfully of the divine Word that became flesh: "In the beginning was the Word, and the Word was with God, and the Word was God. He was in the beginning with God. All things came into being through him, and without him not one thing came into being. . . . He was in the world, and the world came into being through him; yet the world did not know him" (John 1:1–3, 10). Heavenward Christians have a healthy awe of this divinity, and are right to be on high alert for those who would obscure it. After all, salvation itself is at stake: if Christ isn't fully God, then Christ didn't save us.

Yet this heavenward way works against the very Gospel it aims to protect. It shields the Savior in the fullness of his divinity, but keeps him from reaching the very humanity he came to save. If Christ doesn't take on the whole of our humanity but only some of it, or if he doesn't take on a real human nature but only absorbs it, then we remain unredeemable; God can't really make us one with him after all. The desire to protect heaven from earth, however pious and well-intended, seals earth off from heaven.

—

The earthward way is the flesh at the expense of the Word.

The Eutychian fear that talk of two natures would compromise

3. Augustine, *Confessions* 5.10.

Christ's divinity wasn't unfounded; some earthward heretics had done exactly that. The case in point was Nestorius, the superior of a monastery who began his ecclesiastical career as a respected opponent of the Arians and other heretics. Nestorius' zeal would drive him into a heresy of his own—as when Eutyches later rose up to squash Nestorius.

Nestorius' main idea wasn't—as was thought then, and still commonly thought now—that Christ was two "persons," one divine and one human. He admitted two distinct natures, divinity and humanity, coming together as one *prosopon* (person) in Jesus. But Nestorius still drove a wedge between the human and divine in Christ: the two natures were more "conjoined" than unified, and it was the conjoining that mattered. This came into play in how we talk about Jesus, especially—and here was the heart of the controversy—how we talk about his birth. Can Mary be called the *Theotokos*, the "God-bearer" or "mother of God"? Nestorius said no: we have to render to divinity what belongs to divinity. Thus, it wasn't *God*, properly speaking, who was born to Mary; it was Christ, the conjoining of God and man.

To truly be one with us, Nestorius saw, the Word had to become fully human: Jesus wasn't just God donning a man-suit or appearing as a kind of hologram, but truly man in every way. Nestorius also wanted to honor the eternal and unchanging God, and speaking of God being "born" seemed to threaten precisely that. His "conjoining" seemed to solve both problems at once, honoring both God's true divinity and Christ's true humanity.

This emphasis on Christ's humanity, like the emphasis on his divinity, is also firmly anchored in the Gospels, especially the synoptic Gospels of Matthew, Mark, and Luke—symbolized by a man, lion, and calf, respectively. The Jesus of Mark—whose intense, refined Gospel is both the earliest and shortest of the four—is especially concrete: we encounter in those pages a flesh-and-blood teacher and healer on the move. There's no miraculous descent from heaven (as there is in Matthew and Luke) and, in the shorter version, no ascent back to it. The Nestorians clearly saw that any attempt to absorb this human nature into divinity drains the Incarnation of all its power. And salvation was again at stake: if Christ isn't fully human, then humanity isn't saved.

But this earthward way steers us right into the opposite threat to the Gospel: if we can't really understand Christ as God—if God, properly speaking, isn't truly born with us and doesn't truly suffer and die with us—are we really saved in any meaningful sense? If Christ can't be called Emmanuel—"God is with us" (Matt. 1:23)—can we really be made one with God? One heresy fully acknowledged Christ's divine nature, while overlooking the flesh; the other fully acknowledged Christ's human nature, while undercutting the Word; and neither heresy could fully bring man, through Christ, back to God.

+

The Way is both the Word and the flesh.

In this fierce debate, Christians fell into opposite errors, but Christ, through the Church, drew their eyes back to himself. A high Christology emphasizes Christ's divine nature, and a low Christology emphasizes his human nature, but a balanced Christology on the Way emphasizes both, in proper order. The two sides, anxious to stress one nature or the other, found their peace in the God-man.

In the span of twenty years—at the councils of Ephesus in 431 and Chalcedon in 451—the Church condemned both Monophysitism and Nestorianism. Ephesus rebuked Nestorius' teaching directly: "The divine nature and the human nature formed one Lord and Christ and Son for us, through a marvelous and mystical concurrence in unity. . . . Being united from the womb itself he is said to have undergone fleshly birth, claiming as his own the birth of his own flesh. Thus [the holy Fathers] did not hesitate to speak of the holy Virgin as the Mother of God."[4] Chalcedon then cut against Monophysitism: "We confess one and the same Son, our Lord Jesus Christ, . . . born of the virgin Mary, Mother of God according to human nature; . . . acknowledged in two natures, without mingling, without change, indivisibly, undividedly, the distinction of the natures nowhere removed on account of the union but rather the peculiarity of each nature being kept."[5]

Neither overlooking Christ's human nature nor undercutting his divine nature could be the Way. In Augustine's beautiful summary: "Christ is both David's Son and David's Lord. . . . Very Man, Very God; God and man, whole Christ. This is the Catholic faith. . . . Whoever confesses both is a Catholic."[6]

This union brought together the best of two rival schools in the Church: the Alexandrian School and the Antiochene School. The

4. Council of Ephesus, "Second Letter of Cyril of Alexandria to Nestorius," in *The Sources of Catholic Dogma*, ed. Heinrich Denzinger and Karl Rahner, trans. R.J. Deferrari (St. Louis, MO: B. Herder, 1954), 49.

5. Council of Chalcedon, "The Chalcedonian Creed," in *Sources of Catholic Dogma*, 60–61.

6. Augustine, Sermon 42.3.

Alexandrians emphasized the divinity of Christ and a spiritual or allegorical sense of Scripture; their "Word-flesh" Christology was rooted in the Gospel of John. The Antiochenes took the opposite approach, emphasizing the humanity of Christ and the literal and historical sense of Scripture; their "Word-man" Christology was rooted in Matthew, Mark, and Luke. Each side produced its great saints and scholars, and each produced its heretics. The Church wisely held them together: both traditions, and thus both natures of Christ and both senses of Scripture.

This balance wasn't self-evident or swift in arriving; on the contrary, it was hard won through the first four ecumenical councils of the Church. The welter of political pressure, theological controversy, and social disarray in these centuries only highlights the miraculousness of the outcome. The Church passed its breaking point—and didn't break. Looking at the Way, it found the Way.

One of the most fascinating images in the world is the Christ Pantocrator icon—dated to just after Ephesus and Chalcedon—of St. Catherine's Monastery in the Sinai Peninsula. The icon, the oldest of its kind, is both a record of this struggle and a portrait of what was at stake. The power of the image lies in a feature at first hidden from view: its asymmetry. Christ's face literally has two facets: holding up a mirror to each side of the face yields two different countenances. The right side of his face—our left—is gently divine: his right hand is raised in blessing, his hair pulled back neatly, his face filled with merciful love. This is Christ the Word, the Savior and Redeemer. The left side of his face, by contrast, is ruggedly human: his left hand grips the Gospels, his hair is thick and cascading downward, his face burning with righteous indignation. This is Christ the Son of Man, our rabbi and our judge.

This is neither the heavenward Christ nor the earthward Christ, but the very face of heaven and earth—the Lamb of God and the Lion of Judah. To those who remain distant from him, like the doubting Thomas, he says, "Reach out your hand and put it in my side" (John 20:27)—*touch my humanity*. To those who cling to him too tenaciously, like the devoted Mary Magdalene, he says, "Do not hold on to me" (John 20:17)—*behold my divinity*.

CHAPTER 19

God: Transcendence or Immanence

The dilemma over Christ's nature was embedded in a broader dilemma over God himself, one embedded in the dilemma of God's place and ours. Does God repose above the world with the coldness of an authoritative father, or does he draw near to it with the intimate warmth of a loving mother?

Is God transcendent or immanent?

I

The heavenward way is transcendence at the expense of immanence.

In the second century, an austere Christian in Rome so lopsidedly stressed God's transcendence that he split the God of Christianity in two. From one angle, Marcion was a classic Gnostic: he shared the same dualistic cast of mind, pushing for "perpetual abstinence to the extent of destroying and despising the works of the Creator," and rejecting marriage as "an evil and unchaste thing."[1]

1. Tertullian, *On Fasting* 15; *Against Marcion* 29.

But he was also more in tune with the basics of the Christian message. His focus wasn't on knowledge but faith, and not on aeons and archons but on the cross and Resurrection. And his heretical movement would prove to be one of the most formidable the Catholic Church ever faced.

At the heart of Marcion's teaching was the existence of two Gods rather than one. The first, the true God, is a transcendent divinity with no taint of immanence; the second, the Creator, is a more immanent power lacking true transcendence. A series of other sharp divisions follow: God is revealed in Christianity, and the Creator in Judaism; God is alien to the world, and the Creator its overseer; God frees us with the Gospel, and the Creator burdens us with the Law; God is all about mercy and grace, and the Creator all about justice and works; God is glimpsed by faith, and the Creator through knowledge; God draws us into his eternal life, and the Creator will eventually die.

Supporting Marcion's two Gods was a formal canon of Scripture—the first ever compiled. Marcion's Bible included some of the letters of St. Paul and some of the Gospel of St. Luke; the rest—the whole Old Testament and the remainder of the New—he left behind. Like Thomas Jefferson centuries later—whose version of the Gospels redacts the virgin womb, empty tomb, and all mention of the miraculous in between—Marcion carefully curated the sacred writings to reflect his theology. But whereas Jefferson's aim was to purify religion of the supernatural, Marcion's was to purify it of the natural.

Where did this leave Christ? For Marcion, Jesus not only wasn't the Messiah of Israel; he also wasn't God incarnate. Like Jefferson, he clipped out the Nativity from Luke's Gospel, though for the opposite reason: not because it was too spiritual but because it was too physical. Instead, the Marcionite Christ was the sudden manifestation of God on earth, sent not to save us from sin but to buy us back from the Creator. This is the Gospel according to Marcion: for the love of man, "that better god . . . was at the pains of descending from the third heaven to these poverty-stricken elements, and for the same reason was actually crucified in this sorry cell of the Creator."[2]

The Marcionites appreciated the Gospel truth that God is a great mystery: "O the depth of the riches and wisdom and knowledge of God! How unsearchable are his judgments and how inscrutable his ways!" (Rom. 11:33). In fact, contrary to Marcion, this same theme also permeates the Old Testament: "For my thoughts are not your thoughts, nor are your ways my ways. . . . For as the heavens are higher than the earth, so are my ways higher than your ways and my thoughts than your thoughts" (Isa. 55:8–9). Even God's very name is beyond the lips and minds of earthlings: he is the unpronounceable YHWH, "I AM WHO I AM" (Exod. 3:14–15). The theological transcendentalist's desire to honor this loftiness is good and right, aligning with both Paul and Plato.

But Marcion's slashing of the sacred writings leads to a deracinated and disfigured revelation. The New Testament—including the writings of St. Paul and St. Luke—is clearly linked, inescapably, to the Old, because Christ is the "yes" to "every one of God's promises" (2 Cor. 1:20). When we separate the fulfillment from the promise, the Word of God becomes muffled, even incoherent. A Christianity without its Jewish roots isn't Christianity at all, but a mere Gnostic fantasy.

2. *Against Marcion* 1.14.

It's also a return to the Gnostic suspicion of the earthly. The Genesis declaration of the goodness of the world was, for Marcion, nothing but the propaganda of its Creator. This suspicion tended toward the denigration of two incarnational dimensions of the faith in particular: the hierarchy and the sacraments. Marcionism established its own ecclesiastical structure cut off from the Body of Christ. It also set strict limits on the sacraments: water was used on the altar instead of wine, marriage went out the window, and only those in a state of "virginity, widowhood, or celibacy" could be baptized.[3] The Paulicians of the seventh century, an outgrowth of Marcionism, amplified the same tendencies, rejecting the hierarchy and the sacraments altogether. Without the full truth of God's immanence, the here and now again come under attack.

—

The earthward way is immanence at the expense of transcendence.

This earthward way was less of a threat to ancient minds, but we see it emerge in the thirteenth century with a strange, secretive association of mystics: the Brethren of the Free Spirit.

Though loosely connected, the Brethren shared a clear theological trend: the immanentizing of God. The main stage for this immanentizing was the Christian soul: the believer, they taught, is already in God, and God already in the believer—full stop. God and the Christian soul have become one, here and now. St. Albert the Great, the teacher of Thomas Aquinas, catalogued some of their

3. *Against Marcion* 29.

ideas: "The soul is taken from the substance of God"; "a person can become God"; "a soul united to God is made divine"; and "a person may become equal to the Father and surpass the Son"—a teaching Albert rightly associates with Satan (Gen. 3:5).[4] This immanentist tendency reached its summit in Amalric of Bena, who went even further: not only is the soul divine, but *all things* are divine. Whatever is, he declared, is God.

The Brethren are often listed alongside Christian neo-Gnostics of the same century, but they moved in the polar opposite direction: they didn't revile the physical, but embraced it with pantheistic awe; they didn't look to escape the world, but declared that it was already heaven; and they didn't see God as dwelling far away from man, but identified him with the soul. Like the Adamites—an ancient Christian sect that worshiped in the nude and called their churches "paradise"—they lost sight of the primacy of heaven over the earth, collapsing the distinction between the two.

These Christians weren't without some footing in Scripture. In the Old Testament, the Creator and creature are compared to a nursing mother and her child (Isa. 49:15), and God is seen as mysteriously everywhere and filling everything: "Do I not fill heaven and earth?" (Jer. 23:24). This closeness only becomes intensified in the New Testament: St. Paul declares that God is "not far from each one of us," for "in him we live and move and have our being" (Acts 17:27–28); in fact, the body is "a temple of the Holy Spirit," and the community "the temple of the living God," fulfilling the prophecy that God "will live in them and walk among them" (1 Cor.

4. Albert the Great, "The Compilation Concerning the New Spirit (Circa 1270)," in *The Essential Writings of Christian Mysticism*, ed. Bernard McGinn (New York: Modern Library, 2006), 491.

6:19; 2 Cor. 6:16). And his declaration to the Romans of God's transcendence ends in a powerful suggestion of immanence—a line that Marcion conveniently clipped from his Bible: "From him and through him and to him are all things" (Rom. 11:36). The theological immanentist's longing to honor God's presence here and now is well-grounded in Scripture, and is also good and right.

But this earthward path puts us in a very dangerous position, both spiritually and morally. The Brethren were far from Gnostics, but they did resemble the Gnostics of old in one respect: their teachings opened the door to complete moral license. If God and the soul have become one, how can we sin? Can God sin? The Brethren, Albert notes, believed that "nothing that is done below the belt by good people is a sin"; in fact, "nothing is a sin except what is thought to be a sin."[5] Like the early Christians in Corinth who fell into sexual libertinism, the Brethren abused their spiritual freedom, declaring, "All things are lawful for me" (1 Cor. 6:12). An overemphasis on God's presence in the world and the flesh leads us into worldliness and the works of the flesh.

Like the Marcionites, the Brethren also had no need for the Incarnation, and thus for the hierarchy or the sacraments. But whereas the Marcionites rejected these things for interfering with heaven, the Brethren rejected them for limiting the earth: priestly fathers weren't necessary because the Christian was already one with the heavenly Father, and the Eucharist wasn't necessary because the universe was already a Eucharist. Yet the end result was the same: the obsolescence of the Church.

This collapse of the primacy of transcendence leads, in the long

5. "Compilation Concerning the New Spirit," 491.

run, to a collapse of faith. The Brethren anticipated the modern pantheistic movements of Romanticism and Ralph Waldo Emerson's "transcendentalism"—a complete misnomer, as it was really pure immanentism. Emerson, like the Brethren, called on us to awaken to the divine within and all around: "God incarnates himself in man," and man in nature is "part or parcel of God"; "the currents of the Universal Being circulate through me."[6] He reduced Jesus to a great spiritual teacher and emptied Christianity of its incarnational tensions. Why go to drafty churches when we can find God in the warmth of the woods? And Emerson, as it turns out, would go on to become a key influence upon a young Friedrich Nietzsche. Between the transcendent God and the death of God stands the God of pure immanence.

+

The Way is both transcendence and immanence.

The answer to this riddle was, once more, in the face of Christ. In Jesus, the transcendence of God becomes one with his immanence, his sovereignty over the world with his closeness to it. And the Son's whole mission is to reveal his Father: "Whoever has seen me has seen the Father" (John 14:9). Thus, the Father, too, is both transcendent and immanent.

The New Testament God and the Old Testament God are not two Gods but one: "The New Testament lies hidden in the Old

6. Ralph Waldo Emerson, "An Address Delivered Before the Senior Class in Divinity College, Cambridge," and "Nature," in *Nature and Selected Essays* (New York: Penguin Books, 2003), 113, 39.

and the Old Testament is unveiled in the New."[7] And this God is, as Augustine said, "more inward than the most inward place of my heart and loftier than the highest."[8] He's further beyond this world than we can imagine, but also, in a sense, closer to it than we can conceive: "Are you not in every place at once in the totality of your being, while yet nothing contains you wholly?"[9] He's both the great Unknown that we can't grasp and the great Known that we can't avoid.

The Church thus excommunicated Marcion in 144 and battled his transcendentalism for decades after; both the Apostle's Creed and the canon of the Bible emerged out of the backlash. But in 1215, it also condemned the immanentism of Amalric, "whose mind the father of lies has so blinded that his doctrine must be considered not so much heretical as insane."[10]

The heavenward are right to affirm God's transcendence. God can't be grasped by human hands; he can't even be grasped by the human mind: "Si comprehendis, non est Deus," Augustine declared. "If you understood him, it would not be God."[11] And the earthward are right to affirm God's immanence. God draws close to the soul, and even creation itself. "Where is God?" asked the *Baltimore Catechism*. The answer? "God is everywhere."[12] He envelops

7. *Catechism of the Catholic Church* 129.

8. Augustine, *Confessions* 3.6.

9. *Confessions* 1.3.

10. Fourth Lateran Council, "The False Doctrine of Joachim of Fiore," in *The Sources of Catholic Dogma*, ed. Heinrich Denzinger and Karl Rahner, trans. R.J. Deferrari (St. Louis, MO: B. Herder, 1954), 172.

11. *Catechism* 230; Augustine, Sermon 52.6, 16 (PL 38, 360) and Sermon 117.3, 5 (PL 38, 663).

12. *Baltimore Catechism*, "On God and His Perfections."

and permeates all things, from the highest to the lowest: "Where can I go from your spirit? Or where can I flee from your presence? If I ascend to heaven, you are there; if I make my bed in Sheol, you are there" (Ps. 139:7–8).

Belief in a purely transcendent God overlooks the goodness of the here and now; belief in a purely immanent God undercuts his sovereignty over it. The first is too distant to feel for the earth; the second is too chained to it to do anything about it. But the Way is the tension of affirming both at once.

This tension has marked Catholic theology in countless ways. The medieval debate over how we talk about God—his dissimilarity or similarity to creation, related to the pull between apophatic (or "negative") and cataphatic (or "positive") theology—revolved around precisely this paradox. For one side, God is beyond being, and our words are equivocal; he's utterly different from creation. For the other, he's the highest being, and our words are univocal; he's on the same continuum of meaning as creatures. Thomas Aquinas navigated the dilemma with the idea of analogy: God is ultimately *unlike* us, but we can still rightly speak of him being *like* us. The first is greater—"between Creator and creature no similitude can be expressed without implying an even greater dissimilitude"[13]—but a God of love has to be both, because love requires both otherness and closeness. God is neither beyond being nor the highest being but Being itself.

The long debate over icons—the depiction of Christ, the saints, and the angels in art—plays out the same tension. The heavenward—referring back to the Ten Commandments (Exod. 20:4–5)

13. *Catechism* 43.

but forgetting God's immanence—fall into iconoclasm, seeing all use of images, with the exception of a bare cross, as a return to pagan idolatry. On the other side, the earthward—swept up in the use of images and forgetting God's transcendence—fall into the opposite danger of skidding toward superstition. The resolution of the dilemma, led by John of Damascus and affirmed in the Second Council of Nicaea, was a distinction between *latria* (adoration) and *dulia* (veneration). Adoration was reserved for God alone, which honors his transcendence, but veneration could be shown to icons, which honors his immanence. The faithful don't pray *to* icons but *through* them to the higher reality to which they connect us.

There's also the pull between God's mercy, emphasized in the New Testament, and God's justice, emphasized in the Old. But in the one God—and in each Testament, and especially in both received as one—mercy and justice come together: "Steadfast love and faithfulness will meet; righteousness and peace will kiss each other. Faithfulness will spring up from the ground, and righteousness will look down from the sky" (Ps. 85:10–11). God is both merciful and just: "God acts mercifully," Aquinas writes, "not indeed by going against his justice, but by doing something more than justice. . . . Mercy does not destroy justice, but in a sense is the fullness thereof."[14] The same dynamics apply to God's grace and God's law: "The law was therefore given, in order that grace might be sought; grace was given, in order that the law might be fulfilled."[15] The Church is called to dwell in the same tensions: a Jean Valjean is transformed by mercy and grace from above, and an Inspector Javert is affixed to justice and law here below; the people of God—like Eugène

14. Thomas Aquinas, *Summa theologiae* 1.21.3.

15. Augustine, *On the Spirit and the Letter* 34.

François Vidocq, the inspiration for both characters—inhabit both spaces.

Time and again, the Catholic instinct is to honor the distinction between God and the world, but also—in imitation of Christ—their connection: God is beyond the world, and the world is with God.

CHAPTER 20

The Church: The Holy Spirit or the Body of Christ

The Church's understanding of itself, like its understanding of both Christ and God, falls into a dilemma of heaven and earth—in this case, an extension of the spiritual-physical dilemma. On one side is the sense of a spiritual Church—invisible, mystical, charismatic. On the other side is the sense of a bodily Church—visible, practical, institutional.

Is the Church's identity in the Holy Spirit or in the Body of Christ?

I

The heavenward way is the Holy Spirit at the expense of the Body of Christ.

A pivotal figure in this heavenward way was the twelfth-century ascetical abbot Joachim of Fiore. Joachim was not a rabble-rousing street-preacher like Montanus—he spent his days recording his ideas in cloistered solitude—but after his death, he polarized the Church in ways Montanus never did. The Church's greatest philosopher, Aquinas, refuted Joachim's views in the *Summa*, whereas the Church's greatest poet, Dante, had the abbot shining in paradise.

Joachim gave new currency to an old idea, one based on Revelation 20: that Christ would rule over the earth for a thousand years before the Last Judgment. This "millennialism" had cropped up among figures of the early Church—including Montanus—but Joachim gave a robust theory to support it. He divided history into three ages: first, the earthly Age of the Father, which was the age of the Old Testament and the Law, facilitated by laypeople; next, the incarnational Age of the Son, which was the age of the New Testament and the Church, facilitated by the clergy; and third and finally, the heavenly Age of the Spirit, which was the age of the Eternal Gospel, facilitated by "spiritual men." Contemplatives and monastics would not only spiritualize the Church, Joachim thought; they would draw the unbelieving world to itself and usher in a thousand years of love, joy, and peace—a universal brotherhood of man until the end of time.

The abbot's ideas spread like wildfire, particularly among the Fraticelli sect of the Franciscans, also called the "Spirituals." Joachim had predicted that a new Elijah would usher in the Age of the Spirit, and St. Francis seemed to fit the bill: here was a deeply spiritual, Christ-like figure whose radical holiness was—and still is—an irresistible magnet to the world. The Third Age seemed to be at hand, and the Spirituals became increasingly apocalyptic and radical. One, Fra Gherardo, went so far as to say that even the Scriptures themselves were as good as gone, and that Joachim's writings were the new Eternal Gospel. The Body of Christ was a thing of the past; the future belonged to the freedom of the Spirit.

It wasn't just the book of Revelation inspiring the Joachimites; the New Testament—from "the Advocate" (John 14:16) and the Great Commission (Matt. 28:19–20) through Pentecost (Acts 2) and the Acts of the Apostles—speaks frequently and powerfully of the Holy Spirit renewing the face of the earth. The archetype of this emphasis is St. Paul, the impassioned Apostle to the Gentiles beyond the borders of Judaism. The Spirit fills, frees, and flows out of the people of God, with various charisms signaling his work: preaching, teaching, miracles, healings, prophecies, tongues, vision, interpretation—all of them "activated by one and the same Spirit, who allots to each one individually just as the Spirit chooses" (1 Cor. 12:11). The heavenward cooperate with this work and cultivate a healthy contrast with this passing world.

But the Joachimite mentality leads to the same rejection of the hierarchy and the sacraments that dogged the Marcionites: the Fraticelli saw themselves as the narrow, pure, true Church of believers, and the rest of the Church as a broad, carnal, counterfeit Church without valid sacraments. It also leads to the same apocalyptic fervor that dogged the Montanists: the resistance to the here and now is so stressed that it turns into an obsession with the imminent Last Days. Without the grounding rod of the Body of Christ, receiving these spiritually electric charges can be deadly: instead of love, peace, joy, and other good fruit of the Spirit, we easily spread "enmities, strife, jealousy, anger, quarrels, dissensions, factions," and all the highly "spiritual" works of the flesh (Gal. 5:20).

Joachim also bequeathed to the Church—and the West through it—a peculiar enantiodromia: a vision of spiritual apocalypse that would repeatedly flip into secular utopias. First there was the French Revolution, which was energized by, and interpreted through, a ferment of millennialist excitement among French Christians; then there was Hegel, who secularized Joachim's three ages, making the Age of the Spirit the self-manifestation of God in the world; next came Marx, who despiritualized Hegel, dreaming of the classless society to end all history; and finally there was Hitler and the Nazis, whose idea of the "Third Reich"—a "New Order" of Nazi supremacy to last a thousand years—came directly from Joachim.

Even the hippie and New Age movements of the 1960s and '70s—both distinctively utopian in tenor—have the same root. These movements dreamed of three astrological ages: first came the Age of Aries leading up to Christ; then came the Age of Pisces leading to the present; and dawning was the Age of Aquarius, in which harmony would fill the earth and love would steer the stars. The preparation for paradise swung between extremes—from the Dionysian revelry of Woodstock, billed as an "Aquarian Exposition," to the clean living of the Brotherhood of the Spirit commune, which prohibited alcohol and promiscuity and farmed a meager vegetarian diet—but the expectation of the "New Age" was thick in the air.

Again and again, whether consciously or not, the West continues to dream Joachim's dream—earthly paradises imported from the heart of heavenward faith.

—

The earthward way is the Body of Christ at the expense of the Holy Spirit.

Standing opposite the heavenward way is an overemphasis on the visible, institutional Church—not a heresy preached so much as a hypocrisy practiced. And we see an instructive example of this institutionalism, ironically enough, in the first two hundred years of Joachim's Age of the Spirit. These were among the worst years for the papacy in Church history—an era of worldly political entanglement, rank moral hypocrisy, and spiritual sloth.

Among the worst of the "bad popes" was Boniface VIII at the end of the thirteenth century. His reign was marked by an obsession with seizing and wielding temporal power through war, excommunication, and interdicts to cut the faithful off from the sacraments. So vicious was his rule that Dante placed this pope—who "didn't fear to wed by guile the lovely Bride [the Church], then rend and sell her flesh"—in the eighth circle of hell.[1] Whatever his eternal fate, chaos continued well after his papacy: by some estimates, no less than half the Christian world was in a state of excommunication by the 1320s, and his power struggle with the French crown paved the way for the Avignon papacy and the Papal Schism, when a series of antipopes claimed the chair of Peter.

Two centuries later there was Rodrigo Borgia, who in 1492 became, as Alexander VI, the most infamous of the Renaissance popes. The powerful Borgia clan, like the Medicis after them, occupied the upper ranks of the hierarchy and amassed great wealth and influence. But Alexander pushed this corruption to new lows, propagating a culture of sexual libertinism and family favoritism. In the course of his ecclesiastical career, he fathered as many as ten children with multiple mistresses, and promoted his children to important offices—especially his ruthless son Cesare, who inspired Machiavelli's *The Prince*. In the face of all this corruption, an ascetic

1. Dante Alighieri, *Inferno*, canto 19, trans. Anthony Esolen (New York: Modern Library, 2003), 197.

champion of the Spirit named Savonarola began announcing the Last Days, burning worldly vanities in the streets, and flouting Church authority; Alexander VI brought down the institutional fist of the Church in response, excommunicating Savonarola then ordering him hanged and burned.

The New Testament bears witness not only to the work of the Spirit but also to the institutional reality of the Body. Christ gives authority to his Apostles, and the Apostles physically lay hands on their successors—an unbroken chain of visible communion and authority: "Obey your leaders and submit to them" (Heb. 13:17). If the archetype of an instinct for the Spirit is St. Paul, the archetype of an instinct for the Body is St. Peter, the fisher of men who receives the keys of the kingdom from the Lord (Matt. 16:19), and whose chair the popes of the Church have dared to occupy. Institutional men correctly insist on this earthly dimension of the Church, which keeps its members on the rails through tradition and proscription, rules and regulations, laws and penalties, property and money—in short, through an engagement with the world as it is, not as we dream it to be. Without it, the Church inevitably fragments.

But there's a great spiritual pitfall on this path, and not only for popes: in fixating on the Church's temporal authority, influence, and image, we grow deaf to the higher call of God, becoming cynical, swollen, and self-protective. If the heavenward float into otherworldliness, untethered from the Body, the earthward trudge into a dull worldliness, bereft of the Spirit. The former are preoccupied with the end of man's world, the latter with the world as man's end. At the limit, we not only cease to hear the voice of the Spirit; we also begin to lean in to the whispers of the Evil One.

This leads to one of two outcomes, both of which are disasters for the faith. The first is institutional corruption: if everything is transactional, everything is negotiable, and the teachings of the Church become a means to an end. The second is institutional torpor: the faith becomes about checking boxes and jumping through hoops, and is slowly drained of the passion and purpose of the Gospel. In both cases, the Church becomes something worse than an electrical current with no grounding rod: a grounding rod with nothing to ground—a stiff and lifeless thing: "I know your works; you have a name of being alive, but you are dead" (Rev. 3:1).

+

The Way is both the Holy Spirit and the Body of Christ.

The Church is Christ's "Mystical Body," the extension of the Incarnation in space and time. And it's defined by both the Spirit and the Body: "What the soul is to the human body, the Holy Spirit is to the Body of Christ, which is the Church."[2] In an analogous way, it's a universal *sacrament*, drawing together the spiritual and the physical in all things.[3]

This union of Spirit and Body naturally has both invisible and visible dimensions that form "one complex reality": the Church is both a "spiritual community" and a "visible society,"[4] both charismatic and institutional, both prophetic and priestly, both pneumatic and corporate. She is "both human and divine, visible but endowed with invisible realities, zealous in action and dedicated

2. *Catechism of the Catholic Church* 797; Augustine, Sermon 267.4 (PL 38, 1231D).

3. *Catechism* 774–776.

4. *Catechism* 771; *Lumen Gentium* 8.

to contemplation, present in the world, but as a pilgrim, so constituted that in her the human is directed toward and subordinated to the divine, the visible to the invisible, action to contemplation, and this present world to that city yet to come, the object of our quest."[5]

Paul and Peter have their distinct missions, but they flow together: Paul, the charismatic preacher, doesn't overlook unity in the institution, where we find both "one body and one Spirit" (Eph. 4:4); Peter, the institutional guardian, doesn't undercut the pouring out of spiritual gifts, which make its members "see visions" and "dream dreams" (Acts 2:17–18). This doesn't mean that Paul and Peter were without their tensions: Peter cautions about an arcane ambiguity in Paul (2 Pet. 3:16), whereas Paul warns about a pragmatic protectiveness in Peter (Gal. 2:11–14).

But the solution can't be to raze Peter to prop Paul, or rob Paul to pay Peter. Neglecting the horizontal element makes the Church unsteady, and downplaying the vertical makes it unwieldy. It's no coincidence that the statues of both men flank St. Peter's Basilica, the remains of both men lie under the Eternal City, and the feasts of both men are celebrated on the same date.

Thus, the heavenward way of Joachim couldn't stand. Both Augustine and Aquinas had rejected the millenarian view of Revelation, interpreting the thousand years instead as "the whole of the present time wherein the saints now reign with Christ."[6] And while Jesus is "coming soon" (Rev. 22:7, 12, 20), no one knows the day or the hour (Matt. 24:36). Joachim himself was never formally condemned by the Church, but in 1256, the writings of Fra Gherardo—and by association, of Joachim—were. A formal

5. *Catechism* 771; *Sacrosanctum Concilium* 2.

6. Thomas Aquinas, *Summa theologiae* Suppl. 77.1.

condemnation of the Fraticelli with their "two churches," one "spiritual" and the other "carnal," followed in 1318.[7]

The earthward path of institutionalism, because it's more a matter of hypocrisy than heresy, could not be formally condemned. But it's condemned already in nearly all that Scripture and Tradition tells us about the Christian life. Openly flouting the Church's precepts makes a mockery of the Gospel, and will never escape God's notice: "How much worse punishment do you think will be deserved by those who have spurned the Son of God, profaned the blood of the covenant by which they were sanctified, and outraged the Spirit of grace?" (Heb. 10:29).

We see an icon of this unity of Spirit and Body in the very first ecumenical council of the Church: the Council of Jerusalem. What was on the table was the identity of the Church itself: Did new Christians have to follow the bodily prescriptions of the Law of Moses, such as circumcision? Or were they released, in spiritual liberty, from all such laws? The resolution kept the two "wings" in communion: Christians had to keep some essentials, but were otherwise free. And this decision came as much from above through the Spirit as below through the Body: "It has seemed good to the Holy Spirit and to us to impose on you no further burden than these essentials" (Acts 15:28).

Needless to say, these two dimensions make the Church a place of constant tension and painful growth. Spiritual experiences, devotions, and movements are always springing up; the Body looks to "test everything" (1 Thess. 5:21), holding fast to what's good,

7. John XXII, *Gloriosam Ecclesiam* 14, in *The Sources of Catholic Dogma*, ed. Heinrich Denzinger and Karl Rahner, trans. R.J. Deferrari (St. Louis, MO: B. Herder, 1954), 191.

cutting loose what's dangerous, and—with a great liberality—tolerating what's ambiguous. Sometimes this tension becomes fierce: here the charismatic violently lurch ahead, there the institutional violently pull the reins; here one man tests the limits, there another draws a new one. At times, the tightrope snaps, only to be retied in providential ways: the warrior mystic Joan of Arc was burned at the stake by members of the institutional Church—the same Church that would later canonize her as a saint.

No merely spiritual community could ever take root in this world; it had to be grounded in the earth. And no merely human institution could ever spread its branches across it; it had to receive living water from the heavens.

CHAPTER 21

Mission: Contemplation or Action

A related dilemma for the Church—an extension of the spirit-flesh dilemma—is the pull between mystical contemplation and practical action. One side inwardly gazes at the Creator, while the other outwardly provides for his creatures. One is a way of spiritual rest and worship, the other a way of bodily work and service.

Is the Church's mission in contemplation or action?

I

The heavenward way is contemplation at the expense of action.

We see a striking example of the way of contemplation in the Quietist movement, which emerged in Spain in the seventeenth century. The Quietists were pure mystics, teaching an inward ascent into God that stripped away all bodily and worldly things. Even ascetic self-discipline, penitential practices, and mental exercises of all kinds had to be left behind. Any and all activity of the body and the will was superfluous; all that mattered was a state of inner stillness and quiet. The summit of this ascent was a purely passive state of annihilation in God, a "mystical death" into nothingness—the dissolution of the spirit in the ocean of the Spirit.

Miguel de Molinos, the leading light of the Quietists, spoke volumes with the title of his work: *The Spiritual Guide which Disentangles the Soul, and Brings It by the Inward Way to the Getting of Perfect Contemplation and the Rich Treasure of Internal Peace*. Molinos draws a sharp contrast between "two sorts of spiritual persons": one internal, the other external; one a master, the other a beginner; one contemplative, the other meditative; one pure, the other sensible; one rare, the other common. The more a person ascends on the spiritual journey, the more he becomes the first kind of person, and the more his soul is annihilated in God: "How happy and well applied will thy soul be, if, retreating within itself, it there shrink into its own nothing . . . without heeding, thinking, or minding any sensible thing? . . . Let it be silent and do nothing, forget itself, and plunge into that obscure faith."[1]

The Quietists were right to celebrate contemplation and mysticism, a recurring theme of the New Testament that finds its archetype in St. John. The beloved disciple was attentive to Christ's every move: he rested his head on his chest (John 13:23), followed him to the cross (John 19:26), and even rushed to his empty tomb before Peter (John 20:4). So intensely spiritual is John's writing—and so sharp its contrasts of light and darkness, spirit and flesh, God and the world—that one popular theory ties his Gospel to Gnostic movements. As in every distortion, there's at least an element of truth: John's writings are a contemplative crescendo of the New Testament. The heavenward way of contemplation, in

1. *Golden Thoughts from the Spiritual Guide of Miguel Molinos* (Glasgow: David Bryce & Son, 1883), 64–65.

following this trajectory, wisely emphasizes silence and stillness, detachment and docility—powerful weapons against the anxieties, uncertainties, and distractions of this life. Indeed, Molinos himself was initially well received by the Church.

But worrisome tendencies creep in on this heavenward way. First, as on other heavenward paths, we position ourselves beyond the need for sacramental confession, the authority of bishops, or any ecclesial tribunal at all. The heavenly soul, for the Quietists, passes beyond the earthly ministrations of the institutional Church; only a spiritual director could follow it into the abyss of contemplation.

The temptation toward moral laxity also reappears. One of the chief concerns with Quietism—which came out in accusations against Molinos himself—was that it was giving cover to acts of sexual license. It wasn't that sexual acts were encouraged, as they were with earthward libertines; it was that they were seen as meaningless. The Quietist's will was so dissolved in God, Molinos taught, that such outward behavior is the work of evil forces manipulating the body—which, like anything else, had to be passively accepted. Without a corrective emphasis on outward action, we become susceptible to an indifference to sins of the flesh.

Finally, Quietism quite literally turns its back on the Way: among the bodily attachments that contemplatives had to ignore was the human nature of Christ. The flesh of the Word—the very flesh that wrought our salvation on the cross—becomes, like all things physical and worldly, unworthy of the contemplative soul.

—

The earthward way is action at the expense of contemplation.

We see the opposite tendency take off, like so many earthward movements, in the modern world. And a vivid case in point is the radical wing of the "theology of liberation." This movement—first forged in Latin America, but later spreading to Africa, India, the Philippines, and all around the world—drew out the social dimensions of the Gospel: a liberation, in Christ, from economic, social, and political oppression. At the heart of the movement was a focus on the poor—and not just treating the surface symptoms of poverty, but attacking its deeper structural causes.

The radical wing of liberation theology so stressed this attitude of action that it began to undercut the very truths of God at the heart of Christian contemplation. One liberation theologian, Fr. Tissa Balasuriya in Sri Lanka, began throwing into question the Church's dogmas and doctrines, arguing that they were rooted in myth. This included teachings about Mary, original sin, and even Christ himself—a "supreme teacher" who communicated to his listeners a "primordial spiritual experience," Balasuriya wrote, but not the divine Son of God.[2] The Church's formal definitions on such matters were, he argued, simply appropriated over time to serve the self-interest of clerics: "Whatever is in the interest of the power-holders may be proposed as faith."[3] The Church itself, like the world around it, was really an all-too-human matrix of power dynamics with good and bad actors.

Worldly action, like spiritual contemplation, is a recurring New Testament theme, and if St. John is an archetype of the former, St. James the Less is the archetype of the latter. The epistle attributed

2. Tissa Balasuriya, *Mary and Human Liberation* (Harrisburg, PA: Trinity Press International, 1997), 112–113, 119.

3. Balasuriya, 116.

to James stands firmly in the tradition of the Jewish prophets and sages—the very books considered so worthless by Marcion—encouraging us "to do justice, and to love kindness, and to walk humbly" with God (Mic. 6:8). We have to be not only hearers of the word, James exhorts, but "doers who act" (James 1:25); not only religious, but *truly* religious, which means "to care for orphans and widows" (James 1:27). Most famously, he declares that "faith by itself, if it has no works, is dead" (James 2:17). These same themes carry over into the writings of the Church Fathers. In fact, what most impressed the pagans about the Christians wasn't how they worshiped but how they *acted*: "See how they love one another."[4] The earthward rightly pick up on this great scriptural and patristic theme of action, which reaches its high point in Christ's Sermon on the Mount (Matt. 5–7).

But a radical liberation theology neglects the timeless exhortation of the Psalmist: "Be still, and know that I am God!" (Ps. 46:10). It's not just that we forget to be still; it's that we also cease to know that God is God. Indeed, behind Balasuriya's undercutting of Church teaching is one of the great dangers of this earthward path: a drift of the Christian faith into the atheistic ideology of Marxism.

A 1984 critique of "certain aspects" of liberation theology from then-Cardinal Ratzinger drew attention to this creep toward Marxist ideology. As liberation theologians looked out at the world through the lens of class struggle, Ratzinger argued, they were being drawn more and more into Marx's Feuerbachian cry against the world above and the summons to reclaim the world below by violent revolution. What resulted was a subordination of divine truth

4. Tertullian, *Apology* 39.

to pure praxis, and even "a new interpretation of Christianity," one that reduced salvation in Christ to "a purely earthly gospel."[5] In ceasing to gaze at God first and foremost, the Church becomes just another political regime or nonprofit organization, and God himself just a function of its activity.

+

The Way is both contemplation and action.

Jesus wasn't trained as a contemplative mystic or scribe but as a carpenter, passing his "hidden years" in humble toil and labor. But his identity was in returning the Father's loving gaze, and he often withdrew into silence and solitude, even during active ministry, to be refreshed by it. The Word, as Joseph Ratzinger put it, subsists in the tension of a twofold totality: he is both totally "from" the Father and totally "for" man.[6] And in this communion of contemplation and action, the Son simply reflects the Father: "God knows how to be active while at rest, and at rest in his activity."[7]

This is also the lesson of the story of Martha and Mary (Luke 10:38–42), which is often hastily read along heavenward lines as the choice of contemplation (Mary) at the expense of action (Martha). In fact, it's not Martha's activity per se that Jesus calls out; it's her worry and distraction. Likewise, it's not Mary's contemplation per se that Jesus praises; it's her focus on *him* and his words. The

5. Congregation for the Doctrine of the Faith, "Instruction on Certain Aspects of the 'Theology of Liberation,'" August 6, 1984, vatican.va.

6. Joseph Ratzinger, *Introduction to Christianity*, 2nd ed., trans. J.R. Foster (San Francisco: Ignatius, 2004), 210.

7. Augustine, *City of God* 12.18.

story is, in fact, yet another reminder of the Way: without the "one thing" necessary, which is Christ himself, trouble will always ensue, no matter how much we do—or don't do.

The Way is both contemplation and action, both worship and service. Disciples of Christ can neither stand looking up at the sky (Acts 1:11) nor toil in vain under the sun (Eccles. 1:3). Thus, Molinos was formally condemned by the Church in 1687; Balasuriya, for his part, was excommunicated in 1997 for deviating "from the integrity of the truth of the Catholic faith," but the sentence was lifted before his death, and he was reconciled to the Church.[8]

Entwined with this communion is a more elemental both/and: that the love of God, which tends toward prayerful contemplation, and the love of man, which tends toward concrete action, belong together. The two greatest commandments, Christ teaches, are to love God with your whole heart, soul, mind, and strength, and to love your neighbor as yourself. On these, everything else hangs. Like the Ten Commandments, which joined the first tablet about God (the first three commandments) to the second tablet about our neighbor (the other seven), Christ puts first things first: we have to love God above all. But he doesn't tell his listeners to reject or neglect man, or even to treat the love of man as a separate matter; rather, he ties the two loves close together. Indeed, we show our love of God *through* our love of neighbor: "Those who say, 'I love God,' and hate their brothers or sisters, are liars" (1 John 4:20).

Thus, contemplation comes first—Sunday, a day of rest and focus on God, is the first and most important day of the week—but

8. Congregation for the Doctrine of the Faith, "Notification concerning the text 'Mary and Human Liberation' by Father Tissa Balasuriya, OMI," January 2, 1997, vatican.va.

action flows from it and leads back to it. The Church recognizes, Augustine writes, "two states of life": "One is in faith, the other in sight . . . one in active work, the other in the wages of contemplation."[9] The Church fixes its eyes on God with the loving gaze of St. John, yet marches through the world with the blistered feet of St. James. Its hands are for both chalices and callouses, its nose for both the aroma of incense and the stink of the sheep. "One does not live by bread alone" (Matt. 4:4), and without contemplation of Christ, the spirit starves; but whatever we do to the poor we do to Christ (Matt. 25:35), and without bread, the poor starve.

In resisting Quietism, the Church was hardly resisting contemplation itself. In Spain alone, we find two of the greatest contemplatives in Christian history: St. John of the Cross and St. Teresa of Avila, both recognized as Doctors of the Church. But both were also active reformers of the Carmelite Order. Authentic mysticism never devolves into a navel-gazing separatism; instead, it flows back into concrete service, both in the spiritual works of mercy (like counseling the doubtful) and corporal works of mercy (like feeding the hungry). Indeed, sometimes service is more pressing. Even the great mystic Meister Eckhart counsels, "If a man were in an ecstasy, as St. Paul was, and knew that some sick man needed him to give him a bit of soup, I should think it far better if you would abandon your ecstasy out of love and show greater love in caring for the other in his need."[10]

Likewise, though the Church said no to certain liberation

9. Augustine, *Tractates on John* 124.5.

10. Meister Eckhart, "Counsels on Discernment" 10, in *Meister Eckhart: The Essential Sermons*, trans. E. Colledge and B. McGinn (New York: Paulist, 1981), 258.

theologians enamored of Marxism, it never said no to liberation theology itself; indeed, the movement's theme of the "preferential option for the poor" has become a part of the Church's formal teaching.[11] From the patristic era to the present, the Church has a deep tradition of both personal charity and social justice—a term first coined by a Jesuit priest. We see a modern exemplar of action in the Servant of God Dorothy Day, a former communist who converted to Catholicism and co-founded the Catholic Worker Movement. But Day didn't live by bread alone; like all great saints of social justice, she was animated by prayer, liturgy, and contemplation—especially the gaze of Eucharistic Adoration: "Under the form of bread and wine, for my nourishment, lest I faint by the way, his Real Presence."[12]

Pope Benedict XVI argued that the Church has a "three-fold responsibility": *leitourgia*, celebrating the liturgical and sacramental life; *diakonia*, ministering to the poor and suffering with love; and *kerygma-martyria*, evangelizing the world with the Word of God.[13] The first is a Johannine path of contemplation; the second, a Jamesian path of action; and the third, a contemplation-in-action —the concrete mission of inviting others into the presence of God. As the Church is both Pauline and Petrine, it's both Johannine and Jamesian. Contemplation and action, together with charism and institution, commune in the life of the Church.

11. *Compendium of the Social Doctrine of the Church* 182.

12. Dorothy Day, *The Duty of Delight: The Diaries of Dorothy Day* (New York: Image Books, 2008), 271–272.

13. Benedict XVI, *Deus Caritas Est* 25, encyclical letter, December 25, 2005, vatican.va.

CHAPTER 22

Conversion: Grace or Nature

Christians agree that we're converted, or radically reoriented, toward Christ. But how does this happen? On whom do we rely? Here, the Church finds itself again in an extension of the great God-man dilemma. On one side is the Good News of God's grace, which is tied to the Bad News of our wretchedness—the fall of man and all its awful fallout. On the other side is our natural freedom, which is tied to our natural nobility—the dignity of man and all its beautiful expressions.

Are we converted through the way of grace or the way of nature?

I

The heavenward way is grace at the expense of nature.

Grace was the animating principle of Jansenism, an influential movement that started in seventeenth-century France. Cornelius Jansen claimed to have read the works of Augustine ten times over, and agonized over his own theological magnum opus for twenty-two years. He died a son of the Church in good standing, dutifully delivering his *Augustinus*, named after the Bishop of Hippo, into the Church's maternal arms for her judgment.

But this wasn't just *Augustinus*; it was *Augustinus Cornelii Jansenii, Episcopi*—"Augustine according to Bishop Cornelius Jansen." The Bishop of Hippo had passionately raised the Church's arms to heaven; Jansen pulled them out of their sockets. Man wasn't simply wretched, Jansen taught; he was *totally* wretched: "Once human nature has been thrown into the weakness of sin, nothing good at all can remain in man, not a concession of the will, not an inclination or impulse."[1] Instead, our nature is pulled ever downward into carnal pleasure—a pull we can rationalize but not resist. If the flesh says yes, we can't say no. When it comes to human nature, all is wretchedness.

The same totalizing quality applied to grace: those who receive the divine life from above can't possibly resist it. In a kind of divine violence, the will "is so seized by grace that it can be hardly said to act."[2] If God says yes, we can't say no; our sinful nature is overpowered and subdued. We're then pulled out of the whirlpool of lower delights and into a whirlwind of higher delights—away from the irresistible force of the flesh and into the irresistible force of the Spirit. Without our say so, sin enslaved us; without our say so, God liberates us.

For the Jansenists, this story of grace was as rare as it was vivid. They taught that it was only for the elect that Jesus died, and they made this point clear by portraying Christ on the cross in a posture

1. Leszek Kołakowski, *God Owes Us Nothing: A Brief Remark on Pascal's Religion and on the Spirit of Jansenism* (Chicago: The University of Chicago Press, 1995), 15.

2. Kołakowski, 15.

of taut verticality—his tortured arms stretched *upward*, not outward. The great heaving masses of human nature are not a part of the story at all.

The Jansenists rightly acknowledged the truth of human wretchedness, which resounds across the whole of the Bible: "There is no one who is righteous, not even one. . . . All have sinned and fall short of the glory of God" (Rom. 3:23; see Ps. 14:3, 53:3). Indeed, Christ's very first public declaration is a call to "repent" (Matt. 4:17; Mark 1:15). The theme of God's grace is likewise all over the Scriptures—and not as something earned, caused, or controlled by man in any way, but rather as the work of the sovereign God. Though we sinned—even *while* we were still sinners—God brought us back to himself through the "free gift" of his grace: "Where sin increased, grace abounded all the more" (Rom. 5:8, 15–17, 20). This drama of grace, in both acts, is essential to a correct telling of the Christian story. Too often, Christians are tempted to reduce religion to a crutch or to rely on their own powers altogether, making God their second-in-command. Against these distortions, the heavenward rightly revolt; grace makes all the difference in the world.

But the total wretchedness of man occludes our natural goodness, leading back to a grim Gnostic pessimism: human nature is in utter darkness. And the irresistible grace of God occludes our natural freedom to say yes or no, leading back to an equally grim Stoic fatalism: the human will is utterly helpless. In both movements, we're left with a denuded and degraded humanity scrambling to hold on to the hope of the Gospel. The heavenward honor God's side of the ledger, but only by running roughshod over the integrity of his most prized creation.

—

The earthward way is nature at the expense of grace.

We see the clearest example of the opposite path in the fourth-century heresy of Pelagianism. In a familiar pattern, Pelagius, too, began as a heresy hunter, fighting what he saw as a slow drift back into Manichaeism. He even accused Augustine of the same slippery slope, quoting from his earlier texts emphasizing free will to argue against his later texts emphasizing grace.

Christians, Pelagius felt, were more and more treating evil as a rival force to God as the Manichaeans did, and failing to hold themselves and each other accountable for succumbing to it. This was having a disastrous effect on the Church: believers were making peace with sin and falling into moral laxity. Pelagius sought a return to the high moral calling of the Gospel—and he practiced what he preached. Though "Pelagian" is now one of the ultimate terms of derision in Christian discourse, Pelagius himself had a sterling reputation as a man of high moral caliber and great spiritual seriousness. Augustine spoke charitably of "so worthy a man, and so good a Christian."[3]

But his reaction led to an overreaction, sending him careening into the opposite error. In the first place, Pelagius argued that there was no original sin inherited from the first man: we're not born wretched, but good. He didn't mean that there was no sin—*personal* sin had run rampant—but rather that sin wasn't inborn and propagated through human nature. Instead, it was an *imitation*

3. Augustine, *On Merit and the Forgiveness of Sins, and the Baptism of Infants* 3.6.

of Adam's bad example: just as the first man freely chose to disobey God, we, too, freely choose disobedience.

Likewise, he argued that grace wasn't necessary to be converted to life in Christ; human freedom was sufficient. Once again, he didn't deny grace altogether, but he did make it secondary: we receive the grace of forgiveness in Baptism, but it cleanses us of our personal sins, not original sin; and we receive continued grace in the Christian journey, but only as an *assist* in choosing good, not as a sovereign movement from above. Grace largely comes through the imitation of the teachings and example of Christ: just as we can imitate Adam in choosing evil, we can imitate Christ in choosing good. Whichever way we choose—the way of Adam or the way of Christ—the fate of the Christian, for Pelagius, is in his own hands.

Pelagianism is a clear departure from the Gospel, but it's not without its scriptural support. Even after the fall, the human being retains, in part, the nobility of being made in God's image: God made human beings "a little lower than God, and crowned them with glory and honor" (Ps. 8:5–6; see Heb. 2:7). St. Paul goes further, calling man the *doxa*, the glory, of God (1 Cor. 11:7). And central to this *imago Dei* is our free will to choose one thing or another: "Choose this day whom you will serve," Joshua proclaims. "As for me and my household, we will serve the LORD" (Josh. 24:15). Even St. Paul, that great herald of grace, acknowledges the Christian freedom to indulge or resist temptation (1 Cor. 10:13). In fact, the whole of Scripture is difficult to understand apart from the assumption that we can respond freely to God's Word. The earthward seize on these truths of human nature, and often with the good intention of moral and spiritual reform.

But Pelagianism leaves us in a naïve optimism: we so honor the goodness of human nature, and so believe in its ability to perfect itself, that we lose sight of our fallenness and helplessness—qualities that will never completely vanish this side of heaven. Even St. Paul laments the sway that sin holds within him: "I can will what is right, but I cannot do it. For I do not do the good I want, but the evil I do not want is what I do" (Rom. 7:19). At the same time, Pelagianism opens the door to a restless, works-based perfectionism reminiscent of the Stoics—or even the Pharisees, for whom Jesus reserves his harshest words (Matt. 23).

Worse yet, in making the Bad News not so bad, this earthward way also makes the Good News not so good. Christ tells us that even the *least* person inside the kingdom is greater than John the Baptist, who was the *greatest* person outside of it (Matt. 11:11). But Pelagianism obscures this sharp contrast between the grace of the kingdom and our own intestinal fortitude. We're thus robbed of both the darkness and brightness of the Christian faith, returning to paganism's calm light of mild philosophy.

The Way is both grace and nature.

The film *The Tree of Life* opens with a mother reflecting, "The nuns taught us there are two ways through life: the way of nature and the way of grace. You have to choose which one you'll follow." What she refers to, though, is the choice between the City of God and the City of Man, between the Way and the false earth of sinful humanity: "Grace doesn't try to please itself. . . . Nature only wants to please itself." A hasty reading of the film assigns these roles to the "graceful" mother and her demanding husband. But the two represent grace and nature in a more exact way—because in the climactic scene, they embrace in the new heavens and the new earth amid a chorus of "Agnus Dei."

Is our conversion achieved through divine grace or human nature? Naturally—by God's grace—the Church insists that it's both, because "grace does not destroy nature but perfects it."[4] Thus, the Church condemned Pelagianism at the Council of Ephesus in 431 and Jansenism in a papal bull in 1653.

Ontologically, we're fundamentally the "very good" creatures of a good God (Gen. 1:31)—Manichaeism has been left behind—but existentially, we're fundamentally the wretched sons of Adam and daughters of Eve: "The heart is devious above all else; it is perverse—who can understand it?" (Jer. 17:9). We fight the very thing that would heal us: "All human nature vigorously resists grace, because grace changes us and the change is painful."[5] We know our desperate need for help, and if we don't, the Church communicates it: in the Confiteor at the Mass, the faithful ask for the prayers of those present, the Mother of God, and—not to put too fine a point on it—every last one of the angels and saints. Who but the wretched could be in need of such extravagant and constant help?

But our ontological goodness still permeates human existence. Original sin *wounds* us, but it doesn't destroy us. Man is, in Aquinas' metaphor, like a gravely sick man: everything we do is, in an ultimate sense, enveloped in an illness tending toward death, but we can still occasionally act in perfectly healthy ways. And we need

4. Thomas Aquinas, *Summa theologiae* 1.1.8.

5. Flannery O'Connor to Cecil Dawkins, December 9, 1958, in *Flannery O'Connor Collection*, ed. Matthew Becklo (Park Ridge, IL: Word on Fire Classics, 2019), 400.

the "higher force" of grace to do works "proportionate to everlasting life," but not to do the good things "natural to man," like working, eating, or spending time with friends.[6] We're both wretched and great—both desperately disgraced and naturally graceful.

This same balance extends into the question of grace and freedom. We can't will our way into God's own life; instead, the divine assistance has to lead us there. We didn't choose him but he chose us, and "we love because he first loved us" (John 15:16; 1 John 4:19). But we're also not simply passive recipients of God's irresistible grace; we have the freedom to accept or reject his invitation: "See that you do not refuse the one who is speaking" (Heb. 12:25). God "precedes, prepares, and elicits the free response of man," but man assents to, cooperates with, and collaborates in the free gift of God.[7]

Though the Jansenists tried to claim Augustine, and he is indeed the Doctor of Grace, we find in him a robust Catholic balance on this question. Augustine knew, from personal experience, both the darkest depths of the Bad News and the brightest heights of the Good. Out of his own helplessness, he could only cry out for God's help: "Grant what thou dost command, and command what thou wilt."[8] And in his ensuing battles with the heretics—the pagans, the Donatists, and most famously, the Pelagians—he fought to make this Gospel of grace known: "What do you have that you did not receive?" (1 Cor. 4:7).

But what both his overzealous supporters and underzealous detractors miss is his corresponding emphasis on both the goodness of

6. *Summa theologiae* 1-2.109.2, 5.
7. *Catechism of the Catholic Church* 2022.
8. Augustine, *Confessions* 10.29.

nature and the necessity of freedom. Human nature remained, for Augustine, noble and honorable, and not totally wretched; in fact, even the evil we do "shows how great and honorable is the nature itself. . . . The perversion disgraces a nature that deserves honor."[9] Similarly, human beings are truly free, and that freedom has a role to play in conversion to Christ: "God created us without us; but he did not will to save us without us."[10]

This doesn't mean that the Church's discussions on these questions are straightforward or easy; on the contrary, one of the thorniest debates in all of Catholic history was the *De Auxiliis* controversy that unfolded between Dominicans and Jesuits in the late sixteenth century. The two sides—each with their distinctive approach—tried to play the right notes, at the right volume, in the harmony of grace and freedom, but ended up at loggerheads. The question rose to the papacy, and after twenty years of debate and three popes, it was declared that each side could retain its own opinions on the matter. Four hundred years later, this is essentially where the debate remains.

But while the exact mechanisms of grace and nature remain an open and fascinating theological question, the argument unfolds among brothers and sisters of Christ, in whom the absolute primacy of God and integrity of man hold together: "From his fullness we have all received, grace upon grace" (John 1:16).

9. Augustine, *City of God* 12.1.

10. *Catechism of the Catholic Church* 1847; Augustine, Sermon 169.11, 13 (PL 38, 923).

CHAPTER 23

Morality: Rigor or Relaxation

Having been called out of sin by God's grace, how is the Christian to live? Here, the dilemma between values and facts—and behind it, the spiritual and the physical—again takes hold. On one side is an exacting discipline that calls Christians to moral excellence, and on the other a patient bearing with human weakness that meets them where they are.

Is the Christian journey defined by moral rigor or moral relaxation?

I

The heavenward way is rigor at the expense of relaxation.

We see this heavenward way, once more, in Jansenism; in fact, what the Jansenists would be remembered for most wasn't their theology of grace but their moral rigorism. If natural man is racing down the path of depravity, the Jansenists taught, then spiritual man—the man of grace—has to be racing up the path of purity.

His inner life has to be of the highest caliber, his behavior beyond reproach—a sharp contrast with the fallen world.

Along this path of moral rigor, grave sin became an ever-present threat lurking around every corner. Even prayer, in some cases, could be sinful: "The prayer of the impious is a new sin; and what God grants to them is a new judgment against them."[1] One Jansenist, Pierre Nicole, argued that it's a mortal sin for a woman to wear clothes showing her breasts, her shoulders, or even her arms, as doing so was born of a secret corruption, a vanity that—by directly exciting men to wicked thoughts and desires—made her guilty of "spiritual homicide."[2]

This rigorism carried over into the confessional. It wasn't enough that a person have an imperfect contrition based on shame for his sin or the fear of punishment; this just meant that he "commits that evil in his heart, and is already guilty before God."[3] Instead, what was needed was a *perfect* contrition based on the love of God. Unless a person had profoundly lamented their sins in an indisputable movement of repentance, the priest was justified in withholding absolution. Forgiveness of sins was to be a more rare, privileged grace.

The Jansenists, of course, could find backing for their rigorism in Scripture. Doesn't Christ exhort his followers to be not only holy but "perfect," their righteousness surpassing that of the Pharisees (Matt. 5:48, 20)? Isn't the love of God tied again and again

1. Clement XI, *Unigenitus Dei Filius: Condemnation of the Errors of Paschasius* 59, September 8, 1713, in *The Sources of Catholic Dogma*, ed. Heinrich Denzinger and Karl Rahner, trans. R.J. Deferrari (St. Louis, MO: B. Herder, 1954), 350.

2. Pierre Nicole, *Instructions théologiques et morales sur le premier commandement du Décalogue* (Paris: 1713), 486–487.

3. Clement XI, *Unigenitus Dei Filius* 62, in *Sources of Catholic Dogma*, 351.

to obeying his commandments (John 14:15; 1 John 5:3)? And don't Paul, Peter, John, and James—for all their distinct emphases—all call Christians to a high bar of morality? Paul warns of the works of the flesh (Gal. 5:19–21), Peter of the devil (1 Pet. 5:8–9), John of the world (1 John 2:15–17), and James of all three—that which is "earthly, unspiritual, devilish" (James 3:15). The Christian life isn't a game—eternity is at stake—and rigorists rightly refuse to make it one. And such rigorism isn't without its bright spots: the Jansenists were ahead of their time in pushing for more frequent reading of the Scriptures by the laity, including women.

But this heavenward way doesn't err in acknowledging and fighting against deadly sin; it errs in seeing it even in those everyday foibles that sinners struggle to overcome. And it doesn't err in calling people higher; it errs in not being there to catch them when they fall flat, as they inevitably will. In short, it errs in overlooking our need to rest secure in the Father's love despite our weakness. Jansenist rigorism is a clarion call to follow Christ's commands, but one that lacks his compassion.

This leads, in the short term, to pride—a spiritual elitism echoing the Manichaean Elect. The Church becomes a kind of country club, a superior space for the privileged few—a Church not for sinners to become saints but for saints to avoid sinners. We pride ourselves on walking the hard and narrow way, but fail to see how precarious our own state is; we denigrate others as hopelessly adrift, but fail to appreciate how precious their souls are. And we push ourselves, gradually, into a self-perfectionism, trying to prove ourselves before God—the very same impulse that the Jansenists decried in the Pelagians, only now, under the cover of grace.

But "pride goes before destruction, and a haughty spirit before a fall" (Prov. 16:18). We can never, of course, be perfect, and in the long run, the pride that we can do no wrong turns into the anxiety that we can do no right; sanctimony transforms into scrupulosity. For the scrupulous—a religious manifestation of obsessive-compulsive disorder—the spiritual life becomes quicksand: the very struggle for certainty further plunges us into anxiety. The smallest infractions become infernal; the gravest sins—like the unforgiveable sin of blaspheming against the Holy Spirit (Mark 3:29)—become a live threat; and the spiritual life becomes a death spiral of doubt: Do I *really* love God? Am I truly in a state of grace? Did I ever even have it in the first place? God, for his part, becomes a merciless taskmaster overseeing all this anguish, a relentless tyrant who is always out to get us. We're left to lash out at both God and neighbor—for "the one to whom little is forgiven, loves little" (Luke 7:47).

—

The earthward way is relaxation at the expense of rigor.

Jansenist rigorism didn't emerge in a vacuum; rather, it emerged in opposition to certain Jesuits being accused of a backslide into Pelagianism and an unhealthy emphasis on human nature. Among these Jesuits was a group of theologians called "laxists" who wandered the path running opposite the way of rigorism: the way of moral relaxation.

When Rome condemned five Jansenist principles in 1653, the philosopher and scientist Blaise Pascal—a committed Jansenist whose sister had become a nun at the movement's stronghold, the Port-Royal abbey in Paris—rose to their defense with *The Provincial*

Letters. But in this series of scathing letters, written under a pen name, Pascal didn't attack the Jesuits primarily for their views on grace and free will; instead, he viciously satirized the sophistry and relativism of the laxists in their ranks.

The laxists took casuistry—a case-based approach to Catholic ethics applying universal values to particular situations—and turned it into a playground of obfuscation and rule-bending. Deadly sins were massaged into peccadillos, and peccadillos into noble virtues—even divine gifts. There was still plenty of talk of "grace," but it wasn't the costly grace of the Gospel; it was a cheap grace that ran interference for sinners eager to remain in their sin.

"A great many things, formerly regarded as forbidden, are innocent and allowable," Pascal's laxist declares. "We relieve people from troublesome scruples of conscience, by showing them that what they believed to be sinful was indeed quite innocent."[4] Such "innocent" activities detailed by the laxist include everything from making money by consulting the devil through magic to killing a whistleblower threatening to expose scandalous crimes in a religious community. For the Jansenists, a bare arm is spiritual homicide; for the laxists, "intercourse with a married woman, with the consent of her husband, is not adultery."[5] Human freedom eclipsed God's commands, darkening first into mere license and then into pure licentiousness.

As with rigorism, laxity carried over into the confessional—and the bar for absolution was as low for the laxists as it was high

4. Blaise Pascal, *The Provincial Letters*, trans. Thomas M'Crie, in *Pensées; The Provincial Letters* (New York: Modern Library, 1941), 450.

5. Innocent XI, "Sixty-Five Propositions Condemned in the Decree of the Holy Office" 50, March 2, 1679, in *Sources of Catholic Dogma*, 328.

for the Jansenists. Penitents were free to conceal certain sins under certain conditions, and to not really intend to change their ways at all. They could even opt to delay their penance until purgatory—a request their confessors were obliged to accept.

The laxists, like the Jansenists, had their footholds in Scripture. Christ exhorts, but he also promises "rest" to his disciples—"for my yoke is easy, and my burden is light" (Matt. 11:28–30). And imitating his Way, the same four archetypal Apostles—Paul, Peter, John, and James—are relentless in calling for gentleness and patience toward other sinners. We have to be especially patient, Scripture tells us, with new believers taking their first clumsy steps on the Way; they're infants who need "milk, not solid food" (1 Cor. 3:1–2; Heb. 5:12–14). The laxists saw that every Christian—from those alienated from the Church and sunken in sin to those entrenched in its life and wrestling with doubt—needs to find acceptance and encouragement in the arms of Christ; that the Church can offer those arms, rushing out to meet and embrace its prodigal sons and daughters (Luke 15:20); and that none of us, after all, are perfect: "Do not judge, so that you may not be judged" (Matt. 7:1).

But the laxists, as Pascal saw so clearly, were bending over backward to the point of falling over—and pulling their listeners down with them. They didn't "tie up heavy burdens" with a ruthless hand, but they did pacify slaves to sin with a truthless word (Matt. 23:4; John 8:32–34). They didn't make people feel untouchable, but they did make them feel irreproachable—the deadlier of the two errors. And they didn't suffocate Christians with the threat of sin, but they did make every possible excuse for it—and he who excuses himself accuses himself. Following this path of relaxation, we fall from one extreme right into the other: from a vicious pessimism to a blithe optimism, from scrupulous obsessions to unscrupulous shrugs, and from a rigidity that never bends to a flexibility that never resists. God the Father becomes a lenient Grandfather; the Church becomes welcoming and affirming but never demanding or convicting; and the moral life becomes "a most uncommonly comfortable" task instead of spiritual battle.[6] Christ's new commandment is love, and "mercy triumphs over judgment" (John 13:34; James 2:13). But a patience that undercuts the reality of sin and the urgency of fighting it is a counterfeit Christianity of self-love and false mercy.

And the sickness of laxity isn't only a threat to individual believers through subtle winks and nods; it's also a threat to the Church's mission of drawing the world to Christ because of public scandal and confusion. In this earthward climate, the acts that Scripture and Tradition have always regarded as incompatible with the kingdom—the sins of "fornicators, idolaters, adulterers, male prostitutes, sodomites, thieves, the greedy, drunkards, revilers, robbers" (1 Cor. 6:9–10)—come to be taken as "quite innocent"; as a result, those inside the Church who have fallen away are assured they haven't left, and those outside the Church who never entered are assured they haven't fallen. What results is an overemphasis on relaxation and ease, and a half-truth that—ignoring the primacy of rigor and necessity of constant conversion—is so often twisted into a lie: "God loves you just the way you are."

6. Pascal, *Provincial Letters*, 383.

The Way is both rigor and relaxation.

Two devotions of the Church exploded in popularity around the time of the Jansenist controversy. The first was the Stations of the Cross, which underscores the brutal reality of sin and the high cost that was paid for it. The second was the Sacred Heart of Jesus, which underscores a tenderness toward sinners and a forbearance when they fall. The first devotion is, for the earthward, too cold and harsh; the latter—which wasn't popular with the Jansenists—is, for the heavenward, too warm and fuzzy. But the two devotions—one more vertically aimed at rigor, and one more horizontally aimed at relaxation—are inseparable: on the cross, blood and water gushed forth from the Sacred Heart, and on the Sacred Heart, a crown of thorns and burning flame lead upward to the cross. Christ's Passion to save humanity and his passion to embrace humanity are one movement of divine love.

Christ displayed the same communion of rigor and relaxation in his ministry: he protects and doesn't condemn the woman caught in adultery, but he does command her to "not sin again" (John 8:11); he befriends the reviled tax collectors and even calls one into his inner circle, but he also declares them sick and in need of healing (Matt. 9:9–13). An iciness that never comforts and a niceness that never offends are both grave mistakes. And the Church, aspiring to follow the Way, condemned both the heavenward rigorism of the Jansenists in 1713 and the earthward relativism of the laxists in 1679.

It's a testament to God's sense of humor—and to the Catholic both/and—that the first Jesuit pope would issue an apostolic letter in praise of Blaise Pascal.[7] But Pascal was, after all, a deeply Catholic thinker, and his posthumous *Pensées* is a philosophical masterpiece that, at heart, is an ode to the Way. But his satirical *Letters*, however brilliant, were lopsided, not only unjustly tarnishing the Jesuits—and becoming, by extension, a handy bludgeon against the Church itself—but also losing sight of what even the laxists got right.

For the Church, "rigor" is no dirty word; the faithful have to remain alert to the world, the flesh, and the devil, and cling to the rough wood of the cross. At the same time, neither is "relaxation": we have to be patient with ourselves and others, and rest in the tender heart of Jesus. True freedom is in knowing, accepting, and strenuously rising toward God's commands—and knowing, accepting, and comfortably falling back into his hands when we fail. It's in navigating, as Augustine writes, between the "pinnacle of pride" on the right hand and the "whirlpool of indolence" on the left[8]—going, as Scripture says, neither right nor left (Prov. 4:27).

The two elements come together in the Church's teaching on mortal and venial sins, which is rooted in Scripture (1 John 5:17). For a sin to be mortal, it has to meet three conditions: it has to be a "grave matter," committed "with full knowledge" of its gravity, and with "deliberate consent" of the will.[9] Any sins that don't meet all three of these requirements are venial. Inherent in this teaching are guardrails against the extremes of either rigorous anxiety or relaxed indifference. If almost *no* sins are serious, then the faith isn't serious; but if almost *all* sins are serious, then no sins are serious. The two

7. Francis, *Sublimitas et Miseria Hominis*, apostolic letter, June 19, 2023, vatican.va.

8. Augustine, Letter 48.2.

9. *Catechism of the Catholic Church* 1857.

errors about deadly sin—that the danger of falling into it is either horrifyingly constant or happily rare—are both deadly.

This balance carries over, too, into the Church's teaching on confession. Against the Jansenists, it insists that approaching the sacrament with "attrition," or "imperfect" contrition, is enough, and it lavishly communicates reconciliation to whoever seeks it with an open heart.[10] But against the laxists, it also insists that we really do have to confess our sins, be sorry for them, and resolve to change. Catholics conscious of mortal sin have to go to confession at least once a year and before receiving Communion, and those with no mortal sins to confess are still encouraged to go regularly for guidance, strength, and healing. The Church refuses to let us go either too hard or too easy on ourselves, to think that we're either beyond help or perfectly fine. She is a firm but gentle parent, an immovable but living stone.

Should we summon people to conversion or accompany them with tenderness? Should we point them vertically to God's commandments or walk with them horizontally through the messiness of their lives? Should we speak the hard truths of sin with clarity and boldness or soften the hard hearts of sinners with gentleness and charity? Should we be demanding or understanding, doctrinal or pastoral, "co-workers with the truth" or "united in love" (3 John 8; Col. 2:2)?

To all these false dilemmas, the Church in her wisdom responds with Qoheleth, "It is good that you should take hold of the one, without letting go of the other; for the one who fears God shall succeed with both" (Eccles. 7:18). Like the bishop of *Les Misérables*,

10. *Catechism* 1453.

she offers the kindness of love with one hand, but beckons up to the demands of love with the other:

> And remember this, my brother
> See in this some higher plan
> You must use this precious silver
> To become an honest man
>
> By the witness of the martyrs
> By the Passion and the blood
> God has raised you out of darkness
> I have bought your soul for God

Strive to be perfect, but be patient with imperfection; detest wickedness, but rush to embrace the wicked; strive rigorously for the crown, but under an easy yoke. This is the Way of the saints.

CHAPTER 24

The Christian Life: Abstinence or Indulgence

The pull between discipline and passion—and behind it, the same spiritual-physical dilemma—also emerges in the Christian life. What's the ideal texture of being a Christian in the world? How do we deal with the goods of the here and now—not only food, drink, and sex, but also wealth, power, honor, and the pleasures of society and entertainment? Denying these goods as evil or overindulging in them as our greatest good are both off the table. But in general, should we resist them or yield to them?

Is the Way defined by abstinence or indulgence?

I

The heavenward way is abstinence at the expense of indulgence.

We see this way crop up in various heresies in the Church's history, but the Jansenists—especially in light of their opponents—remain a useful case study. While they didn't succumb to a neo-Gnostic rejection of meat and wine altogether, they did tend to see them in highly negative terms. Philippe Hecquet, a Jansenist and physician enamored with Descartes and Porphyry, argued that rich meats and wines were clogging the arteries—both physical and spiritual—of Christian hearts. He wrote a defense of a simple vegetarian diet—one of the first of its kind—a "theological medicine" good for both soul and body.

The Jansenist movement also emerged in a deeply celibate culture of priests and nuns, hermit-like "Solitaires," and unmarried laypeople like Pascal. In itself, this meant little—many Christian movements have similar roots—but infecting that culture was a distorted Augustinianism when it came to sex and marriage. Sex was seen as the work of the fallen desire of concupiscence, and matrimony the work of restraining it and putting it to good use. Pierre Nicole spoke of marriage in precisely these bleak terms: it "checks concupiscence," this "source of poison able to infect us every moment," and "it is not but by force that it keeps itself within the limits that reason prescribes it."[1]

Nicole penned these lines in a treatise on the dangers of the theater, and for the Jansenists, abstaining from such worldly distractions—a prominent theme of Pascal's *Pensées*—was another major preoccupation. Poetry, literature, art, entertainment, fashion, politics—these things were just too riddled with temptation to be handled with anything but the utmost caution.

We see all these forms of abstinence at work in a rulebook for schoolgirls, some as young as four, written by Pascal's sister Jacqueline. The girls were instructed "to eat indifferently," starting with "the foods they like least"; to comb their hair and get dressed as quickly as possible, minimizing the time spent "decorating a body

1. Pierre Nicole, "Of Plays," in *Moral Essays*, vol. 3 (London: 1689), 222–223.

that must serve as food for worms"; to not write "letters, notes, or even sentences to each other" without permission; and to observe, the whole time, either a strict silence or a carefully monitored speech. At recreation, "a few innocent games" were permitted to younger children, but otherwise absent, and a few unserious conversations were tolerated, but guided back toward religion. When a girl broke a rule, she was corrected "in front of everyone" as a lesson to all.[2] Darkness lurked everywhere in taste and touch, the mind and the mirror; self-denial was the way.

This mentality of fasting carried over into the Eucharistic feast—not because the Eucharist was too profane for man, but because man was generally too profane for the Eucharist. At the heart of the Jansenist controversy was a treatise—written by the philosopher and Cartesian sympathizer Antoine Arnauld—arguing against the idea of frequent Communion. "Never have so many confessions and communions been seen," Arnauld roared, "and never more disorder and corruption."[3] Priests imagined they were making whole towns Christian by making Communion common, he wrote; in reality, they were simply adding sacrilege to the rap sheets of unrepentant sinners. In the Jansenist way of thinking, Communion, like confession, had to be a rarer and more privileged encounter—one received only on occasion, only by some, and only after long and careful preparation.

As with grace and rigor, there's much in the Scriptures to validate this Jansenist theme. Indeed, one of the greatest champions of

2. Jacqueline Pascal, *A Rule for Children and Other Writings*, ed. and trans. John J. Conley (Chicago: The University of Chicago Press, 2003), 81, 73, 75, 79, 76.

3. *Port-Royal Education*, ed. Félix Cadet, trans. Adnah D. Jones (London: Swan Sonnenschein, 1891), 61.

self-denial is Jesus himself. He repeatedly encourages fasting—even fasting from attention while fasting (Matt. 6:16)—and lauds John the Baptist, who never drank wine and subsisted on locusts and wild honey in the desert (Luke 7:33; Mark 1:6); he goes out into the desert himself to fast for forty days (Matt. 4:1–2; Luke 4:1–2); and he prophesies that his followers will fast when he's taken away from them (Luke 5:35). He never marries, associating heaven with the celibate state and encouraging celibacy for those who can accept it (Matt. 22:30, 19:12). And he consistently relativizes the goods of the world in comparison with the kingdom to come: blessings are upon those who are poor, hungry, weeping, and hated in this life, and woe is upon those who are rich, full, laughing, and admired (Luke 6:20–26). The heavenward justly recall these themes—and the gravity of forgetting them. How many young lives are tossed around in gluttony, drunkenness, and lust? How many middle-aged souls feast on vanities in a stupor? And how many Christians approach the living God at the altar with indifference, feasting on what they don't hunger for—or even understand?

But a distorted path of abstinence delivers us back into a high-strung Stoicism. This austerity orients us toward heaven, but drains the earth of all its goodness; and our abstention from Communion keeps us alert to our unworthiness, but twists the Eucharist into a "prize for the perfect"—a source not of healing and strength but of dread and terror.[4] We're caught in a double-sided fear of contamination: from below by stooping to the world's bread and circuses, and from above by approaching the bread of angels.

This path also delivers us, once again, into the threat of enan-

4. Francis, *Amoris Laetitia* 305n351, apostolic exhortation, March 19, 2016, vatican.va.

tiodromia. The Jansenist view on sexuality gave rise to a neurosis that psychiatrists later called the *maladie catholique*, the "Catholic malady"—a rigidity obsessed with "authority and purity."[5] But in the following century, French thinkers made a U-turn back toward the embrace of physical pleasure, from the hedonist La Mettrie, who initially studied theology at Jansenist schools, to the Marquis de Sade, the nadir of the libertine movement.

The beginning of the end of Jansenism—the "Convulsionaries" of the 1720s—saw the budding of this enantiodromia. A zealous Jansenist who once went two years without Communion, François de Pâris, pushed heroic self-denial to its limit, flagellating himself, walking barefoot, wearing iron wires, and sleeping without warmth. His excess—like the hedonist La Mettrie, but at the opposite extreme—likely led to his untimely death at just thirty-six. Soon after, his tomb became the site of reported mystical activity: miraculous cures, apocalyptic denunciations of the hierarchy, and ecstatic convulsions. But the Convulsionaries became increasingly sadomasochistic: those in trances made suggestive poses, and their comrades pierced and pummeled their flesh to prove that their spirits had flown. David Hume, who lived in France at the time, derided the movement in his treatise on miracles—the emaciated movement collapsing to the sound of an earthward taunt.

—

The earthward way is indulgence at the expense of abstinence.

The laxists went the opposite way, and in *The Provincial Letters*,

5. Joseph Ratzinger, *Principles of Catholic Theology: Building Stones for a Fundamental Theology*, trans. M.F. McCarthy (San Francisco: Ignatius, 1987), 77.

Pascal lampoons their quickness to indulge in the flesh. At one point, Pascal's laxist ridicules the extremes of a Jansenist ascetic—but in doing so, only reveals his own: "He has no eyes for the beauties of art or nature. . . . On festival days, he retires to hold fellowship with the dead. He delights in a grotto rather than a palace, and prefers the stump of a tree to a throne. As to injuries and affronts, he is as insensible to them as if he had the eyes and ears of a statue. Honor and glory are idols with whom he has no acquaintance, and to whom he has no incense to offer. To him a beautiful woman is no better than a specter."[6]

This Jansenist, at least, retains the primacy of self-denial. The laxist, on the other hand, has completely lost the plot; his Christianity is upside down. Pascal lands a devastating blow in response: "If that is not the picture of a man entirely denied to those feelings which the Gospel obliges us to renounce, I confess that I know nothing of the matter."[7] What the laxist lampoons as severity is, at heart, nothing but good old-fashioned piety, and what he heralds as piety is in fact an indiscriminate self-indulgence.

This general attitude shaped the laxists' own approach to the Mass. To the justified horror of the Jansenists, the laxists encouraged a kind of Eucharistic free-for-all—a buffet of cheap grace for the taking. Christians could take Communion less seriously—they were excused for being mentally absent at Mass—and they could take it more frequently, and without the necessary spiritual preparation. For the Jansenists, infrequent Communion was a sign of predestination, provided one lived as a purified Christian; for the

6. Blaise Pascal, *The Provincial Letters*, trans. Thomas M'Crie, in *Pensées; The Provincial Letters* (New York: Modern Library, 1941), 439.

7. Pascal, 439.

laxists, frequent Communion was that sign—even if one lived like a dissolute pagan.

This earthward theme, like its heavenward opposite, is also a motif of the New Testament. Christ wasn't just a champion faster; he was also a notorious feaster. His dining was so hearty that he was famously accused of being "a glutton and a drunkard" (Luke 7:34); his first public miracle is the transformation of water into wine at a wedding feast; and his earliest followers gathered for "love-feasts," a vibrant sharing of food and fellowship after the feast of the Eucharist (Jude 12; 2 Pet. 2:13). He speaks of marriage in the beautiful and positive terms of Genesis: man and woman join as "one flesh," a lifelong mutual self-gift never to be torn asunder (Matt. 19:5; Gen. 2:24). And while he relativizes the goods of the world, he never denounces them as inherently evil. The earthward tap into this great embrace of life's pleasures, receiving them with joy and without fear.

But the earthward way delivers us into a shameless self-gratification, one that only caricatures Christian joy. In striving to make the Gospel more palatable—to "attract all and repel none,"[8] as Pascal's laxist puts it—we succumb to the very worldliness it warns us about. More importantly, we miss the very discipleship—which shares the same Latin root as "discipline"—that Christ calls us to: "If any want to become my followers, let them deny themselves and take up their cross and follow me. For those who want to save their life will lose it, and those who lose their life for my sake will find it. For what will it profit them if they gain the whole world but forfeit their life?" (Matt. 16:24–26).

8. Pascal, 450.

Laxism also leads us into grave spiritual danger at the altar. In following this path of mindless indulgence, reception of the Eucharist becomes, at best, an empty formality, and at worst, a grave sacrilege. It's enough to point to the sobering words of St. Paul: "All who eat and drink without discerning the body, eat and drink judgment against themselves" (1 Cor. 11:29).

We find a blistering critique of this earthward way in Dostoevsky's "Grand Inquisitor." In the parable, the Inquisitor explains—to Jesus himself, no less, returned to earth—that true Christianity consists in lavishing people with earthly bread, permitting their sinful pleasures, and stilling their unsettled consciences. What Jesus was asking for was just too difficult; the herd of believers, desperate for relief from their own freedom and frailty, had to be excused from the high calling to sainthood. Instead of the scorching desert, they need a bucolic meadow, where they can graze peacefully on the world like cattle.

The Way is both abstinence and indulgence.

In its 1713 condemnation of the Jansenists, the Church refused a distorted self-denial; but in its 1679 condemnation of the laxists, it also refused a mindless overindulgence. The Church, like her Head, celebrates both abstinence and indulgence, though the former—the way of the cross—has to take the lead. The Christian life, whatever vocation it follows, is defined neither by disgust nor debauchery but *detachment*—"for the present form of this world is passing away" (1 Cor. 7:29–31).

Dostoevsky—no fan of the Catholic Church—said that the

Grand Inquisitor parable was meant to expose the worldview of Russian socialists, whom he called "Jesuits and liars."[9] But in the broader Jesuit tradition, we don't find the Inquisitor's stultified humanism; on the contrary, we find the sane balance of the Way. Indeed, it was precisely this balance that equipped the early Jesuits to meet the challenge of modern humanism head on, innovating in the worlds of theater, science, and especially education in a way that the Jansenists never could. The Jesuits both distanced themselves from the here and now and entered tactically into it.

We see this same communion of abstinence and indulgence in the Church more broadly, beginning with the liturgical calendar's union of fasts and feasts. But here—because we feast on the riches of the Lord (Ps. 36:8)—the latter takes on a greater importance than the former. Lenten abstinence, Advent vigilance, and Friday penances remind the faithful to fast on the journey; but feast days, solemnities, and Sunday celebrations glimpse the heavenly banquet to come. The two even interpenetrate, as when the joyful rose of Gaudete and Laetare Sundays appears within the penitential purple of Advent and Lent.

The Church's approach to receiving Communion follows the same pattern. Abstaining from the Eucharist is required for non-Catholics, for Catholics in a state of mortal sin, and for Catholics in a state of grace who have eaten or drunk something besides medicine or water in the hour before receiving. But for those who meet the conditions, receiving is required at least once a year, and encouraged on Sundays, feast days, or "more often still, even

9. Fyodor Dostoevsky to N.A. Liubimov, June 11, 1879, in *New Dostoevsky Letters*, trans. Samuel Solomonovitch Koteliansky (London: Mandrake, 1929), 86.

daily."[10] We have to be properly disposed—the one who shows up to the wedding supper "not wearing a wedding robe" isn't welcome (Matt. 22:11)—but if we are, there's no arguing with the Lord's simple command: "Take, eat; this is my body" (Matt. 26:26).

But what about the ordinary lives of Christians as they unfold outside of the liturgical life of the Church? Should they be lives of salivating or savoring, celibacy or marriage, the sacred or the profane? The Catholic Church makes room for all of the above, so long as each is connected to the other in the Body—and through the Body to the Way.

This is true of eating and drinking: "Those who eat must not despise those who abstain, and those who abstain must not pass judgment on those who eat; for God has welcomed them" (Rom. 14:3). In the Catholic tradition, we find both those abstaining from meat and alcohol and those cooking sumptuous meals of both. We also find those withdrawing from the secular to be sanctified and those engaging with the secular to sanctify it. But these paths are always oriented toward each other and learn from each other—not only through the prayers and good works that flow *between* them, but also, by their share in one Spirit, through a communion with the whole Church *within* them: "We are members one of another" (Rom. 12:5). Even the Desert Fathers—heroic fasters who sought a *fuga mundi* (flight from the world)—appreciated a little indulgence when the time was right; likewise, even those men and women feasting on the world's goods have to retreat at times into abstinence, because "there is no holiness without renunciation and spiritual battle."[11]

10. *Catechism of the Catholic Church* 1389.
11. *Catechism* 2015.

This dynamic becomes especially clear with celibacy and marriage. The Church encourages vocations to the priesthood, religious life, and consecrated single life, teaching that it's "better and happier to remain in virginity or celibacy than to be united in matrimony."[12] But it also encourages vocations to marriage, because marriage remains beautiful and good—the very image of Christ's union with his Church (Eph. 5:21–33). And once again, these vocations are oriented toward each other. In the first place, neither can exist without the other: the laity produce celibates, and celibates minister to the laity; and both—according to their station in life—respond to one "universal call to holiness."[13] And each informs the other from within: celibates are called to be married to the Church as Bride (or, for religious sisters, to Christ as Bridegroom), with many wearing rings to symbolize that union, and the married have to practice the discipline of celibacy with all others except their spouse.

St. Thérèse of Lisieux, a Carmelite nun called "the Little Flower," grew up in the aftershocks of Jansenism in France, and is a beautiful exemplar of this Catholic balance. Her family strictly observed the Church's fasts, but little Thérèse also confessed a great love for its feasts—especially Sunday, the day of rest: "I stayed in bed longer than on the other days; then Pauline spoiled her little girl by bringing her some chocolate to drink while still in bed and then she dressed her up like a little Queen. . . . The whole family then went

12. Council of Trent, "Doctrine on the Sacrament of Matrimony," November 11, 1563, in *The Sources of Catholic Dogma*, ed. Heinrich Denzinger and Karl Rahner, trans. R.J. Deferrari (St. Louis, MO: B. Herder, 1954), 297.

13. *Lumen Gentium* 5, in *The Word on Fire Vatican II Collection*, ed. Matthew Levering (Park Ridge, IL: Word on Fire Institute, 2021), 100–106.

off to Mass."[14] Her parents were daily communicants, but young Thérèse was struck by scrupulosity, and writes movingly of overcoming that "narrow circle" of hellish piety by humbly accepting God's self-offering: "It is not to remain in a golden ciborium that He comes to us *each day* from heaven; it's to find another heaven, infinitely more dear to Him than the first: the heaven of our soul."[15] Thérèse was canonized and later made a Doctor of the Church, in part for helping to "heal souls of the rigors and fears of Jansenism."[16] Her parents, Louis and Zélie Martin, were both canonized in 2015—the first married couple to be recognized together as saints.

The Christian on the Way incarnates both abstinence and indulgence, both fasting and feasting—both inside and outside the life of the Church.

14. Thérèse of Lisieux, *Story of a Soul*, trans. John Clarke (Park Ridge, IL: Word on Fire Classics, 2022), 43.

15. Thérèse of Lisieux, 103, 106.

16. John Paul II, *Divini Amoris Scientia* 8, apostolic letter, October 19, 1997, vatican.va.

CHAPTER 25

Salvation: The Elect or the World

The dilemmas of conversion, morality, and the Christian life all culminate in a dilemma of salvation and the four "last things": death, judgment, heaven, and hell. Here, the God-man dilemma reemerges: on the one hand are the stalwart standing in the Church of God, and on the other, the rest of humanity standing outside of it. Who will be saved in the end?

Is salvation for the elect or for all the world?

I

The heavenward way is the elect at the expense of the world.

Centuries after Jansenism was condemned and faded away, a new heresy cropped up through a Jesuit with Jansenist leanings: Fr. Leonard Feeney. In the 1940s, the one-time editor of *America* magazine began preaching a hardline interpretation of an ancient doctrine: *Extra ecclesiam nulla salus* (Outside the Church there is no salvation). Feeney taught that only those baptized into Christ's death and Resurrection through the Church, administered through the sacrament of water and Spirit, had any real hope of salvation; to live and die outside of that channel was to live and die outside of salvation.

The flashpoint of the debate was the *Baltimore Catechism*, which taught that "there are three kinds of Baptism: Baptism of water, of desire, and of blood."[1] A Baptism of desire would apply to a catechumen who earnestly desires Baptism but dies before he can receive it, while a Baptism of blood would apply to a martyr who loses his life for the sake of the faith without being formally baptized first. For Feeney, these were not being treated as rare exceptions, but rather as increasingly loose and common alternatives—especially Baptism of desire. Is it possible that the whole world, in some vague way, "desires" Baptism? Water Baptism, the Feeneyites argued, was being watered down—and their solution was simply to get rid of the exceptions altogether. Feeney thundered that the catechism was teaching heresy, one concocted to pollute the minds of the young: "Neither 'Baptism of Desire' nor 'Baptism of Blood' should truly be called Baptism. Neither is a sacrament of the Church. Neither was instituted by Jesus Christ."[2] Feeney invoked the words of St. Paul in his defense: "One Lord, one faith, one baptism" (Eph. 4:5).

Indeed, on the deeper question of election and salvation, the Feeneyites had much of the Scriptures in their court. The God of the Bible is a God who freely chooses: he has regard for Abel's sacrifice, but not Cain's (Gen. 4:4–5); he loves Jacob, but not Esau (Mal. 1:2–3); and he forms the people Israel, but not other people (Ps. 147:19–20). This election is oriented toward salvation, which God offers, finally, only in his Son: "There is salvation in no one

1. *Baltimore Catechism*, q. 642.

2. Leonard Feeney, *Bread of Life* (Fitzwilliam, NH: Loreto Publications, 2018), 111.

else, for there is no other name under heaven given among mortals by which we must be saved" (Acts 4:12). And the door to Christ's "one body"—and thus to salvation—is Baptism (1 Cor. 12:13): "The one who believes and is baptized will be saved; but the one who does not believe will be condemned" (Mark 16:16). In fact, Jesus warns about hell more than any other figure in the Bible: "the outer darkness, where there will be weeping and gnashing of teeth" (Matt. 8:12, 22:13, 25:30); Gehenna, "where their worm never dies, and the fire is never quenched" (Mark 9:48). The heavenward rightly pick up on this "scandal of particularity" running through the Bible, and see that a clear boundary of Baptism is necessary to honor it: without it, we may make the faith sound more welcoming, but we compromise its integrity.

But this exclusivist path leads, in the first place, to triumphalism, which overlooks the goodness and beauty of the various other traditions and people outside the Church. We're tempted to dismiss non-Catholics as a horde of lost souls under the sway of Satan, to approach evangelization in an arrogant and aggressive tenor, and to treat those who refuse to convert with outright hostility and even violence. This triumphalism can become especially vicious in the Church's relationship to the Jewish people, where a seething anti-Semitism—under the pretense of fidelity to Christ, who himself was Jewish and declared that "salvation is from the Jews" (John 4:22)—so often takes hold.

This way also distorts our view of God. It's not that the Feeneyites limited salvation to a minority of humanity—an opinion that many great saints and Doctors of the Church have held. It's that there was no door of hope ajar for anyone who dies outside of the visible Church—whether through their own fault or not—to find

God. Even if, being among the baptized, this gives us a sense of satisfaction and even *schadenfreude*, over time, we lose a sense of what the Scriptures call God's *hesed* or "tender mercy." We also fall into an unhealthy obsession with hell, one that undermines the very goodness of the Good News of salvation.

The fire-and-brimstone sermon of Father Arnall in James Joyce's *Portrait of the Artist as a Young Man*—one based on an actual seventeenth-century devotional text by an Italian Jesuit titled *Hell Opened to Christians to Caution Them from Entering Into It*—is a vivid case in point. Father Arnall ruminates at length on hell's endless blackness, unquenchable fire, tortured screams, demonic jeers, and even foul stench—like "millions upon millions of fetid carcasses massed together in the reeking darkness, a huge and rotting human fungus"—all of it "an instrument of Divine vengeance."[3] Such a relentlessly dark view of God often sends people running as far away from the Church as possible and, rather than scaring them away from hell, very possibly leads them right into its open mouth.

This distortion of God eventually turns on us too, because "with the judgment you make you will be judged, and the measure you give will be the measure you get" (Matt. 7:2). Down this darkened path, we wonder: Was my Baptism valid? Even if it was, am I really among the elect—a sheep rather than a goat? Might I be a citizen of that other city and not know it? The sword we triumphantly raise to cut away hope for others eventually cuts away our own, leaving us in despair.

3. James Joyce, *A Portrait of the Artist as a Young Man* (New York: Penguin Books, 1996), 137, 138.

—

The earthward way is the world at the expense of the elect.

Fr. Feeney and his followers were reacting to an earthward threat emerging from the opposite end of the dilemma: the juggernaut of Modernism, which so flagrantly embraced the here and now at the expense of the not here and not yet. Behind Modernism there was also its forerunner "Americanism," which emphasized natural virtue over divine grace.

Modernism's redefinition of religion as an inward experience eventually threw not only the Church's teachings and mission into question, but the Church itself. And once again, it was the incarnational realities of the hierarchy and the sacraments that were at issue. Might the Church's authority be a mere product of the collective conscience of believers, and the sacraments mere signs and symbols to encourage them? And might Christians, therefore, be equally related to Christ according to their particular tradition?

With this questioning of the Church came a broader questioning of the Christian faith. After all, Christianity wasn't, and never had been, the only game in town: from Hinduism to Islam to agnosticism, the experience of the divine varies around the world and down the centuries. Might religion be the fracturing of one divine light into a rainbow of different colors? And might non-Christians be equally related to God through a more fundamental and universal desire for him? The Modernists didn't deny the reality of Christ or the Church—or even the necessity of both for salvation—but they softened and stretched their contours, adapting the faith to a world weary of religious conflict.

Like his free election, God's universal concern for the whole world also runs throughout the Scriptures. In the Old Testament, there's the whole history of God's relationship with humanity before the formation of Israel, from Adam and Eve up through Noah; there are the many non-Israelites that play key roles in salvation history, from Melchizedek to Ruth; and there are God's repeated declarations that he will gather to himself, through Israel, all the world—a theme that echoes across the prophets. And in the New—right beside the emphasis on salvation in Christ through Baptism—we also detect a more global vision and purpose: Christ declares, "I, when I am lifted up from the earth, will draw all people to myself" (John 12:32); St. Paul announces that all people are made alive in Christ (Rom. 5:18; 1 Cor. 15:22), that "one has died for all" (2 Cor. 5:14), and that God "desires everyone to be saved" (1 Tim. 2:4); and the book of Revelation, in its glimpse of heaven, tells us that "saints from every tribe and language and people and nation" will be gathered into God's kingdom (Rev. 5:9). The earthward take seriously this universal concern transcending religious boundaries, and see its relevance for an increasingly interconnected and globalized world.

But this inclusivism leads us into a religious indifferentism standing opposite triumphalism: it doesn't really matter, in the end, how one lives out the faith. Can't you be a perfectly good Catholic and yet only go to Mass on special occasions? Can't we adopt, as the ancient Arians did, an attitude of open "intercommunion" among Christians for the sake of social unity? In fact, does it even matter in the end whether we believe in Christ at all? At the limit of indifferentism is a blasé universalism: Christianity becomes just one of many roads toward salvation—and the uniqueness of the one, holy, catholic, and apostolic Church, and any urgency to belong to it, vanishes. For the heavenward, the masses are damned no matter what they do; for the earthward, the masses are saved no matter what they believe.

Inclusivism also leads to its own distorted understanding of God—a "moralistic therapeutic deism." On this view, God wants us to be kind and happy, extends his merciful help when we ask for it, and gently guides all good people to salvation; otherwise, he's content, just as we are, to live and let live. The God of indifferentism becomes indifferent himself—more a positive energy than the Lord of Israel and Hound of Heaven.

Shrugging at the Church in the face of a shrugging God, we're led, inevitably, into the danger lying opposite despair—namely, presumption. If salvation is all but guaranteed, and the eternal fires of hell just medieval fearmongering, then there's little need of repentance or conversion, contrition or penance, service or conviction. All that matters is that we're decent people; in fact, all that really matters is that we're sincere people. We rashly assume we'll glide up into heaven, forgetting all of Christ's urgent warnings about just how easily we can slip into hell.

The Way is both the elect and the world.

The Church holds to the same tensions that Scripture holds to, keeping both God's election and his universal salvific will in view. Catholics have to be both fiercely particular (Catholic) and fiercely catholic (universal). They have to be both centripetal, moving inward toward God, and centrifugal, moving outward toward the world. The elect are indeed set apart—but not to withdraw from the world and focus on their own salvation, but to hope in God's salvation and help bring it to the world.

The Church does teach that outside of the Church there's no salvation, and that outside of Baptism one isn't in the Church. But it also affirms both Baptism of blood and Baptism of desire, a view that Aquinas, invoking Augustine and referencing the example of the good thief on the cross (Luke 23:43), endorses: "Each of these other Baptisms is called Baptism."[4] The Council of Trent later taught that justification—our being made righteous before God—can't be effected except through Baptism "or a desire for it."[5] And the *Catechism* now puts the teaching this way: "God has bound salvation to the sacrament of baptism, but he himself is not bound by his sacraments."[6] For refusing to accept this, Feeney was excommunicated in 1953, though he was later reconciled to the Church. The words on his tombstone still ring true: *Extra ecclesiam nulla salus*.

But the Catholic balance also means refusing the indifferentism against which Feeney was justifiably reacting. The exceptions to water Baptism are the exceptions, not the rule; salvation isn't automatic or guaranteed for anyone, least of all those who know but refuse Christ and the Church. In 1846, Pope Pius IX condemned the view that "men can gain eternal salvation by the practice of any religion";[7] in 1907, his successor Pope Pius X lambasted the con-

4. Thomas Aquinas, *Summa theologiae* 3.66.11.

5. Council of Trent, "Decree on Justification" 4, January 13, 1547, in *The Sources of Catholic Dogma*, ed. Heinrich Denzinger and Karl Rahner, trans. R.J. Deferrari (St. Louis, MO: B. Herder, 1954), 250.

6. *Catechism of the Catholic Church* 1257.

7. Pius IX, *Qui Pluribus* 15, encyclical letter, November 9, 1846, in *The Papal Encyclicals: 1740–1878*, ed. C. Carlen (Ypsilanti, MI: Pierian, 1990), 280.

fused notion—sometimes only suggested, sometimes admitted "in the most open manner"—that "all religions are true."[8]

We find the Catholic tension emerging even among the Church Fathers. Augustine took a more pessimistic stance: without the Gospel, humanity is a *massa damnata*, a "damned mass": "The fact that a few are saved (they are indeed few in comparison to those who are lost, though their number itself is large) is the work of grace."[9] Yet he also affirms the possibility of salvation for the unbaptized—specifically, for catechumens: "I do not hesitate for a moment to place the Catholic catechumen, who is burning with love for God, before the baptized heretic."[10] He also speaks of our final citizenship as being hazy in this life: "Some predestined friends, as yet unknown even to themselves, are concealed among our most open enemies. In truth, those two cities are interwoven and intermixed in this era, and await separation at the last judgment."[11] And while the *massa damnata* theory became the mainline theological opinion in the West, it was never formally taught by the Church.

A very different perspective arose in the East even earlier than Augustine: all people, in the end, would be gathered back to God. This idea of an *apokatastasis* or "restoration" had roots in both Plato and Scripture: "[Jesus] must remain in heaven until the time of universal restoration [*apokatastasis*]" (Acts 3:21). A form of *apokatastasis*

8. Pius X, *Pascendi Dominici Gregis* 14, encyclical letter, September 8, 1907, vatican.va.

9. Augustine, *Admonition and Grace* 10 (28), in *Christian Instruction; Admonition and Grace; The Christian Combat; Faith, Hope and Charity*, 2nd ed., ed. Roy J. Deferrari (Washington, DC: The Catholic University of America Press, 1950), 279–280.

10. Augustine, *On Baptism, Against the Donatists* 4.21.

11. Augustine, *City of God* 1.35.

was taught by St. Gregory of Nyssa, who picked it up from Origen of Alexandria. Origen's exploration of this idea—an "investigation and discussion," he admits, not a "fixed and certain decision"—still affirms punishing, purgatorial fires for the ungodly until they've "paid the last penny" (Matt. 5:26).[12] Yet Origen's overzealous followers pushed too hard on the idea, and in 543, the Catholic Church drew a line in the sand, condemning it.

Thus, on the one hand, the Church refused to teach that most people are damned in the end; but it also refused to teach that everyone would be saved in the end. It affirmed that hell—not a predestined fate, but one freely chosen—is real, that those who die in a state of mortal sin descend immediately into it, and that its punishments, chief of which is separation from God, are eternal; but it also has never formally declared even one specific person to be suffering that fate.

These same tensions mark the Church's more recent declarations on the question, developments consistent with both Scripture and Tradition. Unbaptized infants, long assumed to be in "limbo," are entrusted to the mercy of God in the hope of their salvation.[13] The possibility of salvation is also extended to those of other religions or even no religion at all who, "through no fault of their own," don't know Christ or his Church, but "nevertheless seek God with a sincere heart, and, moved by grace, try in their actions to do his will."[14] Yet the same passage warns very clearly about how much they have working against them: "Very often, deceived by the Evil One, men have become vain in their reasonings, and have

12. Origen, *De Principiis* 6.1.
13. *Catechism* 1261.
14. *Catechism* 847.

exchanged the truth of God for a lie, and served the creature rather than the Creator."[15]

Thus, the path toward heaven or hell—each of which begins on earth—is open to all of us: "God offers to every man the possibility of being associated with this Paschal Mystery."[16] Dwelling in this tension, the Church calls its members into the theological virtue of *hope*, and teaches that there are two great sins against this hope: despair and presumption. In the first case, "man ceases to hope for his personal salvation from God, for help in attaining it or for the forgiveness of his sins."[17] In the second, man either leans on his own Pelagian strength or "presumes upon God's almighty power or his mercy (hoping to obtain his forgiveness without conversion and glory without merit)."[18] The Way of hope refuses both despair and presumption, and it extends that hope to the whole of humanity: "In *hope*, the Church prays for 'all men to be saved.'"[19] Who knows what evil lurked in the heart of a "good Christian" who seemed to do everything right? And who knows in what profound ways—and for how long—a lost soul might have encountered God in its last moments?

Hope keeps our spiritual focus where it belongs: not on the spiritual state of others, which only God knows, but on the spiritual state of ourselves, which we know all too painfully. We can neither despair of our chances nor presume upon them; we can only strive, with all that we have, to "enter through the narrow door" (Luke 13:24).

15. *Catechism* 844.

16. *Gaudium et Spes* 22, in *The Word on Fire Vatican II Collection*, ed. Matthew Levering (Park Ridge, IL: Word on Fire Institute, 2021), 239.

17. *Catechism* 2091.

18. *Catechism* 2092.

19. *Catechism* 1821.

CHAPTER 26

Reformation: The Solas or the Alsos

On the question of the state of the pilgrim Church and its need for reform, modern Christians fall into a great stand-off that recapitulates the four great dilemmas of heaven and earth. On one side is the way of the five "solas": salvation through faith alone (*sola fide*), by grace alone (*sola gratia*), in Christ alone (*solus Christus*), on the authority of Scripture alone (*sola scriptura*), for the glory of God alone (*soli Deo gloria*). And we can only really understand these five solas in light of five earthly "alsos" standing opposite them: works, merit, submediators, Tradition, and the glory of man.

Should Christians shape the Church along the way of the solas or the way of the alsos?

I

The heavenward way is the solas at the expense of the alsos.

The Protestant Reformation was defined, as a whole, by this heavenward way of the five solas. The first sola, faith alone, is the foundation of the other four, and takes root with Martin

Luther—not with the Ninety-Five Theses, which didn't touch on the idea, but with an epiphany he had two years later. Luther, a pious Augustinian monk, had been desperate to please the righteous God through his own "monkery": "I wearied myself greatly for almost fifteen years with the daily sacrifice, tortured myself with fasting, vigils, prayers, and other very rigorous works."[1] Of course, nothing was ever good enough, and he sank further into doubt and despair in the face of God's wrath, "raging with wild and disturbed conscience."[2] His spiritual life had all the markings of rigorism and scrupulosity: obsessive ruminations, compulsive confessions, disciplined devotions.

One night, while agonizing over Romans 1 in the basement latrine under the monastery tower—a retreat into solitude and a search for certainty not unlike Descartes' a hundred years later—the words of verse 17 leapt off the page and into his troubled mind: "The just person lives by faith." He described this "tower experience" in language still heard in Protestant sermons and music to this day: "All at once I felt that I had been born again and entered into paradise itself through open gates."[3] Works, Luther reasoned, had nothing to do with our salvation; man is justified through faith, and faith alone: "The first care of every Christian ought to be to lay aside all reliance on works, and strengthen his faith alone more and more."[4] It was a resounding declaration of Hebraic faith.

1. Martin Luther, *Luther's Works*, vol. 12, *Selected Psalms I* (St. Louis, MO: Concordia, 1955), 273.

2. Martin Luther, Preface to the Complete Edition of Luther's Latin Works (1545), in *Reformation Commentary on Scripture, New Testament VII: Romans 1–8*, ed. Gwenfair Walters Adams (Downers Grove, IL: InterVarsity, 2019), 48.

3. Luther, 48.

4. Martin Luther, *On Christian Liberty*, in *First Principles of the Reformation*,

The point wasn't that works were evil or unnecessary—Luther still retained a classic heavenward emphasis on "fastings, watchings, labor, and other moderate discipline"[5]—but that they avail us nothing *coram Deo* (in the presence of God). The same is true of the works of the mind: Luther would later famously indict reason as "the Devil's greatest whore"—not to condemn reason itself but to put it firmly in its place vis-à-vis salvation.[6] Only the alien righteousness of Christ—imputed to us extrinsically, in a kind of legal fiction, as if it were our own—can help us. Luther continued to lean heavily on St. Paul, especially his Letter to the Romans; the Epistle of James, on the other hand—that archetype of Christian action—was comparatively an "epistle of straw": "It has nothing of the nature of the gospel about it."[7]

All four of the other solas fold back into faith alone. We're saved by *grace alone*: before grace, our will is in bondage to sin, and after, it remains without any merit of its own. We're saved in *Christ alone*: any submediators on earth or in heaven—especially priests or the saints—get in the way of the "one mediator between God and humankind" (1 Tim. 2:5). This message is infallibly proclaimed in *Scripture alone*: the Tradition of bishops and their priests, under the Bishop of Rome, interferes with the universal priesthood of all believers in the Word of God. And all of this is to the *glory of God alone*: salvation is about the victory of Christ, through the power of

trans. Henry Wace and C.A. Buchheim (London: John Murray, 1883), 107.

5. Luther, 119.

6. Martin Luther, *Luther's Works*, vol. 16, *Lectures on Isaiah Chapters 1–39* (St. Louis, MO: Concordia, 1968), 142.

7. Martin Luther, *Luther's Works*, vol. 35, *Word and Sacrament I* (St. Louis, MO: Concordia, 1960), 362.

the Spirit, to the glory of God the Father—not the victory, power, or glorification of man.

Scripture is brimming, of course, with all five subjects of the solas from start to finish. The Reformers, like so many before and after, rightly reminded Christians of the primacy and power of these heavenly mysteries. They celebrated the power of faith and grace, of a mystical and charismatic Church, and of a vertical and spiritual orientation to God and the saving work of his Son. In many ways, the Reformation is the apex of all the heavenward movements that have roiled the Church across its two thousand years—and all that those other movements correctly saw, the Reformers saw too.

But these stark either/ors lead to devastating problems for the life of the Church, the first of which is fragmentation. Luther tried to keep close to the Way—Catholics and Lutherans share much in common to this day—but the break was decisive. And within just two decades, break after break followed: John Calvin in Geneva, Ulrich Zwingli in Zürich, and Henry VIII in London all founded separate movements on their own authority. With the "Radical" Reformation, there arrived iconoclast rioters in Wittenberg; self-styled end-of-days prophets from Zwickau; Anabaptists ("rebaptizers") and English Baptists challenging infant Baptism; Anti-trinitarians in Transylvania challenging the Nicene Creed; neo-Gnostic "spiritual libertines" and "antinomians" (literally, "against the law") placing themselves beyond the Commandments; and, in a heavenward crescendo, a small sect of radical Anabaptist visionaries who took over Münster as the "new Jerusalem"—a project that promptly descended into chaos. The fragmentation has continued, and while it's wrongly claimed that there are thirty-three thousand Protestant denominations, the true number—about nine thousand—can hardly be called an improvement.

Behind this wild diversity there was a common thread, and it's a second grave problem with Protestantism: "excarnation"—the impulse, in tune with Gnosticism and Platonism, to overlook the here and now and move into the realm of pure spirit. Social life was excarnated: the Reformers cracked down on song and dance at weddings, folksy "Carnival" revelry before Lent, and even Christmas celebrations. Worship was excarnated: the Mass, Luther wrote, was to be stripped of "vestments, ornaments, hymns, prayers, musical instruments, lamps, and all the pomp of visible things";[8] belief in the Real Presence was more and more eroded, first by Calvin to a merely spiritual presence and then by Zwingli to no presence at all, and all the other sacraments besides Baptism and the Eucharist were left behind. Most of all, in the long run, the soul was excarnated: a line from a Quaker periodical in 1892—one falsely attributed to C.S. Lewis, but actually a paraphrase of George MacDonald—shows the long distance traveled from Augustine and Aquinas: "You *are* a soul. You have a body."[9] Since the Reformation, a mentality of excarnation has proliferated through Christian worship, art, and music: "When the shadows of this life have gone / I'll fly away / Like a bird from these prison walls I'll fly / I'll fly away."

A third problem with Protestantism is the strangest: an enantiodromatic pivot into the New Axial Age. The Reformation was a

8. Martin Luther, *On the Babylonian Captivity of the Church*, in *First Principles of the Reformation*, trans. Henry Wace and C.A. Buchheim (London: John Murray, 1883), 162.

9. "Be Not Entangled Again in a Yoke of Bondage," *The British Friend*, July 1892, 157; George MacDonald, *Annals of a Quiet Neighborhood*, vol. 2, in *Collection of British Authors*, vol. 882 (Leipzig: Bernhard Tauchnitz, 1867), 186.

great vertical surge, one that separated the heavenly up and out of the earthly like oil atop vinegar. The medieval era, with its keen sense of the interlocking of the two in a great whole, was left behind, and the face of the earth—Mass and monasteries, holidays and festivals, family life and work life, philosophy and science—was emptied of its intrinsic links to heaven.

At first, a spiritualized Christianity guided the naturalized world: Luther stood against the Church below on his own spiritual authority from above ("Here I stand; I can do no other"); the Calvinists worked below to confirm their citizenship in the kingdom above; kings ruled below through a divine right from above. But the modern world—galvanized by this radical separation—would soon turn its back on the heavens, with only the earth remaining: man would now stand on his own individual authority; capitalists would work to build up the earthly kingdom; and despots would rule through all-too-human dictatorships.

—

The earthward way is the alsos at the expense of the solas.

Like institutionalism, this earthward way is more a covert, informal error than a public, formal one. It amounts to a self-referential legalism, one fixated not on reform but on formalities—and the loopholes around them. This sickness was rampant in the Church at the time of the Reformation. Indeed, the call for reform was far from unique to the Reformers. Similar movements sprang up among Catholics too—not only after the Reformation but also during it and even well before it. Something had gone very wrong indeed, and many pious Catholics knew it. And that something was an overemphasis on the five subjects of the alsos.

The first is the hinge issue of the Reformation: an emphasis on works that undercuts faith. If the guiding logic of the solas was Romans 1:17, the guiding logic of the alsos was a contrasting note in St. Paul: "Work out your own salvation with fear and trembling" (Phil. 2:12). Salvation by works in the manner of Pelagius wasn't an option—the Church had put this heresy in its place—but in the medieval era, an obsession with the rituals of piety began seeping into the Church's bloodstream. The faith was being treated like a magic lamp, and God like a genie.

One work in particular prompted Luther's Ninety-Five Theses: the sale of indulgences—a deeply corrupt practice already satirized by Chaucer a century before Luther was born. An undisciplined spiritual indulgence—like an undisciplined physical indulgence—was wreaking havoc on the life of the Church. But the sale of indulgences was just one symptom of a deeper disease. When Luther visited Rome, eager to pray for his relatives, the pious monk was scandalized by the city's spiritual life. At St. Sebastian, Masses were carelessly rattled off in Latin with the speed of an auctioneer, some as quickly as nine minutes. He even saw two priests saying Mass at the same altar with only a painting for a partition.

A deep moral corruption had also clearly spread through the city. At lunch, Luther heard monks mocking the Eucharist; in the city streets, he saw chaos and filth, public urination and open prostitution. This was a culture of outward acts devoid of inner renewal—one that presumed to buy and sell salvation like a cheap commodity. Writing to the pope a decade later, Luther didn't hold back: "The Church of Rome, formerly the most holy of all churches, has become the most lawless den of thieves, the most shameless of all brothels, the very kingdom of sin, death, and hell."[10]

Also wreaking havoc—not in the streets but in the schools—was an obsession with the works of the mind. Late medieval Scholasticism had become a barren landscape: the nominalism of William of Ockham, whose work dominated Luther's education, reigned supreme, and Catholic philosophy had grown stale and ossified—a kind of self-referential game of logic-chopping that overcomplicated the things of God and distanced Christians from the simplicity of the Gospel. The line about theologians debating how many angels can dance on the head of a pin dates to this period of intellectual decay. Works, whether of the body or the mind, were getting in the way of spiritual basics.

As with the solas, the other four alsos are grounded in the first. There was a distorted emphasis on our own *merit*, undercutting God's grace; on the *submediators* of the Church, especially its priests and saints, undercutting the centrality of Christ; on an apostolic *Tradition* of papal, episcopal, and clerical leaders, many hopelessly corrupt, undercutting the "living and active" Word of God (Heb. 4:12); and on *the glory of man*—his nature, his mind, his will, his power—undercutting the glory of God. Countless Catholics had become "futile in their thinking, and their senseless minds were darkened" (Rom. 1:21): they had lost sight of heaven.

Sola scriptura Christians may often overlook these five subjects, but Scripture itself doesn't (James 2:14–26; Rom. 2:6–11; James 5:14 and Rev. 5:8; 2 Thess. 2:15; 2 Cor. 3:18). And the Church had

10. Martin Luther, "Letter to Pope Leo X," in *First Principles of the Reformation*, trans. Henry Wace and C.A. Buchheim (London: John Murray, 1883), 97.

endured too many heavenward heresies not to stubbornly insist on the goodness of them all.

But this earthward legalism deprives us of living water "gushing up to eternal life" (John 4:10, 14), and leads us, again and again, to worldly wells that only dissatisfy and degrade us. Erasmus, a humanist who remained a Catholic, joined the Reformers in critiquing this stultifying corruption. He lamented how "faith in works" had taken hold of "a good part of priests and theologians and practically all of their followers," undercutting the primacy of grace: "They think heaven is owed to them because of these actions of theirs. . . . What good is it to do good exteriorly if interiorly one's thoughts are quite the opposite?"[11] He lambasted the corruption of the clergy—Erasmus himself being the illegitimate son of a priest—and the superstition of the laity, who took to "certain charms or prayers devised by some pious imposter either for his soul's sake or for money."[12] He created a new translation of the New Testament and longed for the faithful to know and honor the Word of God: "The breakdown was no less in the study of Holy Scripture than in morality. The word of God was forced to become the slave of human appetites."[13]

And the bitter fruit of this degradation was the Reformation itself. The Reformers certainly led the charge, and were supported by political power players who had a vested interest in their success. But we can't understand one without the other: the earthward

11. Erasmus, *The Handbook of the Christian Soldier*, in *The Erasmus Reader*, ed. Erika Rummel (Toronto: University of Toronto Press, 1990), 147, 152.

12. Erasmus, *The Praise of Folly*, trans. Hoyt Hopewell Hudson (Princeton, NJ: Princeton University Press, 2015), 56.

13. Erasmus to Justus Jonas, May 10, 1521, in *The Erasmus Reader*, 206.

excess and heavenward overcorrection were of a piece, and each reinforced the other as both deviated from the Way.

Thus, the grave problems of Protestantism—including the pivot into the New Axial Age—are also, indirectly, the grave problems of legalism. In fact, legalism even provokes the rise of secularism more directly: it's a kind of anti-Gospel, one that makes the Church appear as just another convoluted human institution rather than the inbreaking of God's kingdom into the world. It inspires suspicion and hatred of the Church, not a docile trust in her divine mission: "Believers can have more than a little to do with the rise of atheism. To the extent that they are careless about their instruction in the faith, or present its teaching falsely, or even fail in their religious, moral, or social life, they must be said to conceal rather than to reveal the true nature of God and of religion."[14]

The Way is both the solas and the alsos.

In the Council of Trent, the Church rejected both the heavenward way of the solas and the earthward way of the alsos, beginning with the hinge issue of faith and works. The Church had never taught, contrary to the belief of many Protestants, that we're saved by our works. But the very first canon on justification cleared the fog that had settled: "If anyone shall say that man can be justified before God by his own works . . . without divine grace through Christ Jesus: let him be anathema."[15] Although it took seriously the Reformers' diagnosis, the ninth canon refused their medicine: "If

14. *Catechism of the Catholic Church* 2125.

15. Council of Trent, "Decree on Justification" can. 1, January 13, 1547, in *The*

anyone shall say that by faith alone the sinner is justified, so as to understand that nothing else is required . . . let him be anathema."[16]

The same two-pronged attack carried over into the Counter-Reformation, which is more accurately called the Catholic Reformation. This era saw the rise of new movements and devotions that refocused on faith in Christ; of the Society of Jesus, which not only combatted Protestantism but also cultivated reform; and of the entire seminary system, which targeted both schism and corruption with better-disciplined and better-educated priests. It also saw the end of the sale of indulgences in 1567. The five solas couldn't fly solo, but they did have to come *first.*

Faith comes first: we're initially justified by "the acceptance of God's righteousness through faith in Jesus Christ."[17] Thus, a works-based faith is of no avail: "We cannot therefore rely on our feelings or our works to conclude that we are justified and saved."[18] But we have to freely assent to faith, and this assent is the beginning, not the end, of our justification, which "establishes co-operation between God's grace and man's freedom."[19] God doesn't merely *impute* righteousness to us; he *infuses* it into us, and invites us to respond with good works. This cooperation of charity is a second wave of justification that lasts our whole life long: "The only thing that counts is faith working through love" (Gal. 5:6), because faith is "brought to completion by the works" (James 2:22).

Sources of Catholic Dogma, ed. Heinrich Denzinger and Karl Rahner, trans. R.J. Deferrari (St. Louis, MO: B. Herder, 1954), 258.

16. Council of Trent, "Decree on Justification" can. 9, in *Sources of Catholic Dogma*, 259.

17. *Catechism* 1991.

18. *Catechism* 2005.

19. *Catechism* 1993.

Grace comes first: it's an unmerited gift of God that we can't in any way earn. We're helpless sinners, and "there is no strict right to any merit on the part of man."[20] "In the evening of this life," Thérèse of Lisieux writes, "I shall appear before you with empty hands, for I do not ask you, Lord, to count my works. All our justice is stained in your eyes."[21] But the Little Flower also gave us her Little Way—small acts of love done for love of God—because our human nature also has to come into play. God associates us with his work of grace, and there's a real "merit of man before God in the Christian life."[22] This merit ultimately comes from and flows toward God—"All is grace"[23]—but in a real sense, it becomes ours.

Christ comes first: he's "the way, and the truth, and the life," and no one goes to the Father except through him (John 14:6); thus, everything in Christianity always has to point back to Jesus. But Christ and his Church are one: when Saul was persecuting Christians, he heard Christ say, "Why are you persecuting *me*?" (Acts 22:7). Thus, Christ also "continues his priestly work through the agency of his Church," inviting human beings to participate in his mediation.[24] The saints—especially Mary, his mother—give Christ to the world and resemble him; priests, at their best, do the same. We of course do wrong to worship Mary like Collyridians or idolize

20. *Catechism* 2007.

21. Thérèse of Lisieux, *Story of a Soul*, trans. John Clarke (Park Ridge, IL: Word on Fire Classics, 2022), 279.

22. *Catechism* 2008.

23. Georges Bernanos, *Diary of a Country Priest*, trans. Howard Curtis (London: Penguin Books, 2019), 243; see Thérèse of Lisieux, *St. Thérèse of Lisieux: Her Last Conversations*, trans. John Clarke, revised edition (Washington, DC: ICS, 2023), 29.

24. *Sacrosanctum Concilium* 83, in *The Word on Fire Vatican II Collection*, ed. Matthew Levering (Park Ridge, IL: Word on Fire Institute, 2021), 187.

priests like clericalists; but we do well to lean on their prayers, because Christians "pray for one another," and "the prayer of the righteous is powerful and effective" (James 5:16). It's been said that the Reformation was the triumph of Augustine's doctrine of grace over his doctrine of the Church, but the grace of Christ and its communication through his Church are both necessary on the Way.

Scripture comes first: before the Apostles were sent to preach, they were shaped by the Torah and the prophets, and even after all that their successors have said, apostolic preaching "is expressed in a special way in the inspired books."[25] "All Scripture is inspired by God" (2 Tim. 3:16), and "ignorance of the Scriptures is ignorance of Christ."[26] But Christianity isn't a "religion of the book"; in fact, the Bible itself was formally compiled and canonized by the Church toward the end of the fourth century. It's a "religion of the Word of God"—not a written, silent word, but "the incarnate and living Word."[27] This living transmission of the Word through apostolic succession, which intertwines with Sacred Scripture, is Sacred Tradition. Scripture and Tradition, "flowing out from the same divine wellspring, come together in some fashion to form one thing, and move towards the same goal."[28] Whether written or spoken, the divine Word is expressed in human words and received through a variety of human experiences; it thus needs a living human authority to unify and safeguard human interpretation. This is the Magisterium: the bishops in communion with the Bishop of Rome.

25. *Dei Verbum* 8, in *Vatican II Collection*, 22.

26. *Catechism* 133; Jerome, *Commentariorum in Isaiam libri xviii*, prol. (PL 24, 17B).

27. Benedict XVI, *Verbum Domini* 7, apostolic exhortation, September 30, 2010, vatican.va.

28. *Catechism* 80; *Dei Verbum* 9.

The Word is the bridge between heaven and earth, but the successors of the Apostles, under the leadership of the pope—the *pontifex* or bridge-builder—keep the bridge secure.

And the *glory of God* comes first: "Scripture and Tradition never cease to teach and celebrate this fundamental truth: 'The world was made for the glory of God.'"[29] This is so basic to Christianity that it goes without saying, yet we can never cease to say it: all things are *ad majorem Dei gloriam*—for the greater glory of God. But God's glory is in glorifying man, who attains that glory in glorifying God—"for 'the glory of God is man fully alive; moreover man's life is the vision of God.'"[30] Denigrating man doesn't give God glory; divinizing him does: "God, infinitely perfect and blessed in himself, in a plan of sheer goodness freely created man to make him share in his own blessed life."[31] As it turns out, Jesus links this very theme of mutual glory to Christian unity: "The glory that you have given me I have given them, so that they may be one, as we are one" (John 17:22).

The lynchpin of the five solas and the five alsos, holding them all together, is the Mass. It's the "sum and summary of our faith," but it also engages man's works (*leitourgia* in Greek, meaning "public work"); it's a pure gift of grace, but it also makes Christ's merits our own; it's the Liturgy of the Eucharist, but it also draws on Christ's submediators; it's the Liturgy of the Word, but it also flows out of apostolic Tradition; it's "the sacrifice of praise by which the Church sings the glory of God,"[32] but it's also a "pledge of glory" to man.[33] In

29. *Catechism* 293; *Dei Filius* 5.
30. *Catechism* 294; Irenaeus, *Against the Heresies* 4.20.7.
31. *Catechism* 1.
32. *Catechism* 1361.
33. *Catechism* 1419.

the Mass, heaven leads earth in its hymn, and earth lifts to heaven its prayers. The Spirit comes down like the dewfall, and man offers his meager sacrifices to be transformed and carried on high. The new Jerusalem with its angels and saints descends, and the pilgrim Church with its sorrow and sighing ascends. The once-for-all sacrifice of the Son is re-presented vertically to the Father, and the community is gathered horizontally for a sacred memorial meal. The not here and not yet are glimpsed in all their promise, and the here and now are embraced in all their potential.

"The Eucharist builds the Church," wrote Pope St. John Paul II, "and the Church makes the Eucharist."[34] This Church is on the Way; made up of sinners prone to wander from it, she knows she is "at the same time holy and always in need of being purified."[35] As the formula that comes down to us from Augustine has it, *Ecclesia semper reformanda*—"The Church is always reforming herself." But this reform is never in pulling apart the communion of heaven and earth; any such reformation is always a deformation. Instead, it can only be in drawing closer to that communion, hoping in Christ's own promise regarding his apostolic Church: "The gates of Hades will not prevail against it" (Matt. 16:18).

34. John Paul II, *Ecclesia de Eucharistia* 26, encyclical letter, April 17, 2003, vatican.va.

35. *Lumen Gentium* 8, in *Vatican II Collection*, 53.

CONCLUSION

The Great Either/Or

At the Annunciation, the angel Gabriel said to Mary, "The Holy Spirit will come upon you, and the power of the Most High will overshadow you; therefore the child to be born will be holy; he will be called Son of God" (Luke 1:35). Yet artists have tended to focus either on Gabriel's heavenly message to Mary (the Annunciation) or the earthly birth of the child (the Nativity). A painting of the actual overshadowing of the Spirit—the moment of heaven communing with earth—is rare.

We see a startling exception in Piero di Cosimo's beautiful *Incarnation of Jesus*. It's also as good a visual summation of the Way as we could ever hope to find. At the center of the painting is a resplendent Mary, and at the center of Mary is her pregnant belly. The whole scene has a balance of vertical and horizontal elements, with the rising cliffs flanking Mary contrasting the horizontal row of figures arrayed at her feet. This directional balance appears again at the very center of the image, where Mary's left hand is raised vertically in a gesture of ecstatic praise, while her right hand rests horizontally across her belly in a gesture of maternal warmth.

But this is only the beginning. Above Mary is a pure blue sky with puffy white clouds; under and around her is the pure green of the grass and the dark brown of the earth. Her clothes are a symphony of heavenly and earthly tones: her gray veil, the color of the darker clouds, cascades down a vivid red dress, a symbol of blood, passion, and the "red clay" of man; and her royal blue mantle signals dignity and authority, while its grassy green interior signals growth and fertility. In the top center is a dove surrounded by a great beam of light, a symbol of the Holy Spirit, pouring downward; and immediately under it is Mary herself, a symbol of the Church, looking upward.

On the cliff to the left of Mary's shoulders is a brightened scene of joy: Christ's Nativity. On the cliff to the right is a more shadowy scene of suffering that follows soon after: the flight of the Holy Family into Egypt. To the far left of Mary is John the Evangelist with his eagle, looking, as he often does in Christian art, graceful and feminine; to the far right of her is St. Peter with his key, looking rugged and masculine. To Mary's immediate left is Philip Benizi of the Servites, an order known for their devotion to Mary, especially her sorrows; to her immediate right is Antoninus of Florence of the Dominicans, an order known for their preaching and intellectual tradition. Below Mary, kneeling, are two women: on her left, Catherine of Alexandria, patroness of philosophers, and on her right, Margaret of Antioch, patroness of pregnant women—both of them laywomen.

At the center of all of this—at the center of everything—is God incarnate. Though on the surface this is a painting of Mary, it is, in fact, a painting of the child within her, drawing all of reality, whether in heaven or on earth, around himself in Catholic fullness. Here, all things find their right place in relation to the Lord, who is waiting to be born and usher in his Way.

But Piero's masterpiece of Catholic wholeness also poses a haunting question: *What now?*

We find a modern parable of two final possibilities in the dystopian *Love in the Ruins* by Walker Percy, a former agnostic raised in the Protestant South. Percy tells of a Louisiana psychiatrist, Dr. Thomas More, who invents a "stethoscope of the spirit," a "lapsometer" that monitors two metaphysical perturbations of the soul: angelism and bestialism.[1]

Angelism, a category Percy borrowed from Maritain's critique of Descartes, is an "excessive abstraction of the self from itself."[2] The angelist—whether as a Cartesian mind, a Stoic soul, or a Gnostic spirit—"orbits the earth and himself," cut off from "the lovely ordinary world."[3] Bestialism, on the other hand, is a manifestation of animal pleasure and aggression, a succumbing to carnal desire. The angelic lose their bodies, while the bestial lose their very selves. One side suffers from high blood pressure and succumbs to fits of rage; the other complains of anxiety and is overwhelmed by morning terror. The two conditions are nevertheless of a piece; they can even present simultaneously in a kind of "angelism-bestialism": a man can be abstracted from his body one moment and overcome by his desires the next. More, a self-professed "bad Catholic," suffers symptoms of both conditions.

Indeed, both conditions seem to permeate the whole of society, tearing the social fabric apart: "For our beloved old U.S.A. is in a bad way. Americans have turned against each other; race against

1. Walker Percy, *Love in the Ruins* (New York: Picador, 1971), 62.
2. Percy, 37.
3. Percy, 34.

race, right against left, believer against heathen."[4] Republicans are now "Knotheads" and Democrats the "new Left," the two groups dividing up America's towns and films and raging endlessly against each other. Some people, convinced of world conspiracies, set fire to the dark woods; others form revolutionary militias in the swamp.

The Catholic Church, too, fractures: on the one hand is the American Catholic Church, "which emphasizes property rights and the integrity of neighborhoods, retained the Latin Mass and plays 'The Star-Spangled Banner' at the elevation," and on the other is the Dutch schismatics, who emphasize the freedom for all to marry and divorce and "who believe in relevance but not God." A third group—the Roman Catholic remnant—is "a tiny scattered flock with no place to go."[5]

But this riven world isn't doomed to its division and death-dealing; there remains the forgotten Way that haunts the West. Indeed, the novel ends with More confessing his sins with a just barely adequate remorse, doing public penance with sackcloth and ashes, and eating and drinking the Body and Blood of the Lord. "Some day a man will walk into my office as a ghost or beast or ghost-beast," More muses, "and walk out as a man, which is to say sovereign wanderer, lordly exile, worker and waiter and watcher."[6]

When we turn to the light of Christ, we discover ourselves in the tension of hope: man is *homo viator*, a living Wayfarer; when we turn to our own lights, we lose ourselves in the city divided against itself. "Only in the mystery of the incarnate Word does the mystery

4. Percy, 17.
5. Percy, 6.
6. Percy, 383.

of man take on light";[7] outside of that mystery, we are swallowed up in darkness. The Incarnation is the eucatastrophe—the "sudden joyous 'turn'"—of the story of man, and the Resurrection the eucatastrophe of the story of the Incarnation; to reject them "leads either to sadness or to wrath."[8]

Christ is the Way, and the Catholic Church is "the fullness of him who fills all in all" (Eph. 1:23). What's left? "Either men anchor themselves on him and his Church, and thus enjoy the blessings of light and joy, right order and peace; or they live their lives apart from him; many positively oppose him, and deliberately exclude themselves from the Church. The result can only be confusion in their lives, bitterness in their relations with one another, and the savage threat of war."[9]

The Catholic faith is full of paradoxes, but its greatest paradox is this: that all of its both/ands unleash this ultimate either/or, and all of its communion compels this unavoidable decision—this cutting away of either death or life. Either we are with Christ, or we are against him; either we gather with him, or we are scattered without him; either we enter the perfect peace of the Way of heaven and earth, or we succumb to the endless division of Satan and, in the end, lose everything: "Do not think that I have come to bring peace to the earth; I have not come to bring peace, but a sword" (Matt. 10:34).

7. *Gaudium et Spes* 22, in *The Word on Fire Vatican II Collection*, ed. Matthew Levering (Park Ridge, IL: Word on Fire Institute, 2021), 238.

8. J.R.R. Tolkien, "On Fairy-Stories," in *Tolkien on Fairy-stories*, ed. Verlyn Flieger and Douglas A. Anderson (London: HarperCollins, 2014), 77–78.

9. John XXIII, "Opening Address," in *Vatican II Collection*, 2.

APPENDIX

Illustrations of the Way

This sample of quotations from Catholic tradition—reflecting on the Way itself, reflecting on the four ultimate paradoxes of heaven and earth, and reflecting on other related paradoxes featured in this book—is only a sample. The sea of Catholic wisdom is vast. I have also deliberately excluded Scripture, magisterial teaching, and the writings of Augustine and Aquinas, which are already well covered in the text.

The Way

> Catholicism, somewhat simplistically, has always been considered the religion of the great *"et et"*: not of great forms of exclusivism but of synthesis. The exact meaning of "Catholic" is "synthesis."[1]
> —Pope Benedict XVI

1. Benedict XVI, "Meeting of the Holy Father Benedict XVI with the Clergy of the Dioceses of Belluno-Feltre and Treviso," July 24, 2007, vatican.va.

All not-at-one-ness, all division, rests on a concealed lack of real Christliness, on a clinging to individuality that hinders the coalescence into unity.[2]
—Pope Benedict XVI

Only by circling round, by looking and describing from different, apparently contrary angles can we succeed in alluding to the truth, which is never visible to us in its totality.[3]
—Pope Benedict XVI

It takes two sorts to make a world. One thought without the next, and balancing thought, is as barren as Adam without Eve. It repeats itself; but it cannot reproduce itself. It breeds no new thoughts.[4]
—G.K. Chesterton

Christianity got over the difficulty of combining furious opposites, by keeping them both, and keeping them both furious.[5]
—G.K. Chesterton

Christianity is a superhuman paradox whereby two opposite passions may blaze beside each other.[6]
—G.K. Chesterton

2. Joseph Ratzinger, *Introduction to Christianity*, 2nd ed., trans. J.R. Foster (San Francisco: Ignatius, 2004), 187.

3. Ratzinger, 174.

4. G.K. Chesterton, "The Triumph of the Concrete," *The Daily News*, December 28, 1912, in the Chesterton Digital Library, https://library.chesterton.org/the-triumph-of-the-concrete-15171/.

5. G.K. Chesterton, *Orthodoxy* (Park Ridge, IL: Word on Fire Classics, 2017), 93–94.

6. Chesterton, 149.

Every statement of the faith is twofold; as regards us it necessarily consists of two views, the two apparent objects of which seem at first glance to be opposed to each other, not to say contradictory. These two views tend to coalesce at an infinite distance upon a single object, but the intuition of this unity escapes us. This is why the coherent plenitude after which we aspire can never, in our present condition, be anything but an aspiration.[7]
—Henri de Lubac

Unity is in no way confusion, any more than distinction is separation. . . . "Distinguish in order to unite," it has been said, and the advice is excellent, but on the ontological plane the complementary formula, unite in order to distinguish, is just as inevitable.[8]
—Henri de Lubac

In every man there is a mystery. Contraries coexist in him; he is two, and these two are one.[9]
—Henri de Lubac

This double movement of opposites ends finally at either God or Nothingness.[10]
—Alberto Methol Ferré

7. Henri de Lubac, *A Brief Catechesis on Nature and Grace* (San Francisco: Ignatius, 1984), 73.

8. Henri de Lubac, *Catholicism: Christ and the Common Destiny of Man* (San Francisco: Ignatius, 1988), 32.

9. Henri de Lubac, *The Drama of Atheist Humanism* (San Francisco: Ignatius, 1995), 371.

10. Alberto Methol Ferré, "La Chiesa, popolo tra i popoli," in *Il risorgimento cattolico latinoamericano* (Centro Studi Europa Orientale, 1983), 142; translation

> One tension, for life to be maintained, cannot be resolved by assimilation of one of the poles in detriment to the others, nor by a synthesis (of a Hegelian type) that annuls polarities. The tension . . . must be resolved on a superior plane, that would not be synthesis, but the resolution that contains virtually the tensioned polarities.[11]
> —Pope Francis

> There is something living in the Church which, like the energy that holds together the component parts of the atom, overcomes the tension between the structures and combines them into a whole in a way which, according to all sociological theories, is impossible on an earthly basis.[12]
> —Romano Guardini

> It is not a "synthesis" of two moments into a third. Nor is it a whole, of which the two moments constitute "parts." Still less is it a mixture, in some sort of compromise. . . . Two moments are each in themselves without being able to be deduced, transposed, confused, and yet are inextricably linked to each other; on the contrary, they can be thought of only one in the other and one thanks to the other.[13]
> —Romano Guardini

from Massimo Borghesi, *The Mind of Pope Francis: Jorge Mario Bergoglio's Intellectual Journey*, trans. Barry Hudock (Collegeville, MN: Liturgical, 2018), 96.

11. Jorge Bergoglio, "La Vida sagrada y su mission en la Iglesia y en el mundo," 204; translation from *Pope Francis and the Event of Encounter*, ed. John C. Cavadini and Donald Wallenfang (Eugene, OR: Wipf and Stock, 2018), 212.

12. Romano Guardini, *The Church of the Lord: On the Nature and Mission of the Church*, trans. Stella Lange (Chicago: Henry Regnery, 1966), 4–5.

13. Romano Guardini, *L'opposizione polare: Tentativi per una filosofia del*

The Christian life is the true Jacob's ladder on which the angels ascend and descend.[14]
—St. Jerome

The Catholic Creed is for the most part the combination of separate truths, which heretics have divided among themselves, and err in dividing. So that, in matter of fact, if a religious mind were educated in and sincerely attached to some form of heathenism or heresy, and then were brought under the light of truth, it would be drawn off from error into the truth, not by losing what it had, but by gaining what it had not.[15]
—St. John Henry Newman

One aspect of revelation must not be allowed to exclude or to obscure another; and Christianity is dogmatical, devotional, practical all at once; it is esoteric and exoteric; it is indulgent and strict; it is light and dark; it is love, and it is fear.[16]
—St. John Henry Newman

They are ever hunting for a fabulous primitive simplicity; we repose in Catholic fullness.[17]
—St. John Henry Newman

concreto-vivente (Brescia: Morcelliana, 1997), 163–166; translation from Borghesi, *Mind of Pope Francis*, 114.

14. Jerome, Letter 54.6.

15. John Henry Newman, *An Essay on the Development of Christian Doctrine* (Park Ridge, IL: Word on Fire Classics, 2017), 164–165.

16. Newman, 29.

17. Newman, 317.

In these most profound matters every endeavor of our human intelligence should be bent to the achieving of that simplicity where contradictories are reconciled.[18]
—Nicholas of Cusa

The two contrary reasons. We must begin with that; without that we understand nothing, and all is heretical; and we must even add at the end of each truth that the opposite truth is to be remembered.[19]
—Blaise Pascal

All err the more dangerously, as they each follow a truth. Their fault is not in following a falsehood, but in not following another truth.[20]
—Blaise Pascal

What we need is . . . a philosophy of dynamic polarity. Not subject *or* object, becoming *or* being, person *or* form; not even a static conciliation accomplished once and then considered complete. No: a philosophy of fluctuating movement back and forth between poles, a philosophy of a never-resolved tension between the two poles, a philosophy of a dynamic "unity of the opposites."[21]
—Erich Przywara

18. Nicholas of Cusa, *Of Learned Ignorance*, trans. Germain Heron (Eugene, OR: Wipf & Stock, 2007), 173.

19. Blaise Pascal, *Pensées* 566, trans. W.F. Trotter, in *Pensées; The Provincial Letters* (New York: Modern Library, 1941), 185.

20. *Pensées* 862, 306.

21. Erich Przywara, "Gottgeheimnis der Welt," in Przywara, *Religions-philosophische Schriften*, vol. 2 (Einsiedeln: Johannes Verlag, 1962), 215; translation from Borghesi, *Mind of Pope Francis*, 72.

I choose all![22]
—St. Thérèse of Lisieux

Heaven and Earth

He was made man that we might be made God; and He manifested Himself by a body that we might receive the idea of the unseen Father; and He endured the insolence of men that we might inherit immortality.[23]
—St. Athanasius

By the Word revealing Himself everywhere, both above and beneath, and in the depth and in the breadth—above, in the creation; beneath, in becoming man; in the depth, in Hades; and in the breadth, in the world—all things have been filled with the knowledge of God.[24]
—St. Athanasius

In loving our neighbor in the most ordinary earthly matters, we are encountering Christ in heaven.[25]
—Hans Urs von Balthasar

22. Thérèse of Lisieux, *Story of a Soul*, trans. John Clarke (Park Ridge, IL: Word on Fire Classics, 2022), 28.

23. Athanasius, *On the Incarnation of the Word* 54.3.

24. *On the Incarnation* 16.3.

25. Hans Urs von Balthasar, *Prayer*, trans. Graham Harrison (San Francisco: Ignatius, 1986), 281.

That contemplation is realistic which seeks the reality of heaven, yet not by dissolving or allegorizing away the reality of earth. It endures and holds the tension between the two, which is ultimately a christological tension. Ultimately the only thing strong enough to hold it is the bond between the two natures in Christ.[26]
—Hans Urs von Balthasar

Christian existence calls for two things at once: we must maintain the distinction between heaven and earth which is grounded in creation and will not be overcome until the eschaton; and we must affirm the fact that this distinction has been superseded in principle (though not yet made manifest). . . . This irreducible tension is part of our whole Christian life.[27]
—Hans Urs von Balthasar

For us Christians God is no longer a hypothesis, as he was in the philosophy that preceded Christianity, but a reality, for God "lowered the heavens and came down." Heaven is God himself and he came down among us.[28]
—Pope Benedict XVI

In the man Jesus, God comes at one and the same time in a human and in a divine way. His coming transcends the logic of history, yet concerns all history.[29]
—Pope Benedict XVI

26. Balthasar, 291.
27. Balthasar, 284.
28. Benedict XVI, General Audience, January 11, 2006, vatican.va.
29. Joseph Ratzinger, *Eschatology: Death and Eternal Life*, 2nd ed., trans. Michael Waldstein (Washington, DC: The Catholic University of America Press), 200.

Christian faith really means precisely the acknowledgment that God is not the prisoner of his own eternity, not limited to the solely spiritual; that he is capable of operating here and now, in the midst of my world, and that he did operate in it through Jesus.[30]
—Pope Benedict XVI

The key to the Paradoxes of the Gospel and the key to the Paradoxes of Catholicism is one and the same—that the Life that produces them is at once Divine and Human.[31]
—Robert Hugh Benson

The Catholic Church is the extension of Christ's Life on earth; the Catholic Church, therefore, that strange mingling of mystery and common-sense, that union of earth and heaven, of clay and fire, can alone be understood by him who accepts her as both Divine and Human.[32]
—Robert Hugh Benson

Jesus is the mediator between God and man. In him the union of two natures brings together things divine and human. It marries heaven and earth in perfect peace.[33]
—St. Bernard of Clairvaux

30. Ratzinger, *Introduction to Christianity*, 279.

31. Robert Hugh Benson, *Paradoxes of Catholicism* (London: Longmans, Green, 1913), 23.

32. Benson, 11.

33. Bernard of Clairvaux, "Fragments from a Fragment," in *On the Love of God*, 2nd ed., trans. Marianne Caroline and Coventry Patmore (London: Burns and Oates, 1884), 57.

O depth of love! What heart could keep from breaking at the sight of your greatness descending to the lowliness of our humanity? We are your image, and now by making yourself one with us you have become our image, veiling your eternal divinity in the wretched cloud and dung heap of Adam. And why? For love! You, God, became human and we have been made divine![34]
—St. Catherine of Siena

Star of his morning; that unfallen star
In the strange starry overturn of space
When earth and sky changed places for an hour
And heaven looked upwards in a human face.[35]
—G.K. Chesterton

A mass of legend and literature, which increases and will never end has repeated and rung the changes on that single paradox; that the hands that had made the sun and stars were too small to reach the huge heads of the cattle. Upon this paradox, we might almost say upon this jest, all the literature of our faith is founded.[36]
—G.K. Chesterton

34. Catherine of Siena, *Catherine of Siena: The Dialogue*, trans. Suzanne Noffke (Mahwah, NJ: Paulist, 1980), 50.

35. G.K. Chesterton, "A Little Litany," in *The Queen of Seven Swords* (London: Sheed & Ward, 1926), 14.

36. G.K. Chesterton, *The Everlasting Man: A Guide to G.K. Chesterton's Masterpiece* (Elk Grove Village, IL: Word on Fire, 2023), 279–280.

The work of heaven alone was material; the making of a material world. The work of hell is entirely spiritual.[37]
—G.K. Chesterton

A human being is by nature a finite embodied spirit, in search of the Infinite, in social solidarity with its fellow human beings, on a historical journey through this material cosmos toward its final trans-worldly goal.[38]
—W. Norris Clarke

We are not expecting utopia here on this earth. But God meant things to be much easier than we have made them. . . . Eternal life begins now.[39]
—Dorothy Day

[God] will raise up leaders who will know how to combat the secular, or rather how to integrate the spiritual and material, so that life will be a more balanced one of joy and sorrow.[40]
—Dorothy Day

37. G.K. Chesterton, *St. Thomas Aquinas*, in *St. Thomas Aquinas; St. Francis of Assisi* (San Francisco: Ignatius, 2002), 100.

38. W. Norris Clarke, *Person and Being* (Milwaukee: Marquette University Press, 2008), 41.

39. Dorothy Day, *On Pilgrimage* (New York: Catholic Worker Books, 1948), 102.

40. Dorothy Day, *The Duty of Delight: The Diaries of Dorothy Day*, ed. Robert Ellsberg (New York: Image Books, 2011), 540.

We cannot love God unless we love each other, and to love we must know each other. We know him in the breaking of bread, and we know each other in the breaking of bread, and we are not alone anymore.[41]
—Dorothy Day

The paradise of God, if so it may be said, is the heart of man.[42]
—St. Alphonsus de Liguori

Made of the earth, whose entire history is summed up, prolonged, and transformed in him, animated by a divine breath that makes him eternal, with a "germinal eternity," man must accept his twofold origin, which creates his twofold nature, not as the implacable sign of a twofold oppression, but, on the contrary, as the point of departure for a twofold liberation.[43]
—Henri de Lubac

The Eucharist joins heaven and earth; it embraces and penetrates all creation. The world which came forth from God's hands returns to him in blessed and undivided adoration.[44]
—Pope Francis

41. Dorothy Day, *The Long Loneliness: The Autobiography of Dorothy Day* (San Francisco: Harper & Row, 1980), 285.

42. Alphonsus de Liguori, "Method of Conversing Continually and Familiarly with God," in *The Spirit of Blessed Alphonsus de Liguori: A Selection from His Shorter Spiritual Treatises*, trans. James Jones (Baltimore: F. Lucas Jr., 1800), 130.

43. De Lubac, *The Drama of Atheist Humanism*, 430.

44. Francis, *Laudato Si'* 236, encyclical letter, May 24, 2015, vatican.va.

O admirable heights and sublime lowliness!
O sublime humility!
O humble sublimity!
That the Lord of the universe,
God and the Son of God,
so humbles Himself
that for our salvation
He hides Himself under the little form of bread![45]
—St. Francis of Assisi

I am both small and great, both lowly and exalted, mortal and immortal, earthly and heavenly.[46]
—St. Gregory Nazianzen

It is man's lot to be a living limit, to recognize the fact and to live his circumscribed life. That sets him in the realm of reality. As a result he is free of the fascination of a false, direct oneness with God as well as a direct identification with nature. A chasm, a two-sided cleft, surrounds him.[47]
—Romano Guardini

45. Francis of Assisi, "A Letter to the Entire Order," in *Francis and Clare: The Complete Works*, trans. Regis J. Armstrong and Ignatius C. Brady (New York: Paulist, 1982), 58.

46. Gregory Nazianzen, Sermon 7.23 ("In Praise of His Brother Caesarius"), in the Liturgy of the Hours, vol. 4, *Ordinary Time: Weeks 18–34* (New York: Catholic Book Publishing, 1975), 493.

47. Romano Guardini, "The Meaning of Melancholy," in *The Focus of Freedom* (Baltimore, MD: Helicon, 1966), 89.

The visible and temporal is a manifestation of the invisible and eternal.[48]
—St. Hildegard of Bingen

The world is charged with the grandeur of God.[49]
—Gerard Manley Hopkins

There is only one physician, who is both flesh and spirit, born and unborn, God in man, true life in death, both from Mary and from God, first subject to suffering and then beyond it, Jesus Christ our Lord.[50]
—St. Ignatius of Antioch

For it behooved "the Mediator of God and humanity," by his kinship to both, to lead them back to friendship and concord, and to bring it about that God would take humankind to himself, and that humankind would give itself to God.[51]
—St. Irenaeus of Lyons

48. Hildegard of Bingen, *Scivias* 3.1.1, trans. Mother Columba Hart and Jane Bishop (New York: Paulist, 1990), 94.

49. Gerard Manley Hopkins, "God's Grandeur," in *100 Great Catholic Poems*, ed. Sally Read (Elk Grove Village, IL: Word on Fire, 2023), 267.

50. Ignatius of Antioch, *The Letter to the Ephesians* 7.2, in *Early Church Fathers Collection*, ed. David Augustine (Elk Grove Village, IL: Word on Fire Classics, 2024), 50.

51. Irenaeus, *Against the Heresies* 3.18.7, in *Early Church Fathers Collection*, 223.

The things in heaven are spiritual, while those on earth constitute the dispensation in human nature (*secundum hominem est dispositio*). These things, therefore, he recapitulated in himself: by uniting man to the Spirit, and causing the Spirit to dwell in man, he is himself made the head of the Spirit, and gives the Spirit to be the head of man.[52]
—St. Irenaeus of Lyons

For as the bread, which is produced from the earth, when it receives the invocation of God, is no longer common bread, but the Eucharist, consisting of two realities, earthly and heavenly; so also our bodies, when they receive the Eucharist, are no longer corruptible, having the hope of the resurrection to eternity.[53]
—St. Irenaeus of Lyons

I do not venerate matter, I venerate the fashioner of matter, who became matter for my sake, and in matter made his abode, and through matter worked my salvation. . . . I reverence it not as God, but as filled with divine energy and grace. . . . Is not the ink and the parchment of the Gospel matter? Is not the life-bearing table, which offers to us the bread of life, matter? . . . Before all these things, is not the body and blood of my Lord matter?[54]
—St. John of Damascus

52. Irenaeus, *Against the Heresies* 5.20.2, newadvent.org.
53. *Against the Heresies* 4.18.5.
54. John of Damascus, *Treatise* 2.14, in *Three Treatises on the Divine Images*, trans. Andrew Louth (Crestwood, NY: St. Vladimir's Seminary Press, 2003), 70–71.

Body and soul are inseparable: in the person, in the willing agent, and in the deliberate act, *they stand or fall together*.[55]
—Pope St. John Paul II

Separated creatures are variously united through Christ. . . . He united earth and heaven, demonstrating that the nature of sensible things is one and inclines toward itself. He also united sensibles and intelligibles. . . . According to a principle and mode beyond nature, he united created nature to the uncreated.[56]
—St. Maximus the Confessor

The doctrine of the Incarnation is the announcement of a divine gift conveyed in a material and visible medium, it being thus that heaven and earth are in the Incarnation united. That is, it establishes in the very idea of Christianity the *sacramental* principle as its characteristic.[57]
—St. John Henry Newman

We cannot fail to admit that there are finite beings. So we cannot fail to admit that there is the Infinite. Hence, we admit the coincidence-of-contradictories, above which the Infinite exists. But

55. John Paul II, *Veritatis Splendor* 95, encyclical letter, August 6, 1993, in *The Splendor of Truth* (Elk Grove Village, IL: Word on Fire, 2024), 61.

56. Maximus the Confessor, *On Difficulties in Sacred Scripture: The Responses to Thalassios*, trans. Maximos Constas (Washington, DC: The Catholic University of America Press, 2018), 269–270.

57. Newman, *Development of Christian Doctrine*, 269.

this coincidence is Contradiction without contradiction, just as it is End without an end.[58]
—Nicholas of Cusa

For me it is the virgin birth, the Incarnation, the resurrection which are the true laws of the flesh and the physical. Death, decay, destruction are the suspension of these laws. I am always astonished at the emphasis the Church puts on the body. It is not the soul she says that will rise but the body, glorified.[59]
—Flannery O'Connor

God is pure Spirit but our salvation was accomplished when the Spirit was made flesh. I meant to imply no more than the traditional teaching of the Incarnation as Catholics see it in the Church. When the Spirit and the flesh are separated in theological thinking, the result is some form of Manichaeism.[60]
—Flannery O'Connor

The external must be joined to the internal to obtain anything from God, that is to say, we must kneel, pray with the lips, etc., in order that proud man, who would not submit himself to God, may be now subject to the creature. To expect help from these

58. Nicholas of Cusa, *De Visioni Dei* 54–55, in *Complete Philosophical and Theological Treatises of Nicholas of Cusa*, vol. 2, trans. Jasper Hopkins (Minneapolis, MN: Banning, 2001), 705.

59. Flannery O'Connor to "A," September 6, 1955, in *Flannery O'Connor Collection*, ed. Matthew Becklo (Park Ridge, IL: Word on Fire Classics, 2019), 64–65.

60. Flannery O'Connor, *The Habit of Being*, ed. Sally Fitzgerald (New York: Farrar, Straus and Giroux, 1979), 360.

externals is superstition; to refuse to join them to the internal is pride. . . . The Christian religion alone is adapted to all, being composed of externals and internals. It raises the common people to the internal, and humbles the proud to the external; it is not perfect without the two, for the people must understand the spirit of the letter, and the learned must submit their spirit to the letter.[61]
—Blaise Pascal

Jesus Christ is the beginning and the end, the Alpha and the Omega; he is the king of the new world; he is the secret of history; he is the key to our destiny. He is the mediator, the bridge, between heaven and earth. He is more perfectly than anyone else the Son of Man, because he is the Son of God, eternal and infinite.[62]
—Pope St. Paul VI

The special marks of the Catholic Church [are] the sacraments, especially the Eucharist, which, whatever else they do, confer the highest significance upon the ordinary things of this world, bread, wine, water, touch, breath, words, talking, listening.[63]
—Walker Percy

61. Pascal, *Pensées* 250–251, 88.

62. Paul VI, "Mass at 'Quezon Circle': Homily of the Holy Father Paul VI," November 29, 1970, vatican.va.

63. Walker Percy, *Signposts in a Strange Land*, ed. Patrick Samway (New York: Picador, 1991), 369.

This tree of heavenly dimensions rises up from the earth to heaven. It is fixed, as an everlasting growth, in the midst of heaven and of earth. It is the sustenance of all things, the prop of the universe, the support of the whole inhabited earth and the axis of the world. It holds together the variety of human nature, fixed as it is by the invisible pegs of the Spirit so that, divinely adjusted, it may never more be detached from God. By its pinnacle touching the summit of the heavens, by its foot stabilizing the earth, and by its immense arms restraining on all sides the manifold spirits of the air between heaven and earth, it exists whole and entire in everything, everywhere.[64]
—Pseudo-Hippolytus

In the heart of Jesus, which was pierced,
The kingdom of heaven and the land of earth are bound together.
Here is for us the source of life.[65]
—Edith Stein (St. Teresa Benedicta of the Cross)

He pierced me with an arrow
smeared with the poison of love,
and my soul succumbed,
to be one with its Creator.
Now, I don't want another—
to my God, I have surrendered:

64. Pseudo-Hippolytus, *On the Pasch*, in Hans Urs von Balthasar, *Mysterium Paschale: The Mystery of Easter*, trans. Aidan Nichols (San Francisco: Ignatius, 2005), 58–59.

65. Edith Stein, "I Will Remain with You," in *The Collected Works of Edith Stein*, vol. 4, *The Hidden Life: Essays, Meditations, Spiritual Texts*, ed. I. Gelber and Michael Linssen, trans. Waltraut Stein (Washington, DC: ICS, 2014), 137.

my Love belongs to me,
and I belong to Him.[66]
—St. Teresa of Avila

I want to spend my heaven in doing good on earth.[67]
—St. Thérèse of Lisieux

The rod of Jesse has blossomed;
the Virgin has brought forth one who is both God and man.
God has restored peace,
reconciling in himself the depths and the heights.[68]
—Traditional

Hail, virgin, abyss of honey,
you who drive far away the ancient gall
of death and sorrow,
you who with the needle of providence
joined God with mud
and the lowest with the highest.[69]
—Walter of Wimborne

66. Teresa of Avila, "About Those Words, 'My Beloved Is Mine,'" trans. Dana Delibovi, in *100 Great Catholic Poems*, 184.

67. Thérèse of Lisieux, *St. Thérèse of Lisieux: Her Last Conversations*, trans. John Clarke, rev. ed. (Washington, DC: ICS, 2023), 74.

68. The Roman Missal, Third Typical Edition (Washington, DC: United States Conference of Catholic Bishops, 2011), 1044.

69. Walter of Wimborne, "Ave Virgo Mater Christi," trans. Rachel Fulton Brown, in *100 Great Catholic Poems*, 97.

Other Paradoxes

The Catholic faith is this, that we worship one God in Trinity and Trinity in Unity. Neither confounding the Persons, nor dividing the Substance.[70]
—The Athanasian Creed

The Catholic balance, in the final analysis, is anchored in the supernatural mystery of Christ. . . . In the same way in which we cannot get to the bottom of the relationship between humanity and divinity in Christ, neither can we fathom the relationship, in the Church and thus in ecclesial existence, between institutional "closure" and mystical "openness."[71]
—Hans Urs von Balthasar

Any division of "value" and "being" into two different spheres . . . is not only untenable but is nothing less than a mortal blow to the mystery of being.[72]
—Hans Urs von Balthasar

The Church can only effectively pursue her task . . . if she herself alternates between two impossible poles: preaching to the world purely from without and transforming it purely from within. . . . This paradox, which is baffling at an earthly level, reflects the

70. The Athanasian Creed, in *The Catholic Encyclopedia*, vol. 2 (New York: Robert Appleton, 1907).

71. Hans Urs von Balthasar, *Bernanos: An Ecclesial Existence*, trans. E. Leiva-Merikakis (San Francisco: Ignatius, 1996), 28.

72. Hans Urs von Balthasar, *Theo-Logic: Theological Logical Theory*, vol. 1, *The Truth of the World*, trans. A.J. Walker (San Francisco: Ignatius, 2000), 103.

discipleship of Christ, who comes into the world and leaves it (John 16:28) and yet stays with it until the end (Matt. 28:20).[73]
—Hans Urs von Balthasar

The grace of good works redounds to those who perform them. You gave to the poor, and in so doing you received back even more. For just as seed brings forth an increase for the one who scatters it on the ground, bread cast to the hungry yields considerable profit at a later time. Therefore, let the end of your harvesting be the beginning of a heavenly sowing.[74]
—St. Basil the Great

The Catholic Church is an institution I am bound to hold divine—but for unbelievers a proof of its divinity might be found in the fact that no merely human institution conducted with such knavish imbecility would have lasted a fortnight.[75]
—Hilaire Belloc

Is there not revealed in the unholy holiness of the Church, as opposed to man's expectation of purity, God's true holiness, which is love, love that does not keep its distance in a sort of aristocratic, untouchable purity but mixes with the dirt of the world, in order thus to overcome it?[76]
—Pope Benedict XVI

73. Hans Urs von Balthasar, *Theo-Drama: Theological Dramatic Theory*, vol. 4, *The Action*, trans. G. Harrison (San Francisco, Ignatius, 1994), 465.

74. Basil the Great, "I Will Tear Down My Barns," in *On Social Justice* (Crestwood, NY: St. Vladimir's Seminary Press, 2009), 62.

75. Robert Speaight, *The Life of Hilaire Belloc* (London: Hollis and Carter, 1957), 383.

76. Ratzinger, *Introduction to Christianity*, 342–343.

One draws near to the Lord's radiance by sharing his darkness. One serves the salvation of the world by leaving one's own salvation behind for the sake of others.[77]
—Pope Benedict XVI

The time of the New Testament is a peculiar kind of "in-between," a mixture of "already and not yet." The empirical conditions of life in this world are still in force, but they have been burst open, and must be more and more burst open, in preparation for the final fulfillment already inaugurated in Christ.[78]
—Pope Benedict XVI

Ora et labora. (Pray and work.)[79]
—Benedictine motto

Catholic doctrine and discipline may be walls; but they are the walls of a playground. Christianity is the only frame which has preserved the pleasure of Paganism.[80]
—G.K. Chesterton

Life is not an illogicality; yet it is a trap for logicians.[81]
—G.K. Chesterton

77. Ratzinger, *Eschatology*, 218.
78. Joseph Ratzinger, *The Spirit of the Liturgy*, trans. John Saward (San Francisco: Ignatius, 2000), 54.
79. *Catechism of the Catholic Church* 2834; see Benedict, *Regula*, 20, 48.
80. Chesterton, *Orthodoxy*, 147.
81. Chesterton, 79.

It is true that the historic Church has at once emphasized celibacy and emphasized the family; has at once (if one may put it so) been fiercely for having children and fiercely for not having children. It has kept them side by side like two strong colours, red and white, like the red and white upon the shield of St. George. It has always had a healthy hatred of pink.[82]
—G.K. Chesterton

To be fully a person consists in living out to the full the alternating rhythm of self-possession and openness to others. . . . The two poles can even mysteriously come to interpenetrate one another, without losing their distinctness.[83]
—W. Norris Clarke

Yet, as a wheel moves smoothly, free from jars,
My will and my desire were turned by love,
The love that moves the sun and the other stars.[84]
—Dante

We feed the hungry, yes; we try to shelter the homeless and give them clothes, if we have some, but there is a strong faith at work; we pray.[85]
—Dorothy Day

82. Chesterton, 96.

83. Clarke, *Person and Being*, 113.

84. Dante, *Paradise*, canto 33, trans. Anthony Esolen (New York: Modern Library, 2007), 359.

85. Robert Coles, *Dorothy Day: A Radical Devotion* (New York: Addison Wesley, 1987), 97.

Christianity, in its double aspect—institutional and doctrinal, social and reflective—is, on the one hand, most conservative and, on the other, most revolutionary. It is both, in a supreme way.[86]
—Henri de Lubac

The Church for its part cannot manage to escape. Placed by its founder in the midst of the world, it must there accomplish its task, which is not of this world. Consequently there it remains, always militant, always tormented within. Always loyal yet always estranged. Always here yet always looking elsewhere.[87]
—Henri de Lubac

The grace of Catholicism was not given to us for ourselves alone, but for those who do not possess it, just as the grace of the contemplative life, as St. Teresa understood so well, is bestowed on chosen souls for the benefit of those who undertake the labors of the active life.[88]
—Henri de Lubac

Martha is necessary to Mary, for it was because Martha worked that Mary was able to be praised.[89]
—The Desert Fathers

86. De Lubac, *Brief Catechesis*, 89.
87. De Lubac, 90.
88. De Lubac, *Catholicism*, 240–241.
89. Thomas Merton, trans., *The Wisdom of the Desert: Sayings from the Desert Fathers of the Fourth Century* (New York: New Directions, 1970), 37.

Once two brethren came to a certain elder whose custom it was not to eat every day. But when he saw the brethren he invited them with joy to dine with him, saying: Fasting has its reward, but he who eats out of charity fulfills two commandments, for he sets aside his own will and he refreshes his hungry brethren.[90]
—The Desert Fathers

Not infrequently a kind of opposition is constructed between theology and pastoral care, as though they were two opposing, separate realities, which have nothing to do with one another. . . . Life, then, has no space for reflection and reflection finds no space in life. The great fathers of the Church, Irenaeus, Augustine, Basil, Ambrose, to name a few, were great theologians because they were great pastors.[91]
—Pope Francis

Since we are men we are unable to apprehend being in the way a pure spirit would, but we are able to apprehend being as men, grasping it as closely as possible through the union of our intellect and our sensibility.[92]
—Étienne Gilson

90. *Sayings from the Desert Fathers*, 77.

91. Francis, "Video Message of His Holiness Pope Francis to Participants in an International Theological Congress Held at the Pontifical Catholic University of Argentina," September 1–3, 2015, vatican.va.

92. Étienne Gilson, *Thomist Realism and the Critique of Knowledge*, trans. Mark A. Wauck (San Francisco: Ignatius, 2012), 193.

The Spirit itself was preaching, saying these words: "Do nothing without the bishop. Guard your bodies as the temple of God. Love unity. Flee from divisions. Become imitators of Jesus Christ, just as he is of his Father."[93]
—St. Ignatius of Antioch

Let your first rule of action be to trust in God as if success depended entirely on yourself and not on him: but use all your efforts as if God alone did everything, and yourself nothing.[94]
—St. Ignatius of Loyola

About Jesus Christ and the Church, I simply know they're just one thing, and we shouldn't complicate the matter.[95]
—St. Joan of Arc

As the bread consisting of many grains is made one, so that the grains nowhere appear . . . so are we conjoined both with each other and with Christ: there not being one body for you, and another for your neighbor to be nourished by, but the very same for all.[96]
—St. John Chrysostom

93. Ignatius of Antioch, *The Letter to the Philadelphians* 7.2, in *Early Church Fathers Collection*, 73.

94. Ignatius of Loyola, January 2 reflection, in *Thoughts of St. Ignatius Loyola for Every Day of the Year*, from the *Scintillae Ignatianae*, ed. Gabriel Hevenesi (New York: Fordham University Press, 2006), 15.

95. *Catechism* 795; Acts of the Trial of Joan of Arc.

96. John Chrysostom, *Homilies on First Corinthians* 24.4.

By a Union and Conjoining God the Word and the Flesh are One, not by any confusion or obliteration of substances, but by a certain union ineffable, and past understanding.[97]
—St. John Chrysostom

Faith and reason are like two wings on which the human spirit rises to the contemplation of truth.[98]
—Pope St. John Paul II

A clear and forceful presentation of moral truth can never be separated from a profound and heartfelt respect, born of that patient and trusting love which man always needs along his moral journey, a journey frequently wearisome on account of difficulties, weakness, and painful situations.[99]
—Pope St. John Paul II

It is necessary to keep these two truths together, namely, the real possibility of salvation in Christ for all mankind and the necessity of the Church for salvation. Both these truths help us to understand the *one mystery of salvation*, so that we can come to know God's mercy and our own responsibility.[100]
—Pope St. John Paul II

97. J.R. Willis, ed., *The Teachings of the Church Fathers* (San Francisco: Ignatius, 2002), 314.

98. John Paul II, *Fides et Ratio* blessing, encyclical letter, September 14, 1998, vatican.va.

99. John Paul II, *Veritatis Splendor* 95, in *The Splendor of Truth*, 111.

100. John Paul II, *Redemptoris Missio* 9, encyclical letter, December 7, 1990, vatican.va.

In order that we may follow those things that please him, choosing them by means of the rational powers he has given us, he both persuades us and leads us to faith.[101]
—St. Justin Martyr

I both pray and with all my strength strive to be found a Christian.[102]
—St. Justin Martyr

In Paradise there was no opposition between action and contemplation. We too, if we recover, in Christ, the paradisiacal life of Adam which he has restored to us, are supposed to discover that the opposition between them vanishes at last.[103]
—Thomas Merton

The Coptic hermits who left the world as though escaping from a wreck, did not merely intend to save themselves. Once they got a foothold on solid ground, things were different. Then they had not only the power but even the obligation to pull the whole world to safety after them. This is their paradoxical lesson for our time.[104]
—Thomas Merton

101. Justin Martyr, *The First Apology* 10, in *Early Church Fathers Collection*, 176.
102. Justin Martyr, *The Second Apology* 13, in *Early Church Fathers Collection*, 194.
103. Thomas Merton, *The New Man* (London: Burns & Oates, 1976), 54.
104. Merton, *Wisdom of the Desert*, 23.

The Church has essentially two poles, born of the Spirit of God and of Jesus Christ in the Apostles. It is visible and invisible, in a single, indissoluble breath. Ecclesiologies tend to emphasize one or the other of the poles . . . Spirit without institution or institution without Spirit—both are false oppositions that destroy the Church.[105]
—Alberto Methol Ferré

Christ has done the whole work of redemption for us; and yet it is no contradiction to say, that something remains for us to do; we have to take the redemption offered us, and that taking involves a work. We have to apply his grace to our own souls, and that application implies pain, trial, and toil, in the midst of its blessedness.[106]
—St. John Henry Newman

They alone are able truly to enjoy this world, who begin with the world unseen. They alone enjoy it, who have first abstained from it. They alone can truly feast, who have first fasted; they alone are able to use the world, who have learned not to abuse it; they alone inherit it, who take it as a shadow of the world to come, and who for that world to come relinquish it.[107]
—St. John Henry Newman

105. Alberto Methol Ferré, "La Chiesa, popolo tra i popoli," in *Il risorgimento cattolico latinoamericano*, 148–149; translation from Borghesi, *Mind of Pope Francis*, 88–89.

106. John Henry Newman, "Joshua, a Type of Christ and His Followers," in *Sermons, Bearing on the Subjects of the Day* (New York: D. Appleton, 1845), 148.

107. John Henry Newman, "The Cross of Christ, the Measure of the World," in *Parochial Sermons*, vol. 6 (London: J.G.F. & J. Rivington, 1842), 102.

As God rules the will, yet the will is free—as he rules the course of the world, yet men conduct it—so he has inspired the Bible, yet men have written it. . . . Though the Bible be inspired, it has all such characteristics as might attach to a book uninspired—the characteristics of dialect and style, the distinct effects of times and places, youth, and age, of moral and intellectual character.[108]
—St. John Henry Newman

If you want your faith, you have to work for it. It is a gift, but for very few is it a gift given without any demand for equal time devoted to its cultivation.[109]
—Flannery O'Connor

The Church has always been mindful of the relation between spirit and flesh; this has shown up in her definitions of the double nature of Christ, as well as in her care for what may seem to us to have nothing to do with religion—such as contraception. The Church is all of a piece. Her prohibition of the frustration of the marriage act has its true center perhaps in the doctrine of the resurrection of the body.[110]
—Flannery O'Connor

108. John Henry Newman, *Tracts for the Times*, vol. 5 (London: J.G.F. & J. Rivington, 1840), 30.

109. O'Connor, *The Habit of Being*, 477.

110. Flannery O'Connor to Cecil Dawkins, December 23, 1959, in *Flannery O'Connor Collection*, 162.

What a chimera then is man! What a novelty! What a monster, what a chaos, what a contradiction, what a prodigy! Judge of all things, imbecile worm of the earth; depositary of truth, a sink of uncertainty and error; the pride and refuse of the universe! Who will unravel this tangle? Nature confutes the skeptics, and reason confutes the dogmatists. What then will you become, O men! Who try to find out by your natural reason what is your true condition? You cannot avoid one of these sects, nor adhere to one of them. Know then, proud man, what a paradox you are to yourself.[111]
—Blaise Pascal

If we submit everything to reason, our religion will have no mysterious and supernatural element. If we offend the principles of reason, our religion will be absurd and ridiculous.[112]
—Blaise Pascal

The greatness of man is so evident that it is even proved by his wretchedness. For what in animals is nature, we call in man wretchedness, by which we recognize that, his nature being now like that of animals, he has fallen from a better nature which once was his. For who is unhappy at not being a king, except a deposed king?[113]
—Blaise Pascal

111. Pascal, *Pensées* 434, 143.
112. *Pensées* 273, 94.
113. *Pensées* 409, 129–130.

It is an outstanding manifestation of charity toward souls to omit nothing from the saving doctrine of Christ; but this must always be joined with tolerance and charity, as Christ himself showed in his conversations and dealings with men. For when he came, not to judge, but to save the world, was he not bitterly severe toward sin, but patient and abounding in mercy toward sinners?[114]
—Pope St. Paul VI

By remaining faithful to its original commission, by serving its people with love, especially the poor, the lonely, and the dispossessed, and by not surrendering its doctrinal steadfastness, sometimes even the very contradiction of culture by which it serves as a sign, surely the Church serves culture best.[115]
—Walker Percy

There remains then no other alternative than the completely *open tension* between essence and existence; essence as inward process essentially *within* existence, and yet never as complete essence, essentially *over* or *above* existence: essence *in-over* existence.[116]
—Erich Przywara

114. Paul VI, *Humane Vitae* 29, encyclical letter, July 25, 1968, vatican.va.
115. Percy, *Signposts*, 303.
116. Erich Przywara, *Polarity: A German Catholic's Interpretation of Religion*, trans. A.C. Bouquet (London: Oxford University Press, 1935), 32.

[The Church] affirms the *whole man* in his completeness, body as well as soul, will as well as intellect, heart as well as senses. When therefore the Spirit of God animates a man with its supernatural life it takes hold of him in his entirety, in his catholicity as it were, elevating his intellect by faith, his will by grace, his heart by devotion, his senses by liturgy, his body by sacramentals.[117]
—Fulton J. Sheen

We find [the will] causally conditioned when we feel how a tiredness of body prevents a volition from prevailing. The will is causally effective when we feel a victorious will overcome the tiredness, even making it disappear. The will's fulfillment is also linked to causal conditions, since it carries out all its effects through a causally regulated instrument. But what is truly creative about volition is not a causal effect.[118]
—Edith Stein (St. Teresa Benedicta of the Cross)

The human end in the spirit's greatest reach,
The extreme of the known in the presence of the extreme
Of the unknown.[119]
—Wallace Stevens

117. Fulton J. Sheen, *The Mystical Body of Christ* (Elk Grove Village, IL: Word on Fire, 2023), 69.

118. Edith Stein, *The Collected Works of Edith Stein*, vol. 3, *On the Problem of Empathy*, 3rd ed., trans. Waltraut Stein (Washington, DC: ICS, 1989), 56.

119. Wallace Stevens, "To an Old Philosopher in Rome," in *100 Great Catholic Poems*, 397.

We must never separate the Eucharist and the poor or the poor and the Eucharist. He satisfied my hunger for him and now I go to satisfy his hunger for souls, for love.[120]
—St. Teresa of Kolkata

What is contemplation? To live the life of Jesus.[121]
—St. Teresa of Kolkata

120. Mother Teresa, *No Greater Love* (Novato, CA: New World Library, 2002), 116.

121. Mother Teresa, 12.

Scripture Index

Old Testament

Genesis

Book 3, 14
1 92, 206
1:1 12
1:14–15 13
1:26–27 95
1:28 50, 95
1:28–31 34
1:31 6, 239
2:7 24
2:18 95
2:24 14, 259
3:5 34, 207
3:15 35
3:19 25, 71
3:24 35
4:4–5 266
11:1–9 44
15:5 187
22 186–187
28:10–17 26

Exodus

3:14–15 205
20:4–5 211
24:10 126
25:8 36

Leviticus

26:5 13

Deuteronomy

4:39 34
6:4 94

Deuteronomy *(continued)*
10:14 24
11:11 13

Joshua
24:15 237

1 Samuel
28:13 69

2 Samuel
14:14 70

1 Kings
2:2 62
6:13 36

2 Maccabees
7:28 91

Job
Book 84
19:26 71

Psalms
8:4 38
8:5–6 237
14:3 235
16:11 106
36:8 261
46:10 228
53:3 235
78:24–25 57
85:10–11 212
103:11 25
103:14–16 25–26
115:16 24
116:4 192
116:13 192
139:7–8 211
147:19–20 266

Proverbs
4:27 250
16:18 244–245
27:17 7

Ecclesiastes
1:3 230
1:9 8
7:18 251

Wisdom
11:24 46–47

Sirach
15:14 113
15:18 112–113

Isaiah

1:18	192
6:3	4
14:12	59
30:21	174
40:6–8	70
49:15	207
55:8–9	205
55:10	13–14

Jeremiah

17:9	239
23:24	207

Daniel

3:72	48
12:2	69

Micah

6:8	228

Malachi

1:2–3	266
4:2	77

New Testament

Matthew

Gospel	24, 198–199, 201
1:23	34, 199
4:1–2	256
4:4	231
4:17	235
5–7	228
5:20	243
5:26	274
5:48	243
6:10	45
6:16	256
6:33	47
7:1	247
7:2	268
8:12	267
9:9–13	249
10:16	192
10:34	295
11:11	238
11:28–30	247
13:52	172
16:18	290

Matthew *(continued)*

16:19 219
16:24–26 259
19:5 259
19:12 256
22:11 262
22:13 267
22:23 69
22:30 256
22:37 190
23 238
23:4 247
24:36 221
25:30 267
25:35 231
26:24 67
26:26 262
26:26–29 58
28:18 181
28:19–20 216
28:20 57, 317

Mark

Gospel 198–199, 201
1:6 256
1:15 34, 235
3:29 245
6:3 36
9:24 192
9:48 267
12:30 190
16:16 267

Luke

Gospel 198–199, 201, 204
1:29 194
1:32 36
1:35 291
1:38 36, 194
1:46–55 194
2:19 194
4:1–2 256
5:35 256
6:20–26 256
7:33 256
7:34 259
7:47 245
10:18 59
10:27 190
10:38–42 229
13:24 275
15:20 247
22:19 58
23:43 272
24:39 68

John

Gospel	197, 201, 225
1:1	33, 160
1:1–3	197
1:10	197
1:14	33, 195–196
1:16	241
1:51	27
3:16	47
4:10	284
4:14	284
4:22	267
4:34	160
6	57
8:11	249
8:23	36
8:32–34	247
8:44	34
10:34	36
11:25	69
12:32	270
13:23	225
13:34	248
14:5–6	viii
14:6	4, 287
14:9	36, 209
14:15	243–244
14:16	216
15:16	240
16:28	317
16:33	181
17:11	181
17:15	181
17:16	179
17:18	181
17:22	289
19:26	225
20:4	225
20:17	202
20:27	68, 202

Acts of the Apostles

Book	216
1:11	230
2	216
2:17–18	221
2:46	58
3:21	273
4:12	266–267
8:9–10	21
9:2	4
15:28	222
17:18	188
17:27–28	207
19:9	4
19:23	4
20:7	58
20:11	58

Acts of the Apostles

(*continued*)

22:4 4
22:7 287
24:14 4
24:22 4
26:24 190
27:35 58

Romans

Letter 278
1:17 277, 282
1:20 193
1:21 283
2:6–11 283
3:8 151
3:23 235
4:16 187
5:8 235
5:15–17 235
5:18 270
5:20 235
6:23 35
7:19 238
8:11 68
8:22 46
11:33 205
11:36 208
12:2 179
12:5 262
14:3 262

1 Corinthians

1:10 183
1:13 183
1:22–23 188
2:9 46
3:1–2 247
4:7 240
6:9–10 248
6:12 208
6:13 69
6:19 207–208
7:29–31 260
10:13 237
10:16–17 96
10:16–22 58
11:7 237
11:23–30 58
11:29 260
12:11 216
12:13 267
12:14–26 95
12:27 95
13:2 162
13:6 162
13:13 151
15:6 67

1 Corinthians *(continued)*

15:17 67
15:20 67
15:22 67, 270
15:24–25 46
15:25 179
15:28 46
15:44 67
15:52 179

2 Corinthians

1:20 205
3:18 283
4:7 71
5:7 188
5:14 270
6:16 207–208
7:10 103

Galatians

2:11–14 221
2:20 38
3:28 172
4:4 34
5:6 286
5:19–21 6, 244
5:20 216
5:22–23 107

Ephesians

1:10 4
1:23 295
2:6 181
2:8–9 193
2:14 194
4:3 95
4:4 221
4:5 266
4:10 68
4:13 179
4:15 162
5:21–33 263
6:10–17 103

Philippians

1:21 70
1:23 70
2:5–8 37
2:12 282
3:19 52
3:20 179

Colossians

1:15–16 56–57
1:18 38
1:20 4
2:2 251

Colossians *(continued)*
2:8 188
3:2 179

1 Thessalonians
5:21 222

2 Thessalonians
2:15 283

1 Timothy
2:4 270
2:5 278
3:16 68
4:3–4 59
4:8 46

2 Timothy
3:16 288
4:3 183

Titus
3:9–10 183

Philemon
7 103

Hebrews
2:7 237
4:12 283
4:15 38
5:12–14 247
10:29 222
11:1 125
12:25 240
13:17 219

James
Letter 227–228, 278
1:25 228
1:27 228
2:13 248
2:14–26 283
2:17 228
2:22 286
3:15 244
5:14 283
5:16 288

1 Peter
1:13 103
1:24 70
2:24 37
3:15 190
4:7 103

1 Peter *(continued)*

4:13	48
5:8	103
5:8–9	244

2 Peter

1:4	36
2:13	259
3:16	221

1 John

2:15–17	6, 47, 244
4:2	36
4:8	92
4:16	92, 106
4:19	240
4:20	230
5:3	243–244
5:17	250

2 John

7	21

3 John

8	251

Jude

10	59
12	259
12–13	59

Revelation

Book	3, 25, 58, 178, 216, 221
3:1	220
3:12	46
5:6	68
5:8	283
5:9	270
11:17	181
19:9	58
20	215
21:1	46
21:2	46
21:5	8, 46
21:23	46
22:7	221
22:12	221
22:13	46
22:20	179–180, 221